Crap at the Environment

Mark with Al Gore, who is not crap at the environment

Crap at the Environment

A year in the life of one man trying to save the planet

Mark Watson

HODDER

First published in Great Britain in 2008 by Hodder & Stoughton
An Hachette Livre UK company

1

Copyright © Mark Watson 2008

A CIP catalogue record for this title is available from the British Library

ISBN 978 0 340 95280 1

Typeset in Poppl-Pontifex by Hewer Text UK Ltd, Edinburgh
Printed and bound in the UK by CPI Mackays, Chatham ME5 8TD

Hodder & Stoughton policy is to use papers that are natural, renewable
and recyclable products and made from wood grown in sustainable
forests. The logging and manufacturing processes are expected to
conform to the environmental regulations of the country of origin.

Hodder & Stoughton Ltd
338 Euston Road
London NW1 3BH

www.hodder.co.uk

To my parents.

Contents

Prologue:
Two Snapshots

SEPTEMBER 22, 2006

I was watching a bunch of people trying to stop planes taking off from Heathrow. They'd set themselves up on the runway in a little angry barricade and were talking to news reporters about 'climate change', probably the most used two-word phrase of the year so far, with the possible exception of 'Lily Allen'. I couldn't see things working out well. There were maybe fifteen of them, which is not enough people to stop a plane going anywhere near full tilt. And while they might cause a bit of short-term hassle, it was hard to imagine that the pilot would end up making an announcement: 'Ladies and gentlemen, this is your captain speaking. We're not going to be able to go through with this flight I'm afraid, because these people are concerned about the environment. We recommend you take a weekend break in the UK instead.'

One of the protestors, a downtrodden-looking girl with matted hair, started telling the reporter that because of 'human activity' the planet was becoming dangerously warm. I wondered if she seriously expected this to be reversed any time soon. There are more humans on the surface of the planet every single day, and it is pretty hard to stop them from getting up to 'activities'.

It *was* a very warm September, with a mean temperature which the BBC's weather website described as 'exceptionally above average for the last fifty years'. But then, September 2005 is logged as 'well above average', and so is September 2004. September 2003 appears as 'above average' and September 2002, charmingly, is simply described as 'rather warm'. September 2001 was more or less normal, but September 2000 was again much warmer than most since the war, although it was also 'the dullest summer since 1996' – which seems unusually judgemental for meteorologists.

In fact, browsing the site – which, like any website, very quickly becomes addictive – it's actually hard to find a September in the past decade which *wasn't* unusually warm. Not much to worry about there then, surely?

Of course, I didn't know any of these statistics at the time. Why would I? I had other stuff to think about. Unlike many of these activists, I had a wife, a cat and a career as a stand-up comedian working here, in Australia, and in all sorts of places in between. Now that Michael Fish has gone, who even watches the weather forecast any more, let alone reviews great temperatures of the past? Who, despite the supposed British obsession with the weather, actually remembers or cares what it was like a couple of weeks ago, let alone ten years ago?

And so, as the temperature soared to a supposedly remarkable 3.2 degrees above the average over the past sixty years, I was not only oblivious to the matter – as usual, I'd spent the month of August at the Edinburgh Fringe, so any day when my clothes weren't waterlogged seemed like exceptional weather – but actively irritated by all the talk about it. Al Gore, someone I hadn't thought about once in the six years since he somehow lost the election where he beat George Bush, was suddenly all over the airwaves talking about the film *An Inconvenient Truth*. This movie had chalked up a big success in the USA, despite being, as one reviewer remarked, 'a 100-minute film of a 58-year-old man talking about carbon emissions'. Gore, whom I remembered as a bit of a plodder often criticised for his wooden style, had seemingly been reinvented as some sort of eco-prophet. More than one American reviewer had said it was one of the most important films of the decade so far.

'I don't think we'll go and see that,' said my wife, Emily, when we first walked past a poster. 'I think it might be a bit harrowing.' She has a very low tolerance of harrowing films, along with films which are violent, pretentious, or full of the sort of scenes where someone like Ben Stiller gets his penis stuck in a door and makes a funny face. Like everyone else in the world, I made some joke about how it was a shame Al Gore hadn't done this good a publicity campaign in 2000, and then tried to forget his earnest face with its impossibly smooth slicked-back hair, and his Deep South drawl talking about the consequences of inactivity. It was actually pretty easy. As I said, I had other stuff on.

But as September went by, posters began to appear everywhere on the London Underground for a book called *Heat* by George Monbiot, a prominent environmental scientist whose surname looks like a promising Scrabble rack. The subtitle was 'How To Stop The Planet From Burning', and the posters boasted that Monbiot was 'turning up the heat on politicians'. This seemed an odd way of trying to stop anything from burning, but then, I wasn't a scientist. And not being a scientist I decided to avoid *Heat* as surely as I would avoid the inane magazine of the same name.

Other people were really getting into the whole thing though, it seemed. In the middle of September, when *An Inconvenient Truth* came out, and *Heat* was already starting to appear in bookshops, there was a raft of articles in the press, and a load of discussion in the media, about whether it was ethical to – for example – fly halfway across the world. Luckily, by the time this debate really got going, Emily and I had gone to Hong Kong, where it was much quieter. During the trip – a two-week comedy tour which also took in Thailand, Taiwan and the Philippines – I flew business class for the first time, and at someone else's expense. It was a very enjoyable experience. Looking out of the plane window at the vast, glittering web of lights that made up London by night, I thought how lucky I was to live in an age where international travel was so easy and affordable that it was almost criminal *not* to do it.

And so now, a couple of days after my return, the people trying to stop planes taking off from Heathrow seemed rather silly. The downtrodden girl quoted Monbiot – there he was again – saying that if we did not act now on global warming, we would be risking the lives of 'tens of thousands of people'. This could only be a crass exaggeration; if it were true that environmental disaster on this scale was possible, surely *everyone* would be talking about it. I found myself siding with the burly, orange-bib-wearing men who came onto the runway to chase the students away.

The kettle was nice and full; it had boiled, unnoticed, while I was distracted by the news. I boiled it again and made tea and settled down cosily next to the radiator. I'd been inspired by the news item: it was time to think about booking a holiday for some winter sun.

We were two-thirds of the way into our freakishly warm September. October's mean temperature would be recorded by the BBC weather website as 'exceptionally above average', completing the hottest autumn since records began in 1917. I spent quite a lot of it in the garden, or walking on the heath with my wife, marvelling that anyone in their right mind could imagine this clement weather could be a bad thing. One very mild night in November, I made a joke to this effect at the Comedy Store and the audience laughed quite a lot. Thank goodness, I thought, for people like me with good old-fashioned British common sense.

SEPTEMBER 22, 2007

A year later . . :

I was walking down Brunswick Street with the centre of Melbourne behind me. It was a crisp Spring evening and I had just become a qualified climate change lecturer. Over my shoulder was a black canvas bag which said along its side AL GORE'S CLIMATE CHANGE LEADERSHIP PROGRAM. In it was a certificate with Gore's predictably confident-looking signature, a CD containing all his slides which I was now authorised to use for public presentations, and a thick recycled cardboard folder stuffed with hundreds of pages of notes I'd made from three days of lectures on environmental science.

The sun was setting over Melbourne. It was about forty-five minutes' walk back to where I was staying. A year ago I would have jumped in a cab without a second thought; now I didn't even consider not walking, partly because even this paltry, apparently futile carbon saving seemed worth making these days, but partly also because I'd realised it was usually much more fun to walk somewhere than get there in a car.

Coming out of a café with an organic coffee, I ran into an acquaintance. He asked, 'How are you going?', which, thanks to the flexibility of Aussie slang, can mean anything on the continuum from 'Let's get this unavoidable exchange of pleasantries out of the way as quick as we can,' to 'Please tell me everything that has happened to you since you were born, in as close to the right order as possible.'

'I've just been on a course with Al Gore,' I said.

'Oh right,' said my acquaintance. There was a pause. 'Was it good?'

'It was amazing,' I said. 'I've been trained to give lectures on climate change.'

'Right,' he said again. 'Is that the same as global warming?'

I explained that it was the same concept, but campaigners these days favour the phrase 'climate change' because 'global warming', to a lot of people, sounds less a threat than a quite pleasant prospect.

'Right,' said my acquaintance, 'and do you . . . do you believe all that stuff?'

'Yes,' I said, 'I think, having looked at the evidence, um.' My resolve was faltering. My Aussie acquaintance was looking at me, as Australians often do, as if I was slightly incomprehensible but quaintly amusing; this has been helpful to my comedy career in their country, but it was a bit annoying at present.

Come on, I thought to myself, you have just been trained by Al Gore. You received an exceptionally rare opportunity just so that you could be trained to deal with moments like this.

'I mean, the scientific evidence is pretty convincing,' I said lamely, wondering whether it might be possible to get the slides out and project a couple of graphs onto the wall of a building or something.

'Yeah, but I've heard it's a lot of rubbish,' he said. 'I saw something on the Internet about it. I'll give you the URL.' He pronounced it 'earl', like some computer-savvy people do.

'There's a lot of stuff on the Internet, though,' I countered. 'I was on the site written by a woman who claimed to be married to the Berlin Wall.' This was true. I gave another example, about a website for people who'd 'discovered' that the UK Government had us all under surveillance by means of tiny cameras concealed in squirrels.

'Yeah, but that's just loony tunes,' he said. 'This site I was reading was by actual scientists.'

'Well . . .' I said, shuffling about. 'I think, um, I think most "actual scientists" do agree the world's heating up. The thing is, on the net, everyone's opinion counts for as much as anyone else's.' He looked me as if to say: *and so what? That's a great thing, isn't it?*

'Anyway,' I backtracked, 'I'm still trying to work it all out.'

'Well, fair enough,' said the acquaintance warily. 'Good luck, I guess.'

As I was leaving, we exchanged a look and I had a strange, almost out-of-body moment in which I could see myself as this neutral observer saw me. What he saw was, basically, a fanatic. I had been brainwashed by the greens. I was one of these people who'd got a bit carried away with the latest fashionable 'end of the world' scare. In short, he saw me exactly as I'd seen those people trying to stop planes taking off.

What I felt, as I pondered this remarkable turnaround, was not embarrassment at my about-turn, or chagrin at the prospect of being bracketed with hippies in people's minds, but simply disappointment that I hadn't done a better job of sticking up for what I now believed to be a rather important principle. Somehow, over the past year, the earth and I had become quite good friends. It was still a pretty turbulent friendship, for sure, even abusive on occasion, but it was a lot rosier than I would ever have believed possible. I mean, I had a bag with Al Gore's name on it. I had a certificate that said I knew about climate change. I'd had several conversations that weekend that included the word 'sustainability'. I now possessed an opinion on the viability of carbon sequestration; there was a better than average chance that in the next few months I would appear before a largeish crowd and suggest that they switched to green energy. I tried to work out how the hell this had happened, and what was going to happen next.

Part One
January, February, March:
A New Leaf

It might have been Gore, or Monbiot, or the *Independent*'s almost daily front pages with pictures of desolate polar bears and headlines like 'A FINAL CHANCE'; or maybe it was all these things piling up towards a 'tipping point'. But in any case, by the start of 2007, you would have had to be living on the North Pole – or whatever is left of it – to be unaware of Britain's increasing obsession with the environment.

Not since the golden days of the eighties and the 'hole in the ozone layer' (what happened about that, by the way? We'll find out later) had so many ordinary people been discussing the state of the planet. I noticed at parties, backstage at gigs, even on the London Underground – where people never talk to each other if they can help it – that it was becoming the subject *du jour* previously occupied in this decade by *The Office*, iTunes, blogging, and how Noel Edmonds had managed to get away with having a second career. Not just the *Independent*, but also newspapers with quite a few readers, began to discuss it on a regular basis. My local Waterstone's allocated a bookcase to a new 'Green Issues' section – still, admittedly, quite a lot smaller than their 'Tragic Life Stories' section devoted to the unstoppable genre of memoirs of bad parenting, but a clear acknowledgement of the fact that people suddenly, for some reason, wanted to read about carbon. 'Carbon footprint' was a phrase you suddenly heard every day: getting off a flight from Edinburgh to London I half-expected to see a mucky trail stretching back to Scotland, like when you're a kid and forget to wipe your feet.

There was starting to be a clear divide between people, among them a number of my friends, who thought this was a real, important issue, and people like my dad (a science teacher) who thought it was destined to join SARS on the slag-pile of failed apocalypses. I knew people who were paying for carbon offsets when they went on holiday; recycling properly, rather than just as a sort of hobby, as I did; taking their light bulbs out and replacing them with more efficient ones. I also knew people who thought all this was ridiculous, and they had some powerful role-models in the public eye. Sir David Bellamy had said it was ridiculous, and he knew all about nature. Popular dickhead Jeremy Clarkson antagonised the 'greenies' by bragging about his fuel-hungry car and driving it through as many bits of horrible countryside as he could. The *Daily Express* took a break from pondering the question of whether Princess Diana had been murdered to draw comparisons between the climate change lobby and a religious cult.

Reading back over that paragraph, it sounds like I'm striking a smugly liberal tone and, yes, it's true that if Clarkson and the *Express* were strongly against a cause, I would normally instinctively gravitate towards it. So why didn't I, when it came to this subject?

I suppose the answer is apathy, but that has to be qualified a bit. I wouldn't really describe myself as an apathetic person. I'm interested in 'issues'. I read the papers. I'm occasionally capable of taking a stand on something. I boycotted GAP indefinitely when I found out that there was a large 'gap' between their profits and the wages of their workforce. I spent a large portion of a gig once

ranting about L'Oreal's misleading (not to say horrendously pa-
tronising) advertising, and when someone emailed me to say
they'd stopped buying their skin creams as a result, I felt proud
of myself. I'm certainly good at being interested in current affairs.

But that's the problem. If, like me, you're the sort of person who
is 'interested' in the popular debates of the day, you very often end
up reading so much and in such an even-handed manner, and
having such a good grasp of both sides of the story, that it is
absolutely impossible to have an actual opinion. Throughout my
adult life I've tended to be a neutral on almost every major
question, because the more I immerse myself in the arguments,
the less I can choose between the arguing parties. In 2003, when
many friends of mine were up in arms – to use an unfortunate
phrase – over the proposed invasion of Iraq, I sympathised with
them but, at the same time, Tony Blair really did seem very sure it
was the right thing to do, and he knew a lot more than I did about
what was going on over there. There was a big part of me that felt
that if I joined the crowds marching through London with a T-shirt
saying 'NOT IN MY NAME', I'd look very stupid when the invasion
was cancelled by popular demand and a weapon of mass destruction landed plumb on my roof the very next day.

This same pattern runs through my whole life. If someone
knocked on my door with a gun and said, 'Can you prove that
it is definitely not ethical for me to shoot you in the head?', I would
start off pretty determined, but I'd more than likely give way in the
end. And so, paradoxical as it is, complete engagement with a
debate can somehow turn into the profoundest form of apathy:
being so 'interested' that you do nothing at all.

Of course, eco-conscious friends of mine kept telling me that
global warming *wasn't* a debate, that no one who'd actually
studied the evidence could possibly dispute any of it. Some of
them, like Johann, a columnist for the *Independent,* said it over and

over again. But I found this hard to swallow. For every article I read by someone like Johann, there was a refutation not far away, and since – as ever – I didn't have the expertise to find a definitive answer for myself, I had no real option but to wish good luck to both sides and move on to sit on another fence.

But also, I'm a natural cynic in many ways. My job is to take the piss out of things. Stand-up may only be a job, but it infects your personality and leaves you unconsciously undermining everything you see as a matter of pure professionalism. My friend Paul, who's a doctor, always likes to have a go at diagnosing if he happens upon an ill person in his spare time, and no doubt serial killers see on the news that a body's been identified and think, 'Imagine not even smashing the teeth!' It's inevitable, then, that if something like global warming becomes a big deal to a lot of people, my knee-jerk reaction will be to think of ways to make fun of it. I'd have a limited shelf life as a comedian if I went on stage and said, 'I bought one of those carbon offset packages the other day. (Pause.) I'm not completely sure how much it's just a sop to my conscience, but it seems better than not even acknowledging my responsibility for global carbon emissions. (Pause.) Wow, tough crowd.'

And something I've always been even more cynical about than almost anything else is the notion, which environmentalists are always putting about, that 'if everyone does one small thing, it adds up to something big'. Even if I had been sufficiently alarmed by the Iraq invasion to go out on a protest march, I would have done it out of pure principle, not with any expectation whatsoever that this might actually stop the war from happening. I've just never believed, deep down, that governments can be forced to alter huge policy decisions because people march about it. I was one of the many people left unmoved by Live 8, in 2005, and the accompanying blitz of wristbands, MAKE POVERTY HISTORY adverts and celebrity-endorsed charity drives. I couldn't bring myself to believe that, if everyone in the country texted the Oxfam phone number on the advert ten times every day, it would make a difference to more than a trifling number of people in Africa.

Plus, appalling as this probably sounds, I never believed that anywhere near everyone in the country *would* do that. Even the best-supported public appeal imaginable is up against the fact that the majority of people either don't understand, or more charitably simply don't have time, because they're busy with the millions of more immediate things that make up life, such as getting the kids to school or doing the scratchcards. So I was hardly likely to feel any more well-disposed towards the increasing number of articles claiming that if we 'all' just turned the kitchen light off when we weren't in the kitchen, our grandchildren would have a much better time of it.

However, there is another reason why, as of January 2007, the global warming issue had made virtually no impact upon my life. There is no way of saying this that reflects any credit on me, so I'll be as frank as possible. It is the same reason that probably one in four people reading this sentence is still standing in a shop flicking through the pages trying to decide between this book and a spine-tingling Robert Ludlum offering. The reason is that, of all the possible things you could have a conversation with someone about, 'the environment' is one of the worst. It's boring. Global warming is a tedious subject; climate change might be a catchier name but it won't become a truly exciting prospect until it is re-branded along the lines of 'SuperGlobal Meltdown' or 'Planetfuck 2050'. And all the smaller stuff that fits into the Waterstone's Green Issues section is similarly unpalatable fare. Composting. Water conservation. Ethical trading. Offsetting. Each one of these is, in terms of its usefulness as a social icebreaker, akin to putting

Radiohead on at a party. I'm a stand-up comedian: I don't have any social function other than to be funny. I can't afford to have boring topics in my repertoire – not when my entire career, like the career of any comic, is basically a desperate struggle to persuade as many as possible to love me.

So throughout my life, first as a normal young person wanting to be entertained, than as an entertainer myself, my interest in any environmental cause has been virtually zero. I've been non-plussed by eco-activists right from my first contact with them, in Year 5, when a group of girls gave a talk in class on the importance of not using aerosols for the sake of the ozone layer; I ended up arguing up with them, out of jealousy because the teacher (Mrs Farrell) kept banging on about how impressed she was with them, and pushed one of them into a ditch in an uncharacteristic piece of playground violence.

I make monthly donations to Shelter, the homeless charity, and Oxfam (I mention this, after my earlier comments about Live 8, to emphasise that I am not in fact a monster), mostly because I've been stopped twice by particularly convincing people with clip-boards in the street. However, I've quite literally crossed the road to avoid volunteers with pictures of pandas or other cute animals on their clipboards. I've never lost sleep over the destruction of the rain forest; I've always sort of felt, at the end of the day, that people have been talking about how it's disappearing for a long time now, and there still seems to be an awful lot of it when you look on Google Earth. I've always regarded the Green Party as all well and good, but wouldn't vote for them in my wildest dreams, because basing an entire manifesto on concern for the environment has never seemed any more sensible to me than having an Education Party or a Sport Party. In fact, if you had asked me in January 2007 which was more important an issue, the rising sea levels or the rising ticket prices through the Nationwide Football League, I would immediately have started talking about my plan to reform the national game at grass-roots level.

Some of this probably seems rather crass, and – as I'll go on to discuss shortly when I make my first carbon inventory – I've never been *quite* as flippant about the planet's wellbeing as I might be making it sound. Though I might have poked at fun at 'greens', I've never openly opposed them: I've never deliberately polluted; I've never driven a massive car around, honked my horn at passing wildlife or set alight big piles of plastic; I've never dismissed global warming as a lie. But as of January 2007, I'd certainly never done anything worth calling eco-friendly.

As I was saying, I had no track record of recycling. Oh, I'd been to the bottle bank, but only in the way you go to church a couple of times a year to cover yourself just in case. If I hadn't been cajoled by Emily, who in general has always had more of a social conscience than I have, I probably wouldn't have made even those visits. Fairly often they were motivated less by concern for the earth than concern that there were so many bottles in our kitchen that I kept knocking them over when washing up; my mum would sometimes glance at them during her visits and ask how my career was going.

I rarely bought recycled or Fairtrade goods, and on the few occasions I had done so (again, normally prompted by Emily), I walked home from the supermarket acting as if I'd cycled to Brazil wearing clothes spun from natural fibres and laid down in the path of a logger's truck. I didn't buy local produce, or if I did, it was by pure fluke: when shopping in a supermarket I was as likely to look at where the goods had been 'sourced' from as I was to find out the birthday of the man or woman who did the 'sourcing' and send them a card. Even though my friend, the musical comedian Tim Minchin, had written a cult classic song all about the importance of taking a canvas bag to the shops rather than using plastic bags (you can find it at www.myspace.com/timminchin), and even though I'd walked all over London with this song in my head, and owned a canvas bag with Tim's handsomely rock-and-roll face on it, I rarely took it to the supermarket or anywhere else. I'd worked at Waitrose as a sixth-former when they introduced a 'bag for life' scheme, but all this meant was that I associated economic-al packaging with dark memories of my part-time job – the time my till was missing £50 at the end of the day because of a cash-back mishap, and the time I couldn't identify a fruit and a furious man shouted 'GREENGAGES! They're GREENGAGES!' in my face in front of a long queue.

A particular visit to our local Tesco in mid-January typifies my scattershot approach to 'ethical' supermarket shopping. I recall what time of year it was because I'd just been looking for a present for a friend, whose birthday, exasperatingly, falls close to Christ-mas but not close enough for people to get away with two-for-one gifts. After buying some over-packaged crap which I hoped to redeem with a suitably cute message in the card (I've always been pretty good at birthday cards, poor at presents), I nipped into Tesco to pick up toilet paper, and a bottle of wine for dinner (to accompany dinner, that is; we were planning to have food as well). As often happens, the thought fluttered into my head that it might be nice to go for recycled paper, but there didn't seem to be any. Instead, nearly every brand carried some boast about 'renewable forests'. One packet crowed that for every tree used to produce the 'bathroom tissue' therein, five more were planted. This seemed to suggest that the more toilet paper you used, the more new green-ery you'd be responsible for, and so the most ecologically sound thing possible would be to use as much paper as you could, even if it meant unravelling whole rolls of it at football matches, as fans did in the eighties to take their minds off the hooliganism pro-blem, or going to fancy dress parties as a mummy. There was something wrong with this equation, but rather than try to wrap my head around the ethics of global paper production, I grabbed a big pack – there you go, South America, have a dozen trees on me and the wife – and headed for the checkout, grabbing a bottle of Australian Shiraz on the way.

The checkout clerk, Kevin, began to open up a plastic bag with a pace so lackadaisical and an expression so sullen that one might have thought Tesco's slogan, rather than 'EVERY LITTLE HELPS', was 'WHY DON'T YOU FUCK OFF HOME?' Being a generally jittery, impatient sort of person, I quickly tired of watching his fingers rub at the sides of a bag in the seemingly vague hope of prising it open some time before London hosted the 2012 Olympics. I didn't need a bag, surely. I didn't want to get cocky, but I would back myself to find some way of dividing the two items between my two hands.

'I don't need a bag, thanks,' I said.

Kevin, who was now three-quarters of the way through the process of prising open my plastic prize, looked at me as if I had declared that I didn't need my pancreas, and laid it before him. 'You're all right, I'm just putting it in a bag for you,' he said.

'Well, I don't need one,' I persisted.

'It's fine,' he said, with exaggerated patience, 'I've already put it in the bag.'

And indeed he had, though the wait had stolen away three minutes of my existence. By now the person behind me was sighing, understandably, and it looked as if *I* rather than Kevin were the reason for the hold-up. I abandoned the argument, took the contentious bag and went out into the street, where it was raining so hard that I very nearly got in a cab to take me the few hundred yards home.

This brief exposé of my shopping habits helps to put in context the circumstances in which I finally watched *An Inconvenient*

Truth. I'd had three or four opportunities in the space of five minutes to do something tiny for the planet and given no serious thought to any of them. That was me. I was, and always had been, crap at the environment.

FEBRUARY

I'm ashamed to admit it, but I think it was when he won an Oscar that I finally decided I really ought to think about seeing Gore's film. I hate the Oscars: the spectacle of an already cripplingly self-satisfied industry giving itself an extra pat on the back fills me with the sort of loathing I might feel if there was an award ceremony for the people who had vomited outside the most pubs as I was passing them on my way home from a gig. Nonetheless, there was a docile part of my brain that reacted to the sight of a gong-bearing Gore on the breakfast news with the thought 'wow, now that he's beaten a Czech documentary on hay, maybe I will check out that movie after all'. To give myself a bit of credit, it wasn't so much the fact that he'd actually won – though it was amazing if you thought about it, Al Gore winning an Oscar! Seven years ago you would have said it was more likely John Prescott would win Wimbledon – as the compelling clip of his acceptance speech. That prominent forehead, that slick hair, this man who so obviously never meant to go anywhere near the entertainment industry, saying that reducing our personal consumption was 'not a political issue, it's a moral issue' and being applauded by a crowd of people who would later take goody bags containing thousands of dollars' worth of stuff back to their mansions in one of the most gleefully amoral places on the globe. The whole business was really bizarre. Purely out of curiosity, I was going to have to see how this film had managed to win one of showbiz's biggest prizes for showing highlights of a lecture tour about melting icecaps.

The night we rented it, our first choice was actually *Little Miss Sunshine*, but that was out. So, as an alternative to this charming screwball comedy about a family road-trip, I proposed a documentary about the impending disintegration of all we saw around us. Somehow my pitch failed to impress Emily. She pointed out that we rarely had a night together when we could curl up and watch a film, and she didn't really count it as 'curling up' if she was writhing in misery at a computer projection of flood waters overwhelming a large portion of the globe. I made some flip remark about how it might not be all that different from *Little Miss Sunshine*, since 'sunshine' would still be a feature, only as a potential agent of man-made global catastrophe. The joke didn't go down well and I had a feeling the film wouldn't, either. 'I'm going to stop watching if it turns out to be harrowing,' Emily remarked as I slid the disc into the drive, in keeping with her usual policy. (In the interests of fairness I should record that she has sometimes overridden this policy out of sheer selflessness, for instance sitting through *Monster's Ball* in the cinema with me even though after about the first ten minutes it was clear she would rather be in the electric chair herself than watch any more of it.)

The film began with Gore's voice over some clips of what was unmistakably 'nature'. Then the science began.

Just over an hour later I looked across at Emily's face, half-illuminated by the blueish light from the screen. There was little doubt by this time that you could describe the film as harrowing, but she was absolutely gripped. I was too, and moreover, to my astonishment, I was actually quite moved. I've never cried at a film in my life. Songs often, books sometimes, but not a film, not even

It's A Wonderful Life (not quite). I didn't cry at this one either, but I was certainly shaken. It suddenly seemed extremely odd, inexplicable really, that I hadn't bothered to watch it so far, odder still that I had never come close to engaging with any of the things it was about. Gore himself – did I mention I met Gore? – said at the course that everyone concerned with the environment experienced at some point an 'aha moment', the split second where this suddenly seemed real and important to them (nothing to do with Norwegian pop stars A-ha, who made the 80s disco favourite 'Take On Me'). This was mine.

About ten minutes before the end, though, the DVD got stuck and wouldn't play any more. This meant we missed the part of the film when Gore explained that it was still not too late to make a difference. Our viewing ended instead with a general sense of foreboding, coupled with my first ever genuine pangs of 'eco-guilt', which manifested themselves so strongly that I couldn't put the light on to get the faulty DVD out of the player without glancing nervously up at the sky outside as if I could see the greenhouse gases massing.

The next day, I rented a different copy and watched the whole thing again, this time including the end, which is a gentle, but forceful, call to arms, making the point that the solution to the planet's problems are still, for a limited period, within our grasp. Probably the best moment of the film is one of the final slides, a photo of the earth taken from a distance of billions of miles away. It shows our entire world as an almost invisible blue speck lost in a massive, empty black canvas. Gore's solemn voice says that everything that has ever happened, everything that makes up the sum of what we call history, took place on this blue speck, 'our home'. This potentially rather hackneyed appeal to our protective side in the service of 'Mother Earth' (as it is never referred to in the film) is actually very affecting. Obvious as it might seem, it is a jolt to consciousness to see the world, the totality of everything you have ever witnessed or even heard about, depicted as a tiny, vulnerable smudge in a boundless mass of nothingness. It is mind-blowing to consider that this smudge saw the crucifixion, the World Wars, the rise and consolidation of Ant and Dec; and for some reason you were born onto it and get to stay there for a short while. (In the lecture course, Gore drily remarked that some people argued that we'd simply head for another planet when things became unliveable down here: 'So, what, we're going to evacuate? They didn't even manage to evacuate New Orleans in time.') It makes you feel very, very small but somehow also ennobled, and, above all, as if we are – as Gore says – 'all in it together'.

But 'in' what together? I'd like to give a brief summary of *An Inconvenient Truth* because it provides the backdrop to the rest of what's in this book, and because I'd like you to understand the frame of mind I was in when I came away from it. Ideally, in fact, you would probably go and watch it now, but I can't really ask you to do everything I do in this book: if books worked like that we'd all be running through Paris investigating shady Catholic cartels and being chased by a corrupt cop. If you have seen the film, feel free to skip this bit: I'll put in a Choose Your Own Adventure-style multiple-choice menu so you can pick your path. But it's my experience that most people haven't seen it, either for the reasons mentioned above, or because they assume they know everything that's in it already, or because they like the idea of the film more than the film itself. A friend of mine, when she heard I was going to do the Al Gore course, said 'That's amazing! His film has changed the world!' Had she seen it? 'Nope.'

So here we go.

If you have seen An Inconvenient Truth *and/or are not interested in hearing its content and message grossly simplified, go to page 19. If you decide to stay and listen, read on.*

A *convenient guide to* An Inconvenient Truth

* The planet is extraordinarily beautiful, lush and varied, thanks to
nature. It is easy to take nature for granted and imagine that it
exists independently of us, rather than being influenced by us.
Gore quotes Mark Twain's axiom that what gets us into trouble
is not what we don't know, 'it's what we know for sure that just
ain't so.' It 'just ain't so' that we're not capable of seriously
changing our environment.

* Unfortunately, we are fucking up the planet with greenhouse
gases. In the rest of the film, Gore – in extracts from his more
than 3000 slideshows on the subject – shows how, and what it
means.

* Greenhouse gases (which include carbon dioxide – CO_2 – and
methane) are always in the atmosphere. In the right quantities
they are good because they trap heat from the sun. In excessive
quantities, naturally, they trap too much heat from the sun.

* Since the Industrial Revolution, because of the amount of
carbon-based fuels we burn, the amount of these gases in the
atmosphere has risen enormously. (This is backed up by an
explanation of how they can measure CO_2 by examining ice,
a bit like woodsmen can tell the age of trees from their rings.
The experts are referred to as 'ice scientists' and their group
as 'the ice community', which briefly distracts the viewer by
conjuring up a mental image of a tribe of ice-people.) The
temperature of the planet has also risen. There are all sorts
of statistics showing that the past ten years have been among
the hottest on record.

* Some people deny the correlation between these increased CO_2 levels and the rising temperature, but when you look at the two graphs together, someone like me with a 'B' in GCSE Maths can see that they appear to mirror each other at every point. Gore remarks that in a survey by *Science* magazine of 928 peer-reviewed articles on climate change, not one actually denies that it is happening. This was a surprise to me.

* So we are making the planet warmer. 'But haven't we seen the planet warm up before?' Gore asks, rhetorically. Like in medieval times? Using one of those little pointers you point at graphs with, Gore points out this 'medieval warming period' which sceptics often refer to. It appears as a tiny little upwards prickle on the graph compared with a huge great spike over the past few decades.

* In the film's most celebrated moment, Gore gets in a cherry-picker and goes incredibly high in it, to show what the levels of CO_2 in the atmosphere are likely to be if we continue powering the planet at our current rates and with our current methods.

* He then shows what would happen if we experienced a commensurate rise in the planet's temperature. It is bad.

* The main thing, of course, is that the sea levels would rise (for a number of reasons), swamping cities which are the current home of tens of millions of people. Places like Mumbai and Shanghai would be completely under water. So would San Francisco. Equally worryingly, Hollywood might not be. (That was my bit, not Gore's.)

* And there are all sorts of other potential consequences, none of them heartening, of disturbing the planet's climate as we are doing. Drought, food shortages, and so on.

* The problem has been covered up or understated by scientists under coercion from governments. This bit is more controversial, especially as it's bolstered by gentle reminders that Gore should really have been president, and insights into his private life and history which can't help but make the neutral viewer sympathise with his political standpoint. However, the central thrust of the argument is, once again, pretty hard to take issue with.

* Then we hear how we can still reverse the damage. We could switch to cleaner fuels, heat our homes more efficiently, lobby government for legislation restricting emissions, consume in a less irresponsible way, and so on. There are some surprising bits about how certain people we tend to think of as the real villains have taken steps down this road already.

* We'd better do it now or our children, and theirs, will ask what the hell we were playing at.

* Then there's the really good bit where you see the tiny world.

* It ends with credits over a not-very-good song about making a change, but by then the message is well and truly across.

I thought about the film a lot over the next few days. As luck would have it, just a couple of days after seeing it, I had to venture into nature. I had a gig in Aberystwyth, which meant either about a six-hour train trip or a car journey which would most likely take even longer, not least because I can't drive a car.

The train route is via Birmingham New Street; you change there and get a train that goes across the border around Shrewsbury and just keeps going west through stations with more and more consonants. This means you see some of the worst and some of the best of Britain in one journey. Not far outside Wolverhampton, we passed a huge landfill full of discarded car parts, used-up fuel canisters, tyres, fragments of cardboard boxes lying like amputated limbs on disused pallets, and graffiti offering an insight into what Darren's mum apparently gets up to. I've been past this dump many times on the train: it's one of the most depressing sights for miles around, and in the West Midlands, that really is saying something. Naturally, with *An Inconvenient Truth* still lodged in my brain like a great big blanket of greenhouse gas, I looked at this massive repository of wasted materials with a feeling of deflation and guilt that was quite new to me.

Then, as we got further into Wales and the hilly landscape began to swallow us up, I experienced at least a pale version of the awe of nature which motivates Gore. The sky was full of clouds and as the sun tried to break through, there was a bright, almost solid-looking shaft of light a bit like a picture of God on the cover of a book published in the seventies. For a few moments, half of the hillside in front of us was bathed in golden light, the other half in darkness. I gazed at it for a while and could almost imagine what it would be like to be the only person left in the world. Then, a man came down the aisle with a refreshment trolley, and hot on his heels a gang of eight teenage girls in black hoodies who were returning from a Linkin Park gig in Birmingham the previous night, and my moment of Wordsworthian communion with the earth was cut short in a chorus of ringtones.

Later on, after the gig, as I stood in the teeth of a bitter wind looking over the Irish Sea by night, with the sand crunching beneath my feet, it occurred to me that there was a big gap in my psyche where appreciation of our planet should be. As we'll see shortly, I've always been something of a city-dweller. I was never moved by Wordsworth's poems about a one-on-one relationship with nature; in fact, I found a lot of his poems very stuffy and pretentious, and said so in my 'A' Level exam – a blow from which the poet's reputation has never really recovered. My favourite holidays as a kid were the ones where we went to exciting, garish, carbon-voracious metropolises like New York rather than the one where we went to West Wales: it rained every day, and we locked ourselves out of the cottage and had to break in. Even now, I'd always rather look at the skyline of a great city by night than a mountain or something; I'm more emotionally affected by urban sprawl than by pretty nothingness. Most of the times I have been genuinely 'at one' with nature, like on honeymoon in Kenya, it's still been from the standpoint of a suburbanite, having a look at all the nice trees and rivers and things but knowing a warm room with a proper bed and a broadband connection is only a few days away.

This is quite an important point. Al Gore starts from the assumption that we all have a special place in the world where we feel a special harmony with the elements that make it up, and it's partly to that sense of harmony that he appeals. But I, and I suspect a lot of people, don't really have that special place. We didn't all grow up on a farm harvesting tobacco. For someone whose happiest outdoor times have been spent on patches of grass surrounded by nice, reassuring bits of city, like Hampstead Heath or the Downs in Bristol, it takes a bit more effort to appreciate what it is that we're talking about trying to save.

And there's the weather of course. It's hard to believe the planet is getting warmer when it's late February in Aberystwyth and it's dangerously cold even in your bed-and-breakfast, let alone in the great outdoors. We've all heard people make remarks about how they'd welcome a bit of global warming round our way. It may be a tired joke now (though that doesn't stop certain comedians) but it is true that it's much more difficult to appreciate the threat of a warmed climate when you live in a country where, eight months of the year, you can't go out without a jumper on.

But I was going to have to get past all this.

Home from Aberystwyth, I decided it was time to calculate my personal 'carbon footprint'. I would then make it my mission, over the rest of the year, to reduce this footprint by as much as I could. And maybe I would use what status I have as a comedian to try and encourage other people to do the same.

I used a government website called www.actonco2.direct.gov .uk. The name refers to the need to 'act on' the situation, rather than meaning that the problem of CO_2 is confined to Acton, in West London – an unlovely place, certainly, but not a worthy scapegoat for the whole planet's emissions. On this optimistic-looking website, which has cartoonish graphics of an everyday street to take the mind off the impending end of civilisation, you have to answer various questions about the electrical equipment you own, the journeys you make, the power plants you have constructed in China, and so on. You then get a nice colourful display of exactly how many tonnes of greenhouse gas you are personally responsible for spewing into the already overloaded atmosphere, and some suggestions as to what you might do about it.

I filled out the quiz with some trepidation. In the guilty aftermath of the film, a question like 'How often do you leave unused appliances on standby? VERY OFTEN/FAIRLY OFTEN/SOMETIMES/ NEVER' read like 'How often do you doom the next generation with your selfishness?' I was forced to answer between 'fairly' and 'very' often to a series of these questions, resisting the temptation to give answers which I suspected were the big points-scorers. Other parts of the quiz went equally badly. No, I don't have a microwave (we did, but Emily made me throw it away because I'd allowed it to become encrusted with the residue of baked beans, which she hates with almost psychopathic intensity). Yes, I do take flights to Europe just for a nice break sometimes. No, I do not use a green energy supplier, as we don't own our flat, and our landlady is a stern person with whom we avoid most conversations, including those which begin 'I'm thinking of making changes to the way your property is powered.' And no, 'biomass' does not play much of a part in my heating strategy for the flat, I'm afraid; in fact that is something of an understatement. If a huge ball of biomass rolled down the street after me I'm not sure I would recognise it.

FACTLET: Micro-wave of progress

Microwaves have a pretty bad press because they're synonymous in the imagination with the sort of dinners you cry over while you're eating them. However, they are far more efficient than conventional ovens, converting about 65 per cent of electricity into microwave power. Some people think they can poison you, but there is scant evidence for this and, more to the point, it is outside my jurisdiction, luckily. Do remember to switch the microwave off standby, though: a typical one uses more energy to power the digital clock than to heat your food.

However, I don't have a car, which meant I sauntered through a whole section of the quiz with a smug zero in my debit column. It's not really an environmental decision; it's just that, for someone as clumsy as me, learning to drive would be akin to a normal person learning to fly a spaceship. So I use public transport all the time. And since I'm often out, I can often go a whole week without consuming all that much electricity. But then we do sometimes leave the light on for the cat because he gets a bit twitchy in the dark. And to deter burglars because we were cleaned out while on honeymoon. Hmm.

The computer, like an electronic priest, calmly heard my confessions, crunched all the numbers together and came up with my results, in a best-of-three tournament against the rest of the nation. The game went like this:

CARBON-OFF:
MARK V. THE REST OF THE NATION

	MW EMISSIONS (tonnes of CO_2/year)	NATIONAL AVERAGE (tonnes of CO_2/year)
House	**2.21**	**2.0**
	Mark 0	**UK 1**

Commentary: A close first round ends in defeat for Watson and a morale-boosting victory for everyone else in the UK. Watson had hoped that living in a relatively small flat with just one other person (and a cat) would give him an advantage, but of course, this is all about emissions per capita, not per dwelling, and Watson's inefficiently lit and primitively heated abode inches him above the national average. He can't afford to lose either of the other two rounds.

Electrical	**0.4**	**0.68**
	Mark 1	**UK 1**

Commentary: Watson keeps his cool to secure the must-win second round and set up a tantalising finish to the competition. He had feared that his tendency to leave things plugged into the wall, where they sit all day wasting energy like a truant boy wasting an afternoon, would cost him dearly, but it turns out everyone in the UK is just as profligate. Phew, that's OK then. In the end the deciding factor was probably that Watson's evening job debars him from watching nearly all the good TV that's on, so he has *24* to thank for luring the rest of the country into the carbon trap. Which leads us on to the decider . . .

Travel	3.69	1.80
	Mark 1	UK 2

Commentary: . . . and here Watson's green pretensions collapse like a house of cards. Whatever energy he might conserve by working nights instead of sitting at home with the lights on, watching the TV and overfilling the kettle, the saving is made a mockery of by the enormous balloons of carbon his itinerant lifestyle locks into the atmosphere.

Oh sure, he might not drive a car, but his frequent flights up and down the country, his taste for weekend breaks in Rome, and occasional extravagances like that much-talked-about honeymoon in a drought-ridden area of Africa – not to mention his Anglo-Australian career – produce such emissions that if he were never to drink a cup of tea or watch *The Simpsons* again in his life, it wouldn't do any good. He could probably be one of those people who sit in trees and stop motorways from being built, and it still wouldn't counteract the damage he does every time he hears the words 'please pay attention to this safety video, even if you are a frequent flyer'.

Total	6.3	4.48

GAME, SET AND MATCH TO EVERYONE ELSE IN THE COUNTRY BUT MARK

Commentary: And so a heavy defeat for Watson and a chastening measure of his crapness at the environment. His catastrophic performance in the travel round leaves him with an ugly tally of more than six tonnes of CO_2, which, if you could see them through a telescope, probably spell out 'MARK WATSON' in ominous dark clouds.

This means, if you are reading this as a member of the British public, you have a far better than even-money chance of being less crap at the environment than Watson, certainly as of February 2007. (If you're reading this in Australia, the chances are your carbon emissions are higher and you might even be worse than Watson, but you're so used to victories that you will probably take this with good humour and gain a devastating revenge in the next contest.)

Over 6 tonnes. How can I get a feel for how much that actually is, coming as I do from a generation that mostly doesn't know how many kilograms equate one stone? A male African elephant weighs about five tonnes apparently, so my average annual emissions can be seen as considerably in excess of an elephant's worth of gas. This is a hell of a lot – as I can verify, having, of course, seen an elephant close up while indulging my Western lust for harmful travel; if only I'd known about carbon emissions a year sooner, I could have stopped seeing it as an animal and appreciated it instead as a carbon receptacle. Perhaps there is a case for carbon emissions to be measured in 'elephantfuls'.

In both the USA and Australia, there's been an series of adverts –
which you can watch online at www.climateprotect.org – in which
black balloons, each representing a couple of ounces of CO_2,
squeeze out of electrical appliances in an average home and
cluster in black clouds above the house. The 'average home'
tosses out about two hundred thousand of these black balloons
every year, says a sober voice, and the commercial closes with a
ghastly plume of balloons blacking out the sky above the homely
street. This sends such an arresting message that Gore tried to
show it to us during the course, which led to a tense few moments
as he fumbled around on his laptop, whose operating system was
being projected onto the big screen, and as he typed 'black
balloons' into a search facility we gained the strange insight that
he has a song by the Black Eyed Peas on his computer.

I don't even like normal balloons very much – I'm constantly at
a pitch of tension waiting for them to burst, and I hate things like
balloon modelling where people tweak them into the shape of
dogs with that horrendous screechy noise. I also hate the trick
uncles do at parties where they rub balloons on your hair and then
make them stick to the wall and it's to do with static electricity or
some such nonsense. The image, therefore, of a couple of hundred
thousand balloons waiting to go bang every time I came out of the
house, purely because I'd left my phone charger in the wall or my
TV on standby or gone round the world too much, did an excellent
job of putting me on edge.

But what was I actually going to do?

Firstly, I resolved, I would out myself as being crap at the
environment and begin an organisation with that name to attract
similarly incompetent but willing people to my little crusade.
Actually, my original choice was the harsher-sounding Shit At
The Environment, but I didn't want to scare off the sort of people
who dislike what my dad might call 'industrial language', and also

replacing 'shit' with 'crap' resulted in the more elegant acronym CATE. As well as making my organisation sound like a nice girl you might like to get to know, it also raised the tantalising possibility of celebrity endorsement from Cate Blanchett, a public relations coup which no other green organisation was likely to match, at least until the rise of a celebrity called Todd Greenpeace or Samantha Climatecrisis. Having established a MySpace page and other 'web presences' for this organisation, I would set about trying to attract the attention of other crap people, and we would strive together to do something to counteract our crapness.

It was with this aim in mind that I wrote the following blog on the last weekend of February and put it on my web page.

I've decided to sort out the environment.

At the moment, everyone's banging on about the environment. You can't pick up a paper without reading about ice shelves melting, the earth's atmosphere warming up to disastrous levels, entire nations having to be re-homed, and so on. It's really depressing: especially if, like me, you're Crap At The Environment.

The habits of the huge group of people who are, like me, Crap At The Environment can be summarised in some, or all, of the following ways:

- Never being absolutely 100 per cent sure whether to believe environmental campaigners, even really famous ones like Al Gore who have lots of impressive slides, because there are always sceptics saying things like 'no no, it's just liberal propaganda designed to hurt the Bush administration, big business, etc.'; 'no, humans have little or nothing to do with climate change, the planet has its own 10,000-year heating/

cooling cycle'; 'oh, greens are all just hysterical scaremongers who should get proper clothes'.

– Half-understanding the scientific side of it but not confidently enough to fully grasp the scale of the problems; and lacking the imaginative capacities to engage with the idea of climate change because Britain is mostly still quite cold and shitty most of the time.

– Not being sure what an individual can actually do anyway; half-heartedly doing a bit of recycling and going to the bottle bank while being uncomfortably aware that there are much bigger things which you Could Do But Aren't; therefore, after a while, not even having the heart to do the small things.

– Feeling instinctively that, whatever you do, it's absolutely futile, because the world's most powerful economies can do more damage to the earth in a minute than you could erase on your own in a lifetime.

– Being moved by the obvious argument that we have a clear obligation to safeguard our beautiful planet for our children's children and so on, and yet somehow, when it comes down to it, not being able to resist going to Prague on a cheap energy-guzzling flight because it's really fun.

– Above all, finding the whole topic of the environment disheartening, doom-laden and largely monopolised by grim-faced people with statistics, or groups with placards doing unimpressive protests outside Parliament. Hence, preferring to think about other, more immediate and manageable things such as the FA Cup. In a situation where the topic of the environment is unavoidable, forced to sing

'la-la-la' mentally to oneself as others solemnly discuss
Kyoto.

So.

I've been talking to some people who are going to help me set
up a kind of project where someone like me, a comedian/writer
who's Crap At The Environment, explores the issues,
experiments with changing his life for the better, and attempts
to inspire other Crap At The Environment People (CATEs) to do
the same.

It will start as a daily or weekly blog here on MySpace and the
'spaces' of a few dedicated others (see below). And it will aim to
develop – hopefully – into a word-of-mouth campaign with
things like special themed comedy shows, fun-having, madcap
stunts, and so forth.

If you've ever been to one of the 24/36-hour shows I
sometimes do in Edinburgh, the idea is to try something which
is, in spirit, slightly like that, i.e. a tiny little community that
manages, in its own way, to affect the real community a bit –
but over a year rather than a single day, and with bigger goals
than merely dicking around for an incredibly long time.

But the key thing is, it has to be fun. Most attempts at 'green'
initiatives on a massive scale fail, not just because of the
complexity of the issues – after all, people aren't idiots, or at
least 75 per cent of them aren't – more because appeals to
action are always presented in terms of negatives. Give up this.
Don't do that. If you keep using plastic bags you may as well be
a war criminal. And so on. Whereas, I've got no scientific
credibility at all and absolutely no moral high ground to speak
from, and I really only read the papers to provide me with

material for jokes, and because of the sport section. So, in short, I'm hoping my massive unsuitability to be an environmental crusader might make me exactly what the environment needs.

And on the question of whether one person, or even one person backed by an energetic group, can actually make any difference to the planet's immense problems, my answer is: no, quite possibly not, but as a rule it's better to try things and then afterwards say 'well, that was over-ambitious' than never try at all. And also, it will be fun. Remember? I was talking about that just the other paragraph.

Just to mention one more time, what I've got in mind is fun; plus if we do save the planet, it will look pretty smart on all our CVs.

I posted this on a Friday afternoon at about 4pm. The first enthusiastic email came little more than ten minutes later, from someone I sort-of-knew called Sarah, who, unlike me, had a history of trying to do good – she used to spend her weekends in a cage outside Bristol Zoo, a protest which narrowly failed to force that institution out of business – but, like me, didn't really know what to do about the planet. Her blogs – starting below – will pop up occasionally to give you a different, often better-informed, view of events.

By teatime, I had had quite a lot of responses. People were offering me help, saying it was great that I'd decided to set a positive example, confessing that they too were Crap At The Environment and they were looking forward to joining me in whatever ecological crusade I had in mind.

I didn't know what the hell I had in mind.

But I was buoyed up by people's initial enthusiasm. It had confirmed my belief that this feeling of concern, but helplessness, was shared by the man on the street, and that that man or woman was keen to do something about it – in spite of Sid Vicious's famous assertion 'I've met the man in the street, and he's a c**t.' I wanted to believe that, in spite of my cynical instincts, it was possible for small people's small actions to make a decent-sized difference. I was confident, as I said in my blog, that my total lack of credentials wouldn't hinder me from being an environmental mentor, provided my charges were all equally crap, and anyway flawed activism is better than apathy, isn't it? And I wasn't particularly bothered about looking silly or compromising my social standing; at least one of those things is more or less in my job description. I mean, I used to play Radiohead at parties all the time.

Towards the end of February, I was due to fly from Gatwick to Glasgow Prestwick for a show in Kilmarnock. About three days beforehand, it dawned me that perhaps I could go by train instead. I checked out the price; it would almost have been cheaper to establish a new settlement in Scotland and announce that the gig would take place there instead. Of course, the £120 or so would be a pretty good investment if it was the difference between sea levels staying constant and rising to the stage where they could overwhelm our flat, but I fobbed myself off with the excuses that had always sustained me in the past: well, the plane's going to take off whether you're on it or not, some people say high-speed trains are just as bad as planes, I'm too tired to think about this, etc.

On the plane itself, though, I did begin to experience a repeat of the faint but definite guilt that had hit me during *An Inconvenient Truth*. The whole process was markedly inefficient. The plane was so far short of even being half-full that the crew could hardly get through the here's-how-you-fasten-your-seatbelt rigmarole without giggling and exchanging funny looks. In a reversal of normal roles, I almost wanted to tell *them* to give the safety announcements their full attention: 'Look, chaps, I know there's not many of us but we'll be just as dead if this thing *does* crash.' Then, after an extremely short time in the air, during which I bought a farcically over-packaged bag of Maltesers, we were deposited in the fancifully named Glasgow Prestwick airport – which is so far from Glasgow itself that it's a bit like having an airport called London White Cliffs of Dover – so that an 'airport shuttle' could drag us twenty-nine miles to our actual destination.

So with Gore's hard eyes boring down on my brain, I passed up the option of a taxi to the gig and walked from my hotel instead. Then, later that night, rather than pump up the heating to the level I'd have liked on a bitter night, I left it about a third of the way up the dial. Of course, this, and the short walk I'd made instead of jumping in a cab, were actions too small to make a discernible difference to my carbon footprint, but they were a start. They'd made a discernible difference to my mood, though; I was cold and grumpy. If I was going to get Good At The Environment, I would need to find ways to make it a bit more enjoyable than this.

Back in London, the next time I was in Tesco I took the opportunity to resume the bag-related battle of wills with Kevin. Choosing an 'eco-friendly' washing-up liquid, a British apple rather than one flown in from New Zealand and an Australian wine (not much progress on the wine front yet), I had my cry of 'I don't need a bag' ready almost before Kevin had uttered his toneless 'next customer please'. At my zealous pre-emptive strike, Kevin's face twisted into what was almost a sarcastic grin, but a lack of energy prevented his bottom lip from making the necessary contortion. I seized my purchases and went on my way. It was one-all in the bag game and I had struck my first tiny blow for the environment.

On its own this sort of gesture was pretty much futile, of course, and I sensed that, for a while, the same feeling of futility would hang around a lot of what I did. But this didn't concern me too greatly. Lots of things we do in life are pretty much futile; to take just a few examples: watching the Eurovision Song Contest; entering the Lottery; spending most of your childhood learning to play the recorder; getting to the quarter-finals of Wimbledon. The futility doesn't automatically mean it's not worth doing (except in the case of the recorder, which I think we can now almost definitely say was a waste of time). It's a better moral position to be optimistic. Better to be the band playing uplifting ditties on the sinking *Titanic* than the grumpy old man rolling up his trousers as water coursed onto the deck and muttering: 'Told you. Holidays always end up with people dead.'

END OF FEBRUARY REPORT CARD

Credit: Came to terms with own crapness; began campaign to change; walked instead of taking cab; rejected plastic bag after tense stand-off.

Debit: Took short-haul flight; still leaving things on standby; still largely ignorant of most areas of subject.

Savings: (compared with February 2006) Minimal.

Status: Crap At The Environment.

SARAH'S BLOG: INTRODUCTION

Hello. My name is Sarah. Like Mark, I am a left-handed, 28-year-old Aquarian from the West Country. We're practically the same person – in fact, I sometimes think Mark is the man I would be if I'd worked harder, gone to Cambridge, had the love of a good wife and indeed been born a man.

I first met Mark at the BBC in 2004, when a mutual producer friend of ours thought we'd make good writers for a new sitcom.

We got on well, although the project was as untenable as trying to write a light-hearted 8.30 p.m. BBC1 sitcom about Goebbels, and never got off the ground. Mark went off to be a stand-up comedian, author, and panel game pundit, while I got a job writing challenging quizzes about handbags for a glossy fashion magazine. We sort of stayed in touch, in an Internetty kind of way, mainly through Facebook updates ('Mark is having his tea,' I'd think, 'that's nice') and the odd game of online Scrabble.

One day, though, I was sitting at my nice fashionable desk in my nice fashionable office, procrastinating on the Internet before a tough afternoon of trend-setting, when I got an email from Mark saying he'd decided to save the world, and did I want in? 'These trends will have to set themselves, there's a planet to save!' I thought, and fired off an email along the lines of 'hey I'm crap too! How can I help?'

I've always suffered from a gnawing sense of guilt at the back of my soul about the environment – but it seemed to be something that was so easy to get wrong. So much information seems to be conflicting. One time I spent a whole day tied up in knots because I read that Alan Bennett, one of my all-time heroes, was having a fund-raising event to STOP a wind farm being built near his home. Now, like all right-thinking people, I love Alan Bennett. But I'd always thought that wind farms were a great idea, environmentally. Why would the lovely Alan Bennett not like them? Did he have some insider knowledge on the inefficiency of renewable energy, or was it a poncy aesthetic thing about ruining his view?

These sorts of unanswered questions are always rearing up if you take even a casual interest in the planet. I remember being gobsmacked when someone told me that it's actually better for the environment to run a dishwasher (full, on an eco-setting) than it is to do normal washing up. This just doesn't sound right to me. It's a moot point, as I don't even have a dishwasher, but am I supposed to feel guilty about *that* now?

It's often seemed to me that to be truly interested in the environment – rather than someone who blithely skims the green section in the *Guardian* and thinks they're good for buying organic teabags – you have to do hours and hours of homework. Washing up, going to the toilet, buying a hat, it's all an eco-minefield, and one I've tended to see as a nice idea in theory but too complicated for my small, distractable brain, like chess or *Question Time*.

But here I'm being offered a free pass – it doesn't matter (at first) if I get things wrong, or ask stupid questions, as long as I'm trying. Everyone on the CATE site is saying the same thing, 'I'm crap. Is that okay? Will someone shout at me if I don't know the answer? No, phew, then I'm in.'

The first thing I've done is to work out my carbon footprint, using the same government website as Mark. I was fairly confident here, as living in London makes it quite easy to live greenly, because it's so bloody expensive that it's not really a lifestyle choice, more necessity. Public transport is a way of life, plus most boroughs have a pink bag recycling scheme. I live alone in a one-bedroom flat, which is quite a selfish waste of electricity and heating, but it means I can't afford to go on holiday for the rest of my life, so it kind of evens out.

So I was quite smug when it came to ticking all the boxes on the website – I've been abroad twice in five years, both times for work; I cycle whenever possible; I recycle; I have a Yorkshire-ish mother who would walk around the house flipping off lights with a cry of 'What is this, Wembley Stadium?' long before anyone knew what a carbon emission was, so I'm naturally careful about wasting electricity. My total, then, is pleasingly low, a mere 2.73 tonnes a year – and while this doesn't exactly paint me as the fun-time gadabout I'd always thought myself, it does mean that ostensibly I am doing a lot better at the environment than the national average (and a lot better than Mark – in your face, Watson).

What I didn't take into account, though, was all the other stuff besides leccy and gas that I was consume. Clothes, DVDs, music, food, the trappings of being a semi-hip twenty-something living in the big city.

Plus, there's my job, which is basically telling people to buy stuff. I really want to be less CATE and more GATE, but I hate the idea that I could technically be accused of gross hypocrisy, along the lines of 'How can you say you want to be better at the environment when it's your job to get people to buy clothes and handbags they don't even need by decreeing they're "trendy"?' and I'll have to say 'Don't know sir, sorry sir.' Luckily this kind of nagging in your head can easily be drowned out by the acquisition of a shiny new pair of shoes, at least for a little bit.

So Mark has suggested I start simple, and just write a blog about how to dress stylishly without damaging the planet. I swallowed something hard and jagged and realised I was going to have to make some sacrifices. Gulp.

MARCH

Over the next couple of weeks I received a considerable amount of support for CATE, the brave initiative I had launched to prevent the world from overheating. Indeed, as Emily sardonically pointed out, most of the work I did on the CATE MySpace page in the first couple of weeks was to reply to emails from people congratulating me on its existence.

It seemed I had struck a chord by outing myself as crap. Everyone knows how much British people dislike ambition, achievement and energy in others – that is one of the reasons we are wary of Australians – and would rather back a cheerful, probably doomed underdog than someone who, say, actually knew something about the environment. Actually, the Australians are probably just as familiar with the phenomenon, as it was they who coined the phrase 'tall poppy syndrome' to describe the resentment of people who seek to tower over others in society. By truthfully making myself out to be quite a small poppy, really just a cardboard one used on Remembrance Day, I had garnered a bit of initial goodwill. But unless I actually started doing something useful, and more to the point at least tried to persuade other people to do something too, even the tallest of poppies would be underwater before too long.

Not everyone who got in touch was as crap as me. One, Robert, wrote that, as someone who already recycled most of his household waste, he was torn between getting involved with CATE and 'letting things slide until the end of the world so I can use my survival skills to be one of the handful of humans still populating the earth'. A more community-spirited response came from a girl called Sian. She was the sort of person I would have been unlikely to meet even a few weeks before: she lived in a complex of eco-friendly flats in Manchester, had a picture of some nice trees on her webpage, and had a better than even chance of going to an allotment at some point in her lifetime. Sian told me she'd begun a petition suggesting that rather than renewing Trident, the defence programme which invests a staggering amount in having nuclear missiles ready off the West Coast of Scotland, the government should be spending their money on developing sustainable energy. Although she did not point this out herself, she had mounted this campaign not, like me, as a knee-jerk reaction to a scary film, but because she was the sort of person who not only bothered to apprise herself of current affairs, but was ready to try and affect them. As we have heard, this mentality had only just stopped being alien to me and I hoped I might catch some of it off her.

Sian asked me to bring this petition to the attention of members of CATE, who, at this early stage, already numbered 500. Admittedly, with it being MySpace, some of these new recruits were unlikely to join in much beyond 'adding' us as a 'friend', but I had done at least basic screening on those who signed up, to filter out as many as possible of the goth bands, lunatics and people offering 'INCREDIBLE COCK, SHE WILL LOVE IT' who make up a vast sector of the MySpace universe. I thought this would be a nice first test of my new online community in action, and it wouldn't be a bad thing to do as a small first step along my new road of activism in the green-fuel-powered car of my newly found social conscience. I asked the people of CATE to sign the petition if they felt like it, stressing that I was not planning to make this into a *Fight Club*-style cult and manipulate them into a taskforce to hit each other and trash Starbucks. More than fifty people did it almost immediately. It is unlikely Tony Blair was alarmed enough by this to discuss with Cherie ('Why do you keep tossing and turning?' 'I've been petitioned again, darling'), but it was a tiny contribution to a very large struggle and that, of course, was a good description of what I was trying to do here.

Good.

That weekend, though, there was a protest against Trident in London. I didn't join in – though I'd had a sarcastic text message from a friend asking why I wasn't there, since I was 'into changing the world these days, apparently' – but since I was gigging in Central London, I did get the chance to watch it in action. It was certainly a good-sized rally, compared with those forlorn people on the airport runway, but in some ways it was a rather depressing affair. There were people with banners about legalising cannabis; people with T-shirts with Tony Blair's name changed to 'Tony B. Liar' (a play on words which stopped being funny in 1997, only eight minutes after it began being funny); and people chanting things you couldn't hear. To the onlooker it had the appearance of a gathering of slightly, but not very, angry people who had each been given a different thing to protest about. My taxi driver that night (yes, I know, but it was still early days) lamented having had his day disrupted by 'this save the whales nonsense or whatever it was'. I said it was Trident actually. He said 'oh you're into all this as well, are you?' Hesitantly, like a semi-committed Christian trying to chat to Richard Dawkins, I began talking about the environment. He muttered for a bit, then it went quiet and I ended up giving him a bigger-than-warranted tip because of some sort of subconscious desire to show that I wasn't one of these anti-capitalists.

I still felt instinctively opposed to the renewal of Trident, but witnessing the protest had, if anything, made my sympathies drift towards those who thought it was a nice plan for us to have fifty weapons of mass destruction lined up around our shores. There must be something I could learn from this. I got home feeling that perhaps I should be a bit more careful about aligning CATE with bigger causes that could spill over. A couple of people had left messages on the website saying the same thing. It was my first lesson in benevolent dictatorship and I responded to it with what had become my answer to all life's challenges: I wrote a blog.

. . . The question is, how do you stand up for something you believe in without having your name attached to other 'good causes' you don't agree with?

This ties in with one of the major reasons behind CATE which is, basically, that smallish groups are consistently much better at getting things done than bigger ones. As soon as you have a big group organising a protest march, you'll attract loads of people who are actually just into the idea of protesting about things. At any march like the anti-Trident one on Saturday, you'll find not just anti-nuclear demonstrators, but also 'TROOPS OUT' people, people who want 'THE TRUTH ABOUT 9/11' which they think is a 'GOVERNMENT CONSPIRACY', people who want to legalise cannabis and walk about puffing 'defiantly' on a spliff, people who want the Government to give way to a Marxist coalition, people who think we should concentrate on freeing political prisoners, and people who just want to kick a policeman's helmet around and daub paint on Winston Churchill's statue or something.

Some of these might well be excellent causes but you can't protest about eighteen things at once. If you do, it becomes very easy for the authorities to say 'aha, there are those funny people who do a protest march every three weeks'. Any time a load of people march through Central London you can see the police grinning at each other thinking 'ah, I remember that guy with the headscarf from last time'. This means, however well-intentioned, large-scale demonstrations in this country are destined not to make a great impact. Even the celebrated 'Don't Attack Iraq' march of 2003 was bedevilled by so many dozens of other interests that its central message was fatally diluted.

Now I'm not demeaning any attempt to do good by marching or protesting or anything, and I'm not taking a *Daily Mail*-type 'oh these awful layabouts with their protests, why don't they go down a mine' standpoint. But I think there's a need for small groups who seek alternative ways to improve the status quo. Positive actions, of the kind we are going to do with CATE, are harder for society to ignore than more conventional protests. And they don't run such a great risk of being hijacked by people who largely go on marches because it's a good thing to do on a Saturday.

Sorry if I sound a bit preachy today. It's a year to the day since we came home from honeymoon to find our house burgled. Bloody criminal underworld. I'm going to start a march.

These were all fine words but anyone can sit in an inefficiently heated flat talking about 'positive action', and many do. I had to start working out how I was going to tackle my own, shameful, 6.3 tonne CO_2 count; a count which, if anything, was likely to rise this year, as I had more journeys scheduled than ever before and I would probably have slightly more money to buy electrical goods. Various people who'd read my blog suggested that the figure was a bit ungenerous, because many of the journeys I'd made, which bloated that 'travel' carbon section and lost me the decisive third round of the emission-off against the rest of the UK, were business trips, if you call comedy a business. In particular, my environmentally ruinous shuttling between Australia and the UK could easily be taken off the record (these kind people argued) because it was pure professionalism that made me spend a part of my year at festivals Down Under; it was pure good fortune that Australia was quite a lot like Paradise. I looked at the figures and had a brief wrestle with my conscience, which ended with my conscience dumping me on the canvas with my arm twisted behind my back. The idea that 'work'-induced global warming was somehow less of a problem than holiday damage was obviously absurd. If floods overwhelmed New York City in thirty years it would be very little consolation to my children if I said, 'but you see, in 2007 Daddy played the Adelaide Fringe with Ardal O'Hanlon. Well you *should* know who he is.' If I chose to make my living by endless dashing around the globe, then – unavoidable as this dashing might be – I had to put my hands up and take the rap. It wasn't as if anyone had forced me to be a comedian. It's not the sort of job where you see a feature on *Panorama* telling you the country is desperately short of funny men and faces a bleak future with millions starved of frivolous observations on life.

This said, of course, it was going to be nearly impossible for me to bin these flights, which would, again, be by far the biggest producer of greenhouse gas in my year. I was due to leave for an extensive tour of Australia the day after my UK tour finished, in about three weeks' time. If I were to leave now on a boat I would be lucky to get there in time to fulfil even a quarter of my run. Australians pride themselves on being laid-back but, like people elsewhere in the world, they like a show to take place if they've bought a ticket for it. Nope, I was still going to have to make an enormous flight and, depending on how things went, quite possibly another one later in the year.

And there was more discouragement as I started to think properly about what it would mean to reduce my emissions. Because of the archaic wiring of our house, we shared our electricity with our next-door neighbour, so to change supplier I would have get his permission and the landlady's. This wasn't a huge ask, but it was going to mean hassle, and my life already contained plenty of hassle. Also, most of the light bulbs in our house were those little ones sunk into the ceiling, which can't be replaced by more efficient bulbs because they're the wrong shape, and which waste a large amount of energy lighting and heating up, almost exclusively, a patch of floor about the size of a 20p piece directly below them.

Then there was the simple but serious problem of my unbelievable incompetence, a theme which we shall be forced to return to periodically through this book. For example, and here we come back to one of the great disgraces of my twenty-seven years, I had never learned to ride a bike. That's right. This iconic skill of the environmental movement, mastered by most people about the same time as they learn to walk or play Connect 4, had eluded me all my life. Admittedly I hadn't literally been trying *all* my life; to be accurate I gave it a go when I was eight, failed, and realised, to quote Homer Simpson, 'if something's hard to do, it's not worth doing'. About fifteen years later I had a token go at it again, under the tutelage of my patient wife (then girlfriend) who made it her mission to teach me on a quiet road near her parents' house in rural Essex. But again, no joy; at one point I nearly, very nearly, got both my feet off the ground at the same time but had to stop because I was about to hit a tree. I say 'about to hit it' – it was actually nearly twenty yards away but I am prone to panicking and have virtually no spatial awareness. Neither of these quirks lends itself well to bike-riding. On this occasion I was discouraged even further by a birdwatcher who chuckled at my poor efforts before going merrily on his way, binoculars in hand. In general if a birdwatcher finds your behaviour ridiculous, your credibility is dangerously low.

Now I was going to have to steel myself for a third attempt to master this task, seemingly second nature to almost everyone else in the world, yet for me as arcane and intractable as snake-charming. But even if I could finally conquer my bike-itis, it wasn't going to happen any time soon. So the 'ride a bike instead of taking a car' adverts which had started to spring up all over London were – to me – not so much a message of hope as a jeering reminder of my inadequacy. To me, the phrase 'It's like riding a bicycle' doesn't mean 'You never forget how to do it' but 'It is a humiliating ordeal and your dad wonders why he wasted money on a bike.'

And this incompetence made many other green activities much harder for me than they would be for most budding carbon-cutters. To some people I know, 'grow some of your own food' sounds like an exciting challenge to re-connect with the earth; to me it sounds like a tedious and difficult endeavour to produce what would probably be about two carrots in six months, and moreover, disappointingly un-orange carrots at that, because I'm so used to supermarket-processed fruit and vegetables that the sight of home-grown food is always something of a shock. Composting, gardening, planting trees, the thought of all these rural activities made me wish for a brightly lit room in the city and a nice big computer screen with perhaps, at most, a screen-saver with a bit of nature on it. I couldn't imagine, any time between here and a famine brought on by nuclear winter, attempting to produce more than a pathetically meagre proportion of my own food.

Plus, no sooner had I proudly announced that I was going to be principled and take responsibility for my business as well as personal flights, than it was brought to my attention that, in fact, my actual carbon emissions were probably somewhat *higher* than I had credited (or debited) myself with.

A man called Rick, who, although he didn't say it, was quite obviously – like Sian – Good At The Environment (GATE), sent me a very polite email to point out that the carbon calculator I'd used gave a rather simplistic analysis of my lifestyle. Among other things, it didn't factor in my share of the energy which had been used to manufacture the dozens of goods with which I, as a typical Westerner, surrounded myself compulsively. For example, if I bought food or wine that had been carted halfway across the world just so that Nigella Lawson could publish, in January, a recipe which required a pawpaw to be placed atop a kangaroo meringue, I was partly responsible for a transaction which wasted a vast amount of energy, and – by extension – for supporting an industry which pulled off thousands of these transactions every day. If I bought ludicrously over-packaged products (which I did), threw them away again with as little regard for recycling as I have for actual cycling, if I patronised restaurant chains that had paid for massive deforestation, and so on, then my 'theoretical carbon footprint' was a lot bigger.

This was depressing. I loved eating meat; the vague knowledge that the 'meat industry' caused a surprising amount of CO_2 emissions was for me overwhelmed by the counter-argument that sausages are tremendous. I liked wine from California and Australia and other countries which had enough sunshine to actually grow grapes. I much preferred baths to showers. And so on.

The more I analysed my lifestyle, the less ambitious I felt about possible carbon savings.

Still, there were things I definitely *could* do, among them:

* Replacing as many of my flights as I could with train or bus journeys;

* Offsetting the remainder of journeys so that my travelling was 'carbon neutral';

* Walking or using public transport instead of making short car journeys;

* Switching electrical appliances off when they weren't being used;

* Also, using them less often, by discovering the pleasures of outdoor life;

* Trying not to waste water;

* Refusing to use plastic bags, especially when offered them by Kevin.

That would be a good start on a personal level. In the meantime I would advertise on the CATE site for 'officers' who would each take responsibility for one of these areas of small-time environmental action, and set challenges which we would all do together. And I announced that during the Edinburgh Festival, in August, I would do a 24-hour show on the (broad) subject of the environment.

Very quickly, little sister-sites of CATE started shooting up like I imagined plants did, if you were into that sort of thing. Quite excitingly, various people quickly set up their own initiatives 'inspired by' mine. One of the most exciting was dreamed up by a friend of mine, Nicola, who announced a project called Pimp My Plant Pot with the aim of encouraging CATE people to get into gardening. (In case you are behind the lingo of the times, you should note that to 'pimp' something these days means to make it look nice. It was popularised by the mind-numbing TV show *Pimp My Ride*. According to online slang dictionaries it can also be used as an adjective: as in for example 'that is a pimp car', or 'that is a pimp Botticelli you have hanging in your bathroom'. You should also note that no one says 'lingo' any more.) Participants in Nicola's scheme just had to send her their name and address and she would send them a plant – with instructions – and a pot, which they could decorate before putting pictures up on the site as an inspiration to others. There were in excess of seventy volunteers in the first week, and soon I began to have trouble getting hold of Nicola other than texts that said 'POSTING PLANTS x'.

All this was demonstrating that, if a lot of people of my generation were Crap At The Environment, they were not at all Crap At Organising Themselves Into Online Groups (luckily, as that would be a much tougher acronym). But I was so busy trying to marshal all this promising activity into a coherent group, I had hardly managed to do anything myself. It was time to take my first proper personal carbon-busting step.

The most obvious and pressing target was my tour schedule. I was meant to be flying from Bristol to Glasgow for gigs in Scotland, then from Glasgow back down to London, before getting on the plane to Adelaide, which I would leave on a plane bound for Melbourne two weeks thereafter. And thanks to a quirk of scheduling I was meant to go out to Japan for a week of gigs just a couple of weeks after returning to the Northern Hemisphere (after I'd flown to Kilkenny to do the festival there). These flights were all booked and it would cost me money and perhaps cost other people inconvenience to change them, but it suddenly felt like if I flew that many times in the space of a month, I might as well round off my trip by nipping down from Australia to the Antarctic and personally slicing a huge chunk off an ice shelf.

For a start, I could scrub the internal flights. It would mean a six-hour train journey from Bristol to Scotland and then a seven-hour trek on the sleeper train back to London to take the flight to Australia that evening. This was an unappetising prospect, but www.actonc02.gov.uk had assured me it was one of the best ways I could make a quick difference to my carbon footprint. Actually, they advised that 'buses and coaches are even better' but I wasn't a complete lunatic. I booked train tickets.

As for Adelaide to Melbourne, I would sort that out when I got there. I hadn't been to Adelaide before so I wasn't sure how long it would take on the train, but how long could an interstate journey across one of the world's most massive countries possibly take?

I've been something of a critic of the rail network, in my career and, tediously for my wife, in my actual life too. Because of the amount of travelling my job requires, I feel I've spent around a quarter of this decade waiting on a platform for a delayed train, very often with what David Cameron might describe as 'youths' mooching about threateningly on the platform. Or, sitting stationary on the train in the middle of a tunnel, for so long, and with so little explanation, that you start to think perhaps you have in fact arrived: 'Well, maybe this formless darkness *is* King's Lynn.' Or being frustrated by the endlessly confusing pricing structures whereby a ticket is valid on the 5.09 train but you can more or less be hanged for using it at 5.11; or by the fact that after having paid seventy quid because it's 'peak hours' between three and seven, you quite often don't get a seat at all. Try persuading some people who've been squashed together for three hours in the pungent vestibule of a Virgin London-Newcastle 'express', listening to each other's repetitive mobile phone conversations and catching each other's germs, that it would be 'good for the planet if more people travelled by train'.

Because of these irritants, and their effect upon my blood pressure, I had been cutting back on my train use for the past couple of years, in favour of hitching lifts with other comedians, or flying. Now it was time to go back the other way.

The Bristol-Glasgow journey was actually to get me to Stirling, where I was playing that night; if I'd stuck to the plan and got the plane like a normal person, I would have been picked up and driven to the gig. Now that I was getting the train, I might as well change trains and get a second train straight to Stirling and cut out another little journey's worth of carbon. I felt buoyant at this prospect. On the other hand, rather than the 1 p.m. flight time which was originally on my itinerary, I'd have to leave the house at 8.30 to catch the train; half past eight in the *actual morning*. When the alarm went off, I briefly cursed Al Gore.

Strangely, though – and there's no way of recording this without sounding sentimental – I noticed a very short way into the journey that I was in a good mood, something I scarcely ever am when taking flights. It helped that the train was very empty; it helped also that I was filled with a refreshing (and probably quite smug) sense of 'doing the right thing' which I couldn't remember having experienced since giving my seat up to an old man some months ago. After a couple of hours, there could no longer be any doubt about it: I was actually enjoying myself. It occurred to me that I had got so carried away complaining about trains over the past few years that I'd forgotten the many thoroughly enjoyable trips I had taken on the rails. It was nicer than flying. And yet so many flights were taken to places easily reachable by other means. I could see what they meant about how everyone could make a small difference.

I'd intended to pass the time by writing a blog on my 'sacrifice'. Such was my mood of almost aggressive good spirits that I decided to turn it into an evangelical sermon on the merits of train travel versus nasty, polluting planes.

CATE CHALLENGES: MARK MAKES A FUN SACRIFICE

I'm on the 9.29 train from Bristol to Glasgow. We'll arrive in Glasgow in just under six hours. After that, I have to change and get another train to (historic) Stirling, where my show is tonight. All in all, the trip will have taken me from breakfast until teatime.

I was meant to be undertaking this journey by air, but in the hope of beginning to lower my 'carbon footprint', and setting a captain's example to the CATE public by taking on my own challenge, I've vowed not to take another internal flight for the foreseeable future. Aviation is, famously, a large (and the fastest-growing) source of carbon emissions, and while some of it's essential, a lot of it clearly isn't. The two most popular destinations from Heathrow are Paris and Manchester: places you could reach by train just as quickly, but also, much more pleasantly.

But train travel has had a bad press recently, what with the fatality a fortnight ago on the same type of train I'm on now, and a much-publicised report in *Which?* Magazine, which seemed to show that it's cheaper on average to fly than to take to the rails (though this was pretty misleading, as I'll go on to discuss). Rail companies have done themselves few favours in the past decade, many of them running inefficient services at high prices and pissing off a lot of potential travellers.

Nonetheless, gliding through towns and countryside remains a nicer way to get around the country than hurtling through the sky at an ungodly speed. For this blog I've decided to do an A to Z of things I notice during this journey which make trains better than planes.

A is for ambulation. On trains, you can walk about and go about your business; you can hang out on your own in the vestibules, you can stretch your legs. It's healthier than being in a box in the sky, and psychologically better.

B is for budget. Speaking as someone who spends a lot of time scheming to save money on travel, it's something of a fallacy that 'these days it's cheaper to fly'. Sure, train travel *is* expensive if you're caught out by it, but book ahead and you can travel very cheaply, particularly with a railcard. Recently I went from London to Aberystwyth (nearly a week away) for fifteen quid. This Bristol-Glasgow trip is costing me £40, without a railcard – it could have been £25 if I'd got my act together. When an ITV News reporter says 'I paid £117 to go from London to Manchester!' he's deliberately travelling at peak time and buying the ticket about two minutes beforehand, for rhetorical effect. It's not really a fair representation. I mean even if you buy the day before, you can save money. Who actually just thinks 'ooh I'll get a train to Manchester' on the spur of the moment, at the busiest time of the day? An idiot, that's who.

I'm not denying that train travel can be maliciously expensive but it doesn't have to be, if you plan your life a little bit ahead. And after all, budget airlines are themselves only cheap if you plan ahead: try turning up at the airport on the day you want to fly and saying, 'So guys, where are these £5 flights I keep hearing about?'

C is for conversations. You get to overhear much more interesting chats on the train; people are more relaxed, and not as intent on blocking everything out. Just now I went to the buffet car and the two staff were looking out of the window wondering whether the train might be on fire, or whether they'd just never noticed how much smoke it produces normally. 'Well, no smoke without fire, they do say,' one of the women remarked quite seriously. It was fun to imagine that this was perhaps how the phrase was invented in the first place.

D is for dozing. Much easier to doze on a train, with the rocking-rolling motion, and without the periodical feeling that you're about to leave the sky at a tremendous velocity.

E is for eccentrics. There is a lady three seats down with an animal carrier of the sort you would put a cat or dog in. Every now and again she glances solicitously into it to check on the pet's welfare. I spent a bit of time trying to guess if it was a cat or dog, or something more exotic. But now, having looked, I'm pretty sure there is actually nothing in there at all.

F is for France. Come on, who doesn't like the idea of getting the train to France? 'I'm on the train. Next stop . . . France!' It's amazing. Just getting on at St Pancras and breezing straight into the centre of Paris. Compared with spending an hour and a half getting to Stansted, queuing in security for forty-five minutes, and eventually landing at an airport that's still a bus ride away from the actual Arc de Triomphe. And a horrible bus ride at that.

G is for geography. A shocking number of people don't have a clue about the layout of the country and if challenged to point to Leeds or Taunton or King's Lynn on a map, wouldn't even get close. It's always pissed me off that people in this country lampoon Americans for their ignorance of the wider world, yet frequently those same people consider Birmingham 'the North'. This is a regrettable thing because, for all its faults, one good thing about the UK is the distinct character of its towns and cities, the regional variations, the way you can see the whole country in a week but it would take a lifetime to etc. etc. All this is wasted if you just hop on a plane, disappear into the clouds and get out at the other end not even being 100 per cent sure which direction you flew in. See the country.

H is for hassle. Plane travel becomes more of a hassle more or less every day. The ever-escalating security programme means you can often wait an hour to get into a departure lounge these days, having taken your laptop out of your bag, put it in again, taken it out once more, forgotten it, panicked, gone back, and had to wait behind a man who's intent on getting to duty-free as quick as possible before jetting off on his skiing holiday. Add in the taking-your-shoes-off, the did-you-pack-this-yourself? ('nope, actually, thinking about it, a suspicious-looking man volunteered to do for me . . .'), the pointless rush for seats, and it's a stressful process indeed. Well worth putting up with if you're going to Australia, but if you're just nipping up to Manchester, why put yourself through all this, rather than just getting on a train (like I did a couple of hours ago) and getting off again?

I is for ice-cream. You can get all sorts of snacks on a train – Virgin ones also have Fairtrade coffee. Try getting a bacon roll or a smoothie, or a coffee that didn't result in the premature death of a South American under-age worker, on Easyjet.

J is for jokes. The woman doing announcements on this train (more of her in a moment) just said: 'we'll be here for a few moments, so please stretch your legs on the platform or have a cigarette if you like . . . but don't be tempted to explore Lancaster or we may leave without you!' OK, not Groucho Marx, but not Grouchy Old Pilot Telling You To Do Up Your Seatbelt either. Train drivers are much better at homely banter.

K is for kleptomania. You can collect some amazing things that people leave behind on trains. That's how I got my copy of *War and Peace*. I often wonder whether someone thought 'Right, I've finished the bloody thing, I'm not carrying it for a moment longer', or whether they got to about page 700 and forgot to take it with them, and are still walking around cursing, thinking 'I can't be bothered to buy it all over again, but if I don't finish it now, I'll have wasted three months of my life . . .'

L is for lavatories. Even Virgin trains, notorious for their foul-smelling corridors, have much better toilets than the ones you get on planes. And less of a wait; for some reason that's never been clear to me, people on planes take an unbelievably long time in the toilet, despite the fact they're the last place in the world you would want to spend time. It's not uncommon to wait twenty minutes outside one. What are they doing in there? They can't *all* be having sex.

M is for murder, as in . . . On The Orient Express. There's always an outside chance you might get drawn into a murder drama when you travel by train; it's still got a faint trace of that Hitchcock-era, I-could-stab-you-then-disappear-at-the-next-station unpredictability. Murders on planes tend to be bigger affairs with more explosions, more victims, and only the one suspect.

N is for Norwich. While we're in the business of comparing trains with other means of transport, I should point out that there are many places in the UK that are much better reached by trains than by car. Driving from London to Norwich, for example, is a lethal combination of flat-out motorway boredom and sick-making windy roads when you get lost ten miles from your destination. On the train, it's a short hop and you get to see more of the flats of East Anglia.

O is for Oh! Sometimes on a train you get a view so breathtaking you actually make a tiny noise. As I write, we are rattling up the north-west coast towards Carlisle and we've just slipped through a valley dotted with tiny white houses nestling in the pockets of jagged little slopes, with a big thick grey sky hanging low over the whole thing. You don't often get these sorts of views in everyday life and you can't see much detail from a plane; on a day like this, you'd be swallowed up in cloud in any case.

P is for productivity. If you work on a laptop, like I am now, you can be writing from the minute you get on the train till the minute you get off; a four-hour journey becomes four hours of 'office time', so travelling can be seen as a pleasantly varied part of the working day, rather than an interruption to it. That same four hours on an internal flight yields, at best, maybe two hours of actually sitting doing useful stuff.

Q is for quiet. OK, commuter trains are rarely quiet, but cross-country ones very often are. You can get your thoughts together. It's hard to do that on a plane.

R for rural Britain. Another positive aspect of the picturesque nature of train travel is that it provides a slice of the country without actually having to live there. A lot of CATE people probably feel that, much as they like the great outdoors and the simple life and so on, they wouldn't actually want to spend too much time on farms. Gliding past on a train allows you to feel you appreciate the country, you're doing your bit to preserve its greenery, yet when it's over you can still be in a city and go to a film or something.

S is for Scottish accents. It's been worth the £40 just to hear the woman say 'we're scheduled to arrive at twelve minutes past three' and 'the buffet car is located near the rear of the train' every time we stop at a station, in a typically irresistible Borders accent. All right, perhaps some planes have sexy-voiced Celts on board, but you can't rely on it. And it's not the same. You're on the plane, you're off the plane, it's all so brutally quick and cold. You don't get to *know* the woman like I know this one now.

T is for talking. 'Oh, boo hoo, I'm so bored on the train.' Shut up. No one should ever be bored when they're not doing a job. We're alive for a few seconds in cosmic terms, then we're all going to be dead for all eternity. Why not make the most of this time to phone someone you've not spoken to for a while? Go out into the vestibule where you won't disturb anyone and just surprise someone with a call. Phone home. Tell your wife you love her. Revive a lapsed friendship. Share banter with your brother. You cannot do this on a plane.

U is for umbrellas. I just saw someone on the platform at Penrith with an umbrella that said 'RAIN RAIN RAIN' all over it. A bit like those faux-50s biscuit tins that say 'BISCUITS' on them. It tickled me. Like the person thought 'Yep, this is the umbrella for me, the manufacturers clearly knew exactly what they were about.' You notice lots of tiny, unimportant but rewarding things by gazing out of the window of a train for a bit.

V is for viaduct. When'd you last see a proper viaduct? Get on a train, fucker!

W is for walls. Here in Cumbria you can see those dry-stone walls from the age of the Romans, which you learned about in school. When you see them for yourself you can just about imagine people building them, so long ago that it makes your mind fizz and you do an eager-student face like the kids on those idealistic billboards trying to attract teachers.

X is for X-rated. An acquaintance of mine once successfully executed a blowjob on a train without being noticed by the other passengers. Not easy, but easier than doing it on a jumbo jet I'll be bound.

Y is for yoghurt. I've got half a mind to pick up a yoghurt at Glasgow – like a Fruit Corner or something, you know – and eat it on the way to Stirling. You'd never do that on a plane. You have to be pretty relaxed, and have plenty of space, to eat a yoghurt, especially one with different compartments that need mixing. You need to have no one next to you, and to be able to lean back contentedly, and say 'mmm' once or twice. None of this is normally possible on a cramped Ryanair plane. People look at you as if to say 'Why didn't you go for a shitty dry packet of peanuts like the rest of us?'

Z is for zzzzzzz, the traditional shorthand for sleeping. On Thursday I'll be completing stage two of my Rail Blogs as I travel on the sleeper back from Glasgow to London. What could be more fun or adventurous or romantic than going on a train through the night and waking up to look at the dawn over a new city? Yet sleepers are never very popular, because people would seemingly rather get up at 5 a.m. to check in at 7 a.m. for the 8.30 flight and get in at the same time, but much more miserable and further out of London.

I think that this is one area where CATE-style 'people power' *can* theoretically make a difference, because of the nature of the market. The only reason budget airlines triumphantly advertise 'LONDON TO NEWCASTLE 8 TIMES A DAY!' is that so many people are bonkers enough to catch these flights. If a sufficiently large number could be weaned off it, by being persuaded of the niceness of trains, a lot of flight schedules would be pared back dramatically. (BMI's Bristol to Norwich service, for example, was withdrawn altogether recently, because people just realised it was silly and stopped going on it.) It's a big task, but there's no harm in trying. Like with everything else we're doing.

I'm just cruising over the Scottish border, I feel relaxed, I've got loads of work done, I've read a bit of a book, listened to four albums, and 'that woman' is going to pipe up again any second now. Trains are ace! Toot toot!

It was with a certain euphoria, as you can tell, that I arrived at my destination and went about my day, going straight to the 'green issues' section of Waterstone's in Central Glasgow to buy four books on global warming and the environment for my trip to Australia. Even on the train to Stirling, where I had to stand, I looked out of the window and thought how much better it was than being inside a cloud.

It had begun as a sacrifice, but ended up being fun. I could only describe it as a Funrifice. I felt that I had perhaps stumbled upon a truth which would be quite important to my efforts with CATE: making small changes to my lifestyle didn't have to mean depriving myself of heating, or walking in the rain, or anything else that involved so much internal muttering that it was exhausting to go through with. Something which you entered into reluctantly could actually end up being enjoyable or, at the very least, enough fun to counteract the inconvenience ('fun-neutral', if you will). Even if it meant I was becoming a hippy, I couldn't help thinking about the ways in which simplifying my life and reducing my consumption would be entirely painless; it might even make my life nicer.

I didn't need absurdly over-packaged products like the scissors I had recently bought which were vacuum-packed 'to ensure security', so efficiently that I needed to buy another pair of scissors to get into the packet. I didn't enjoy sitting motionless in cars which were themselves sitting motionless in lines of traffic, listening to taxi drivers' alternative immigration policies, or, worse, having to enter into a two-way conversation with them. (Once, when I stupidly let slip that I worked 'in entertainment', a cabbie reached into the glove compartment and handed me a 70-page handwritten film script he'd been working on, which he invited me to pass comment on.) I didn't feel particularly clever walking around with a single plum in a carrier bag, like a six-year-old with a crappy packed lunch at Alton Towers, just because I couldn't muster the feeble initiative required to take a re-usable bag around with me. I didn't need to have my phone charging all night on the extremely remote off-chance that I was forced to field a three-hour call at four in the morning. (Indeed, more than once, and as a result of having my phone on charge, I'd been woken up by a text saying something like 'are you asleep?') A part of me knew also, without fully acknowledging it, that strawberries would taste much nicer if I waited for them to come into season here rather than stuffing myself with them all year round until they became as commonplace as peas. And I would be just as happy buying wine that had been brought over from France as bottles that had undergone a 10,000-mile trek from Australia; it was just that, as a non-connoisseur, I usually ended up going for the Aussie brands because they often had brash green and yellow labels and confident Australian names like 'Success Valley Shiraz' or 'Hot Fuckin' Cab Sav, Mate'.

Also, I certainly did not need to have my house full of appliances on standby all night and all day, their little yellow lights gleaming like alarm signals. On 'standby' for what, anyway? There wasn't going to be a war between TVs and DVD players into which household appliances might be drafted without notice. The days when a television set had to be 'warmed up', like a hibernating monster, an hour and a quarter in advance of *Coronation Street*, were some way behind us, as indeed was the convention of calling it a 'television set'. Hard as the BBC had tried with *Two Pints Of Lager* and *Little Miss Jocelyn*, there had not yet been a TV show so compelling that the nation's screens had to be poised in permanent readiness for fear of missing a single second. Indeed, in the case of these and many other shows, the moments before the picture formed on the screen were often the most enjoyable.

Yes. There were loads of ways in which my lifestyle burned energy quite unnecessarily and even undesirably. It was time to get my act together.

The more I announced my intention of doing this, though, the more I found myself drawn into conversations on the subject which exposed my still-unsteady grip upon my new hobby horse.

Cynic: I hear you are interested in global warming these days.
Mark: Yes.
Cynic: Do you not realise that the planet has its own natural laws which play out over thousands of years, and which we can't possibly interfere with by driving our cars around? Isn't it just that we're coming out of an Ice Age and the polar ice-caps are going to melt whether we are here or not?

Mark: Um. I don't think that's true. I'm pretty sure it's not still the Ice Age, it feels too warm (nervous laugh). But I'm not actually . . . I'll have to get back to you.

Well-intentioned watcher of *Channel 4 News*: I was all set to get into this environmental question after seeing an article on the *Channel 4 News* about the melting of the ice shelf Larsen B. But then shortly afterwards, Channel 4 screened something called *The Great Global Warming Swindle* which seemed to trash the arguments for human-influenced global warming. What are we to make of this discontinuity?

Mark: Um, well there are a lot of arguments . . . it's complex . . . I don't quite know at the moment. Um. Do you always talk like this?

Mild xenophobe: What's the point of old Gore banging on about global warming when it's his bloody country causing more pollution than the rest of us put together?

MARK: *(thinks)* Well, it's an enormous generalisation to put every American in the same boat. That's like saying because Fred West was born in the same country as me, I am a hypocrite if I condemn chopping up women.

Mild xenophobe: Why are you thinking things and not saying them? Do you want a slap?

Mark: Er, no, no thanks. Sorry. I . . . yes, you could be right. Those Yanks, eh! (Nervous laugh)

Indecisive sort: Won't planes continue to take off whether or not you board them personally? Or am I wrong about that?

Mark: Um, yes, yes I suppose they will. But hopefully . . . mmm. Well. I'm off now, actually.

Hardcore environmentalist: Cycling, I hope?

Mark: Er, no . . . in a, er, someone's giving me a lift. Sorry. I'm an awful example of a person. Sorry. Bye! Bye everyone!

I had quite a lot of time to wrestle with some of these puzzlers, as – to complete the train-based Funrifice – I had of course to get the sleeper back from Glasgow to London. You've already seen that in my train blog, and in my head, I had somewhat romanticised the idea of this overnight cross-border gallivanting. As the 'M for murder' in the blog suggests, I had in my subconscious a definite association between sleeper trains and adventure or romance, planted by a youthful taste for Agatha Christie novels in which one could not safely board any form of public transport without a chain of murders breaking out. When I originally clicked the little blue bed icon on the Trainline website and ticked boxes next to evocative words like 'berth' and 'sleeper', I think I had considered it more or less a certainty that I would end up supplying a detective with a crucial clue to the disappearance of an Austro-Hungarian princess.

As I boarded the train – being checked off a special list of 'sleepers' by a man in a blue hat, as if we were all going on a school trip together – it occurred to me that the reality of sleeper trains was likely to be somewhat different. Rather than spending the night before my Australian flight in a proper big bed in a hotel, then cruising straight down to Heathrow and on to Adelaide, I would be sleeping in a cabin only just larger than a phone box, quite probably with a person unknown to me. I would wake up cramped and sore at Euston, possibly having slept in my clothes because of the cold, and then spend the next night after *that* on a jumbo jet, where night and day mean nothing, and you can't really get into pyjamas without causing a bit of a scene. I had to perform my first show in Adelaide the same day I landed, so, even by the standards of someone noted for doing marathon shows, it was going to be a gruelling period. I was likely to set a world record for the longest time a comic had gone between sleeping comfortably and doing a show. Why was I doing this to myself?

Because of the planet, I thought hastily as these treacherous anti-Gore thoughts began to cluster like greenhouse gas in my brain. Because of the environment. I squeezed down an alarmingly narrow corridor and found my dormitory. There was nobody else in it yet, but there were two ticket reservation slips, so I was going to have a travelling companion of some kind. I took the bottom bunk. I hadn't shared a bunk bed with anyone since youth hostelling in Canada, where I met a Swedish man called something like Karl who'd been able to recite all the American Presidents in sequence, but, unfortunately, insisted on doing so to impress every new person who arrived in the dormitory. Would I meet another European polymath on this trip?

I settled down as best I could and began to read one of my recent green purchases, *Six Degrees* by Mark Lynas. This ominous book predicts the changes to the world that would occur if the average global temperature rose by one degree, by two, and so on – as it would indeed do, according to Gore and all the rest of them, if I failed in my Crap At The Environment quest. Once again, the picture was not exactly rosy. Even at one degree, droughts began to ravage Africa and, yes, also Australia; in other words, people could die in *English-speaking areas*. At two degrees there was widespread flooding as the sea levels rose. I could feel my previous cynicism, or apathy, whatever it was, being overwhelmed by all this. Once again I wondered how it was that everyone wasn't talking about it.

By now we had pulled out of Glasgow Queen Street and I'd started to hope that my single occupancy of the cabin would last all night, but no, here was my companion. He was a short man with a briefcase. We made extremely awkward small talk as he readied himself for bed. Luckily he was a football fan and we got onto the subject of why Rangers were so far adrift of Celtic this season. Not for the first time in my life, nor for the last, sport was allowing me to side-step the reality of being at close quarters with another man's genitals.

As he was climbing the ladder up to the top bunk, he came to a stop on the second-to-last rung, only his legs visible to me, as in *Tom and Jerry.* 'Six degrees of separation?' he said suddenly.

'Sorry?'

'Is it six degrees of separation, the book?' he asked. 'You know, like how there's six degrees of separation between for example you and Marlene Dietrich.'

I was charmed by his example but tried to explain. 'No, it's about . . .'

'Because the thing is,' the man went on helpfully, now shuffling onto his bed – I heard the creak of the springs above me – 'you see, you are connected to someone, who in turn is connected to someone, and . . .'

'Yes, I've heard about that,' I said, 'but, um, no, this is about global warming.'

'Oh,' said my companion. 'Aye. It's really happening is it, eh?'

'I think it is,' I said. There was a pause.

'And what are we meant to do?' the stranger asked me.

To my own surprise as much as anyone's, I began to describe what I personally was doing: scrapping my flights, switching things off, setting up a little organisation and so on.

'Well, that's great, that's a great thing to do,' said the man. He took the address of the website.

I was cheered by the success of this tiny evangelical effort, and more pleased still when he went off to sleep and I realised I wouldn't have to talk about it any further. I turned my attentions back to Lynas's book. There was a little lamp by the side of the bunk but I thought I'd read it by the meagre light of my mobile phone to put a cherry on the locally sourced cake of the journey's carbon savings. In Lynas's vision of the future, the rising temperatures continued to wreak exponential havoc on the planet. It was the dozenth time I'd read this sort of thing since watching Gore's film. If it was all bollocks, it was certainly a widely held and well-substantiated lot of bollocks. I kept on reading with the faint hope that the book's narrative was going to take an audacious twist and, when we got to a rise of six degrees, everything would be all right again. But no. It was more a case of planet-wide devastation. I went to sleep hoping that my thirteen hours of train travel over the past couple of days might do something to stave off the apocalypse.

When I woke up, the man on the top bunk was talking on the phone to a woman called Julie about business. An announcement came over the tannoy saying that we would be asked to vacate our cabins in fifteen minutes. It was then that I realised we weren't moving; we'd arrived at Euston some time ago but, rather sweetly, they allow passengers to doze for half an hour on the platform before being kicked out. If you tried *that* on an Easyjet flight you'd be back in Glasgow before you knew it. I drank a cup of complimentary coffee, which was like oil, and went on my way, after a final exchange of pleasantries with the stranger whose life had overlapped with mine for those strange few hours.

Checking the website for the last time before I got on the plane to Australia, I found a huge collection of comments expressing support for my train campaign. Correspondents pointed out a number of other ways in which training it was superior to going through the sky. 'You can see the white horse carved into the hill 'twixt York and Darlington,' said Lou, lyrically. Janine described the joy of watching someone get momentarily stuck in the train doors. Others extolled the London-Norwich and Newport-Birmingham routes. A handful of people went so far as to say they were going to join me in abstaining from internal flights from now on. This was very encouraging. I'd influenced people. Things had got off to a good start.

In the afternoon leading up to the flight I ran into Johann, the *Independent* columnist who was properly 'into' the environment. Johann is a big-hearted, effusive gent who regularly bellows things like 'JOY, JOY!' where others might say, 'Nice to see you again.' On this occasion he yelled, 'ALL HAIL, MARK!' across a tube train at me. We discussed climate change. He told me that people who denied the reality of it were either 'professional contrarians', or plain ignorant. I asked him if he thought that amateur efforts, like mine, had any chance of actually making a proper difference.

'There are two kinds of amateur environmentalism,' said Johann, 'one of which is essential, one of which I LOATHE!' A number of people looked around and there was a sense of anticipation in the carriage; then the doors opened and I realised it was my stop. I said I would email him. In the meantime I would have to hope that I wasn't doing any of the things Johann loathed.

At Heathrow Airport, without even thinking about it, I ate New Zealand lamb to give me strength for the journey. My senses were slightly disarranged by the emotion of saying goodbye to Emily, so it was only halfway through the meal it dawned on me that the lamb participating in this feast had been flown across the world purely so I could eat it at an airport and convey it in my innards most of the way back to New Zealand. As an example of the wastefulness of modern consumerism it would take some beating.

On the plane, I became still more inclined to the view that we were all living, in global terms, beyond our means when the person in the seat behind me on the plane started trying to negotiate over the origin of the wine he was going to have with his meal. 'Do you have a Spanish wine?' he asked. 'No,' said the Singaporean air hostess wearily; after a laborious consultation of the label, they only had French. The man gave a contemptuous sigh. We're on a plane! I nearly said to him. By rights we shouldn't be able to drink *any* sort of wine from tiny little bottles! By rights we should just be sitting here feeling sorry for the gas we're helping to pump into the atmosphere, not griping over the wine list that accompanies our orgy of destruction! I tried to convey this by turning around to glance at my fellow traveller and making a small noise with my teeth, but I wasn't sure if it hit home with quite the impact it had in my brain.

As I was trying to get to sleep I heard the wine fan discussing the plane's choice of films with his wife. *An Inconvenient Truth* briefly entered the discussion. 'Think what our carbon footprint is!' said the man with a sort of delighted horror in his voice. 'In the past year we've been to Australia twice . . . New York . . . Thailand . . .'

'Japan . . .' said the woman and I remembered with a guilty shiver that I was going to fly to Tokyo almost as soon as my flight back from Australia touched the tarmac in June. They started talking about a friend or associate called Keith who'd made even more journeys over the past twelve months than they had: he had been to Dubai for three days to play golf, for example, and flown to New York just to attend a party. The more they talked about it the more it amused them. 'Keith's going to cause acid rain!' the man chuckled. For the first time in my life I felt something like genuine anger at someone else's eco-behaviour, as the middle-aged couple chortled over their massive carbon consumption. (I also couldn't help reflecting that people who flew that much could surely have racked up enough frequent flyer points to be in business class, where they wouldn't have to stick their feet in the back of my seat any more.) This used to be me, I reminded myself, I used to think the environment was a quaintly amusingly topic. Now it felt real and important. I might be Crap At The Environment but I had completed the psychological transformation necessary to overcome the crapness. Now I had to convert thought into more action and take more people with me, even if the Inconvenient Truth resulted in my having a slightly Inconvenient Life from now on.

END OF MARCH REPORT CARD

Credit: Binned internal flights in favour of train travel.

Debit: Faffed about with admin rather than actually doing much; boarded long-haul flight.

Savings: Minimal, but vow to avoid future flights promises better performance in months to come.

Status: Crap At The Environment.

SARAH'S MARCH BLOG

Two facts:

1) I really love my clothes. I know this makes me sound shallow, so: I also like intelligent conversation, the smiles of children, genuine human experiences, people who are into something that is too big to be expressed through their clothes, nature in all her myriad forms, and people with eyes that shine from inner strength and loveliness (reckon that'll do it). But I really love my clothes. Since I don't earn enough to wear head-to-toe designer labels, I buy a LOT of cheap, disposable, fleetingly-fashionable stuff from high street shops, wear it for a couple of months and then give it to the charity shop.

Cheap, disposable clothing is a massive growth industry – UK clothes purchases have increased by a THIRD in the last five years, with the average Brit buying fifty bits of clothing a year, and this is due to the rise of cheap 'n' cheerful stores like H&M and Primark. Primark in particular have recently become quite the hip and trendy thing recently. In fashion circles it's a 'cool thing' to say 'Oh this? Primark, darling. Oh you spent £7000 on yours? Ah, well no, that's fine, I wrestled mine off a crack whore with a pushchair in Hackney but I'm sure your trip to Bond St was fraught with gritty urban peril too.' Primark is the incredibly depressing mothership that calls me home.

However . . .

2) Cheap, disposable clothes are ethically and environmentally quite iffy indeed. To quote from an article in the *Independent*, on 28 January 2007 called 'Chic & cheerful (but not so great for the environment)': 'the new rapid turnover of clothes increases environmental harm at every stage from growing cotton, through burning energy to make and transport them, to disposing of them in landfill waste dumps.'

And this is before you even start considering the thorny issue of how clothes can be produced so cheaply using overseas labour.

So as my first Funrifice, I decided I was going to give up crap clothes. From now on, I said to myself, I won't buy any new gear unless I am completely certain it was produced with as little ethical and environmental evilness as possible.

As is the point of a Funrifice, there are many perks to giving up un-green clothes. I should going to stop getting that pit-of-the-stomach feeling every time I went in Primark; I'll have far less chance of running into someone wearing the same dress as me; I'll save money, as long as I keep away from the more designer-y end of eBay. I'll stick to charity and vintage shops and only buy new things from companies that could prove their ethical credentials.

This in itself, though, is a minefield. Organic cotton T-shirts can still be air-freighted miles to shops, something made with

Fairtrade labour can be dyed with polluting chemicals, and frankly, it's a damn headache. So I made a sidebar to my funrifice – some things I'd have to buy new. (The Ian Dury album 'New Boots and Panties!!' was named after the only two things Dury thought shouldn't be purchased second-hand.)

Here's a handy summary of some of the tricks I have picked up after the first month of this Funrifice:

Five useful tips for a greener wardrobe:

1) Rent a handbag. Remember, if you just heart-poundingly *must* have 'the latest IT bag' on your arm, you're not a monster. Millions of pounds are spent on advertising, marketing, schmoozing journalists and giving freebies to celebrities to make you want a designer doo-hickey hanging off your arm, so don't feel bad. Bag libraries exist so you can rent a darling little something-something for a couple of months and then pass on to the next girl, minimising its environmental impact. Go to www.bagaddiction.co.uk.

2) Have a 'swishing' party or, as the Americans call it, a 'switch and bitch' do. What this means is, you and a group of pals get together with clothes you don't want any more, and swap. Simple and entirely eco-friendly way to get a wardrobe full of new schmutter. Those with no friends, or friends with crap dress sense, can swap clothes online at www.whatsmineisyours.com or www.iswap.co.uk.

3) Donate old suits and other formal clothes to www.dressforsuccess.org, a global organisation that provides disadvantaged women with clothes for job interviews and so on.

4) Go to charity shops in the posh part of town. Rummaging in your local ones is all well and good, but you get the best clobber

in the shops where rich people donate stuff but wouldn't deign to shop. Wherever well-paid sportsmen live with their WAGs, there will be an Oxfam shop nearby full of designer goods only a season out of date.

5) Pimp your particulars. I'll admit, I'm crap at this. I can't sew for toffee; like streets-full of people die if I sew, but weirdly, I find something incredibly satisfying about haberdashery shops. It may be the word 'haberdashery'. Anyway, making and updating your old clothes has moved on since the days of *Pretty In Pink*. In fact, it's quite hip and I'm a bit miffed that my fat-fingered crapness keeps me from joining in. For instance, in London there's Knitflicks, a club where knitters knit in front of a, um, flick, and www.punkrockknitting.com, for all your anarchist craft needs.

Part Two

April, May, June:

An Inconvenient Life

APRIL

ustralia was experiencing one of its worst droughts in years, which was very bad for agriculture, for rural communities, and ultimately for the infrastructure of the whole country; but it was very handy for making people get interested in the environment. The first time I put the TV on in my hotel room, there were a couple of experts in suits talking about climate change. One of them, who was even more of an expert than the other one, said of the current bone-dry conditions that 'the way our climate is changing, we shouldn't think of this situation as drought, but as normal'. Oh good, that's OK then, I thought, and then realised what he meant. Since it was Australian TV, he had barely got to the end of his apocalyptic sentence before they cut away to an advert made for $15 with a man shouting into a tape-recorder about a special offer on beds, so the message might have been lost on some viewers. Perhaps I was getting too much into the whole 'less is more' thing, but I couldn't help seeing even this lurch between serious programming and garish advert as a sort of metaphor for the fatal distractedness of our society. I had to get out more.

So I did. In my first week in Adelaide I consumed virtually no electricity other than the hour of computer power I spent maintaining the CATE site (of which more in a moment). I walked everywhere. I went running on the beach. Rather than endlessly browsing the Internet I browsed actual, physical shops and markets (trying to buy local produce wherever possible). I lay in parks and gardens marvelling at how much space there is in Australia. I played football and beach volleyball. On my third night I amused barmen in the Garden of Unearthly Delights, the focal point of the Adelaide Fringe, by asking them which of their wines had been produced closest to here. Then I drank too much and, while pissed, publicly claimed to be ranked in Britain's top ten tennis players. As a result of this insane claim, my reputation as a foreign eccentric grew rapidly and the way was clear for me to start talking about carbon.

'It's important not to drink Australian wines,' I said half-intelligibly to one of the bar staff. 'I've given it up.'

'But we're in Australia, mate,' said the guy, mildly.

'Yeah . . .' I said, 'so it's important for *you* not to drink *British* wines.'

'But there aren't any British wines, are there?' he asked.

'Well, not really.' I was confused. 'Just keep doing what you're doing.'

Of course, just as it's easier for Australians than for British people to focus on the importance of climate because they can see, with their own eyes, lakes drying out to dustbowls in the time it takes to get your swimming trunks on, it is also easier to enjoy outdoor pursuits in a country where 'outdoors' tends to be warm and pleasant, towns have parks which aren't just enormous dog toilets, and a trip to the beach doesn't mean sheltering on the pier feeding the 2p machines while your dad says 'I think it's brightening up out there.' It's also easier for Aussies to consume their own country's goods, since with their fertile soil and varied climate they can grow and produce more or less anything one might desire. On the other hand, banana crops in Queensland had been destroyed last year by freak weather, farm animals were perishing from lack of water in New South Wales, and of course the Barrier Reef was dying away faster than you could say 'gap year'. In some respects, then, Australian environmentalists were in a much stronger position to get themselves heard; on the other hand the situation was a lot graver and more urgent here.

In any case, in the mother country, the CATE community continued to grow. We now had around eight hundred members. It was time to put into practice the first CATE Challenges. I had by now elected the 'officers' who would set various fun, easy weekly environmental tasks that we could all do together. Some of these officers were crap like me but had an interest in some area of green living which they were keen to share; others had some kind of expertise and gave us some sort of coherence and reputability, meaning that if – as seemed fairly likely – we supplanted the Green Party and ended up running for office as a political party, nobody could question our credentials.

The initial officers were as follows:

Andy and Dave (Officers for Self-Sufficiency). These Bristol-based identical twins got in touch with me shortly after CATE had been set up. For three years they'd been running a website, www.selfsufficientish.com. Self-sufficient-ish-ism, they explained, had its roots in a similar sort of compromise to CATE. It was a living plan aimed at people who liked the idea of living on a smallholding, brewing their own wine from straw, growing every-thing they ate and so on, but didn't have the time, money or flexibility to spend their whole life slogging it out.

Of course, Crap At The Environment was quite a few rungs down the ladder of enlightenment, as it was largely aimed at people who *hated* the idea of providing for themselves and only visited the countryside because of a malfunctioning sat-nav system, but were reluctantly embracing the need to consume less of the planet's resources. Indeed, I felt somewhat out of my depth exchanging environmental emails with someone like Dave. His 'favourite activities' on MySpace included 'foraging for wild food' – something I thought I'd never read until we reach the terrifying moment when animals became sufficiently well-evolved to have their own MySpace pages – and his website also divulged that 'I'm writing this on a computer made of things people threw away', an awesomely Womble-like achievement to someone like me so used to purchasing pre-packaged commodities that it would not occur to me to make up a bed if I discovered a mattress, a pillow and a duvet in a skip.

Luckily, Andy and Dave were extraordinarily un-smug for people who managed to 'live off the earth' even a little bit. I asked them to set a weekly challenge to do with living a tiny version of 'the good life': the quite good life, as it were, or the not-quite-so-crap life. Because they often signed their emails 'Andy and Dave', there was the additional fun of not knowing which of them I was addressing at any time. This gave our dealings an enjoyable element of mystery and confusion. I resolved that when, on the back of CATE's success, I became Prime Minister, I would appoint as many identical twins as possible to my cabinet.

Cathryn (Officer for Abolition of Unnecessary Packaging). A cheery individual from Wales, Cathryn had long had a bee in her bonnet about the profligate use of plastic bags. Now, inspired by the inchoate CATE movement, she decided to launch an official campaign, Carry On Carriers!, to encourage people to tote their own receptacles to the supermarket rather than going through their days with plastic bags containing a single pack of Polo mints or a carrot. In support of this campaign, she would publish a bag-related challenge each week.

Lily (Officer for Disgusting Areas of the Environment). It was Lily's vow to take on 'the icky, unpleasant areas of green living that other people don't really want to talk about'. She would set a weekly challenge which was 'not for the faint-hearted', 'helping you become a bit greener and possibly in need of a wash'. She adopted the acronym TED (The Environment is Disgusting) as a name for her mini-campaign. I thought it was a good idea to confront the muckier aspects of eco-living, as it might save us from the fate of being cosseted middle-class dilettantes dabbling in 'ethical living' as this year's fashionable craze, even though, arguably, that is exactly what I was. Nonetheless, I was slightly alarmed by what Lily might have in mind. I've never liked getting dirty at all. Once, during a pottery class when others were leaping on the chance to get filth all over their hands without fear of reprisal, I asked the teacher if I could write a poem about a pot instead.

Sian (Good at the Environment Officer). Sian, whom I've already mentioned as the initiator of the Trident protest, was given the job of acting as an ambassador from the world of the already-quite-good-at-the-environment. Along with her boyfriend Sam, she would set tasks which might not have occurred to the rest of us. Sam corresponded with me through my Hotmail account rather than through MySpace like everyone else, because he was boycotting MySpace to make a stand against Rupert Murdoch. Really, it was amazing how some people managed to give a shit about things.

Howard (Officer of Water Conservation). This man was so enthused by his role that he renamed himself 'Captain Howard' and decorated his mini-site with fake celebrity endorsements, featuring, for example, a doctored Phil Collins album cover ('No Jacket

Required; Water Conservation Compulsory), and a David Hasselhoff design ('turn HOFF the tap') – although so ubiquitous was 'the Hoff' in this period that, for all I knew, he might well have lent his support to our campaign without my knowledge.

In addition to all this, I would set my own challenge each week, and I also invited anyone who had a particularly good idea during the week to pitch in with it.

All in all we were set for an orgy of challenging on a scale not seen since Anneka Rice grounded her helicopter. A core of perhaps a hundred people, among the almost one thousand who were now signed up to the MySpace community, indicated that they were primed to take on the challenges. This was all quite exciting.

I mean, we were only getting started. In addition to the MySpace site we by now had a proper website, www.crapattheenviron-ment.co.uk, designed by my brother-in-law and featuring a graphic of me based on my first author photo, in which I have the docile expression of a cow. The MySpace page was getting a lot of 'traffic', as web savants say. It would surely be possible to build upon this foundation and, over time, mobilise a large number of people to join in with challenges and write blogs about their experiences – large enough that we even collectively made some sort of a dent on the public consciousness.

This may seem fanciful, but at the time we are talking about, MySpace had close on one hundred million registered users: more users, in other words, than eBay and cocaine put together. Even if you conceded that as many as half of those were either time-wasters, miscellaneous wrong 'uns, or simply people who would never be persuaded to get interested in the environment, that would still leave fifty million. Even if we went on to admit that 99 per cent of those would never hear about Crap At The Environment, that was STILL half a million people. Subtract Tom, who runs

MySpace, because he would probably be pretty busy for the foreseeable future, and famous MySpacers the Arctic Monkeys, because I knew for a fact they were tied up recording their second album, and that was 499,998. If I could get even a thousandth of *these* heavily filtered people to pay attention to the environment, I would have done considerable good.

Of course, when you put it like this it all sounds a bit facetious, but I genuinely did think at this point – however over-ambitiously – that my little project could become something of a movement. Over the past year or so, I'd become obsessed with the idea that the exchange of ideas over the Internet was changing the world. Bands like the aforementioned Monkeys were the best-publicised example of an Internet seed that grew into a colossal oak, but there were smaller stories everywhere on the web. Its capacity to bring people together was astonishing and unprecedented. On the day I joined Facebook, there was a Group called 'I Love Gaffer Tape' which boasted 113,000 members; about 65,000 were claimed by an organisation named 'I Fucking Hate Bono And His Fucking Face', presumably to differentiate it from groups for people who hated the singer but also found him rather easy on the eye. Yes, you could look on this as proof that the Internet was simply a vast arena of corporate time-wasting, but what if you looked at it the other way around? What if the vast potential of all these people, who were bored enough to set up appreciation societies for cheese, could be harnessed to do some good?

Or was I being an idiot? Perhaps, but the signs were encouraging as, after a short period of planning, the Officers unveiled their challenges for Week One.

Andy and Dave: Make a newspaper pot. The idea of this challenge was to make a plant pot out of newspaper, which would then degrade into the soil, not contaminating it apparently. Along with the challenge, the unnervingly eco-savvy twins posted a link to a video in which Andy demonstrated the process. This challenge filled me with dread and unease. But it wouldn't have been a challenge otherwise, would it?

Cathryn: Take a bag around with you everywhere. This was a nice simple, but important, task which everyone could do without disrupting their daily routine very much at all.

Howard: The Phantom of The O-pee-ra. In this ambitiously titled challenge, CATE members were dared to leave toilets unflushed where possible, conserving potentially large amounts of water which would have been pumped away purely for the sake of propriety. The 'phantom' element referred to the need for the non-flusher to remain anonymous, in the interests of retaining friendships, jobs and civil liberties.

Lily: Stick a Sticker. Lily's first disgusting crusade was to popularise the use of mooncups, a re-usable alternative to tampons without the landfill-clogging consequences. Rather than out-and-out asking people to use one – which would be something of an intrusion for Week One – Lily asked people to find creative ways to make environmentally-friendly stickers about mooncups, and stick them to things.

Sian: Walk up and down stairs instead of using a lift. According to Sian and Sam, an astounding amount of electricity was burned keeping lifts going up and down, up and down, all day long. Necessary perhaps in a seventy-storey monster in Canary Wharf, but how many lift journeys are a simple matter of one floor up or down? Rather a lot, is the answer. Using stairs more would have the additional benefit of sharpening one's taste for walking in general, which could only have positive knock-on effects for other environmental endeavours; plus, by using stairs you avoid the crippling embarrassment of social intercourse with strangers. And lift music. And there's no chance of getting stuck on a staircase; unless you are crippled by existential horror and can't take another step. Which does happen, but a bit less often than lift failure.

Mark: Make a funrifice. I've already explained the thinking behind this new concept, the fusion of sacrifice and enjoyment. I invited CATE members to find their own ways of effecting such a fusion.

The challenges were posted and I stood back and waited for an explosion of amateur environmental activity.

In the meantime, and to a degree which seemed absolutely ludicrous for someone with my absolute lack of credentials – I was already beginning to be regarded in some quarters as a kind of spokesperson for the cause. I was invited to speak on ABC radio (which is broadcast nationally in Australia) and made solemn pronouncements about the need to act 'now, rather than later', all the while wondering whether I might have left the light on in my hotel room, and would return to find the Charlatan Police ransacking the premises. I wrote an article for the *Big Issue* about the value of community action on the environment, and enthusiastically told CATE members that it 'should be on the shelves any time now', before pausing to remember that the *Big Issue* doesn't work like that. I was approached by the British Library to speak on environmentalism in the workplace at their 'company fun day' in June, and agreed, even though I still knew hardly anything about environmentalism and had never really been in a workplace. I was asked by an audience member in Adelaide, who'd heard me on the radio, if I would try to use my 'clout' to help persuade Australia to ratify the Kyoto Protocol. It is fair to say I wouldn't have expected to be asked that question two months before.

Each of these media appearances brought more visitors to the CATE websites, especially as I was tentatively beginning to mention the environment in my stand-up set, and had developed no less than just over a minute of material on the subject. This in turn meant that every day, people kept proposing new projects for CATE members, new websites I should go to, new mini-organisations to function as off-shoots of CATE.

Miriam suggested a fundraising-and-awareness night with music, comedy and so on, provisionally entitled Green Feet, and set about organising it with gusto. Her friend Clare set up a site where people could share ideas about making recycled costumes for the event. Sam proposed having a village fete (the CATE fete) some time in the summer. I had emails about planting trees, getting celebrities involved, organising a clothes swap, and performing at environmental charity events of every description. If I had had the power and resources, I would at this point have appointed a personal assistant to co-run the project for me. Instead, I started getting up earlier and feeling tired, edgy and paranoid, a tactic that's never let me down in the face of adversity.

Pimp My Plant Pot, CATE's first sister movement, was having a similar effect on the life of Nicola, who set it up. The milestone of one hundred plant-pot-pimpers had long been passed and CATE members were already starting to post photos of imaginatively decorated pots and, in a couple of cases, even the green shoots of budding potatoes. Of course, this was not going to save the planet but it was heartening to think of all these people spending a little bit of their day growing vegetables, and it seemed a perfect working example of CATE's ethos that doing a small thing, not very well, is nonetheless better than not bothering. Unfortunately for Nicola, it was also becoming something of a drain upon her time and resources. After having sent out in excess of one hundred and fifty plants and pots without recompense, she was forced to post a poignant message asking for donations. Pimp My Plant Pot now had four hundred MySpace friends, which was a lot of members for a gardening society, most of whose members didn't like gardening and would never meet.

The surprising success of this amateur-green-fingers initiative gave rise to another idea, called Pimp My Patch. In this scheme, initially mooted by a lady who called herself Serendipity, Nicola would build upon the momentum she'd gathered and use it to mastermind a mass gardening campaign by CATE members. We would find a grim, urban area which was in need of some greening, and volunteers from the CATE community, under Nicola's leadership, would go and give it a crap-but-lovely makeover. This sounded a lovely idea to Nicola, apart from the 'under Nicola's leadership'. 'I don't know anything about gardening!' she wrote in a text message; I never would have thought such a sentence could come out sounding so fraught, unless it was uttered by someone trying to cheat in a pub quiz.

Unfortunately, by this time, I had written a blog asking for volunteers.

Recently Nicola celebrated her 100th 'pimper' and there's no sign of it stopping any time soon. This has led to the idea that it would be nice to harness the MySpace community's evident taste for horticulture, to some bigger end.

It was pointed out by one CATE member recently that the UK is full of awful, cheerless towns where once-fertile ground has succumbed to urban decay. Sixties building schemes now abandoned, neglected waste ground, piles of discarded industrial crap, or just miserable town planning: there's many a place in the UK with very little pleasant vegetation of any sort. Kids are obliged to hang about with their bikes on the pavement, spitting, distorting the language and trying to kill people; dogs fight on scrubby patches of turf in lieu of having actual parks; everyone walks around feeling miserable and being ill.

So, what if, under the leadership of Nicola, and with the backing of some sort of Green-Fingered Celebrity, we decided to Pimp A Patch? In other words, turn up in a quite unpleasant place and plant the fuck out of some seeds.

There are already people who do something like this, most famously the Guerrilla Gardeners who turn up and just garden places that weren't expecting to be gardened. What we'd aim for is a bit less lofty than this, in keeping with the overall spirit of CATE. We would liaise with the local community, get keen sorts to help, and in short make sure that people were pleased that we were coming to try and do something nice in their town, rather than patronisingly arriving to make unsolicited changes to the landscape.

So I'd like two things:

Firstly, we need people who might be prepared to join a group making a day trip, some time in the summer – most likely July – to a place yet to be determined, and spend some time clearing space, planting, generally getting involved with some greenery. You don't have to have any expertise.

(And if anyone thinks this might just make us an ineffectual band of jokers, only a few hours ago on daytime TV, a semi-proper environmental person was saying how depressing the 'eco scene' often is, because people are always slagging each other off for not being green enough, and so forth. And a lot of people have said the same since CATE began, which gives me confidence that it is worth approaching these things from a non-expert standpoint.)

So: do you know, or better still, live in, a place that could benefit from some pimping? What we want is for people to nominate candidate towns, or in fact settlements of any size, which would then go 'head-to-head' in a sort of *X Factor* scenario, with the most deserving 'winner' receiving the CATE treatment.

This – both the search for a suitable town and the pimping itself – is the sort of malarkey that would probably get a bit of publicity, be fun, do a little bit of good, and perhaps inspire other people to do their own little bit of good: the essence of CATE.

So please suggest your favourite plant-starved shit-hole, here or at the usual email addresses. And in the meantime keep directing people to Pimp My Plant Pot.

Let Advanced Pimping Planning begin in earnest.

I apologised to Nicola for destroying her leisure time and peace of mind, and reassured her that I would put any large-scale 'pimping' project in the hands of other people so that she wouldn't be called upon to 'do a Titchmarsh' (in the sense of being a gardening mentor to the masses, that is, although at the time of writing, Titchmarsh's empire is becoming so broad that 'doing a Titchmarsh' may soon mean writing a sentimental novel, hosting a chat-show, or, for all we know, manning a mission to Mars).

There was no shortage of volunteers for the proposed mass gardening experiment, and two CATE members even emailed me to say that they'd bought a Young Person's Railcard in readiness. There were also plenty of nominations for top 'plant-starved shit-hole'. JC wrote that 'there is some awful abandoned space here right behind my house. I have a big problem on my hands and officials just aren't listening.' It sounded perfect; it was only on the second reading I noticed that JC was in the States and even our highly motivated taskforce might struggle to co-ordinate pimping stateside. 'I'm just back from a little tour,' said Corry, 'and, holy fuck, Sheffield could do with some flowers, or at least something to soak up the spit of the people queuing outside Ladbrokes at 8.50 a.m.' But by far the most nominations went to Manchester and its environs. 'I reckon if CATE would like to come up north to do the patch pimping,' wrote the ever-industrious Sian, 'we'd not only be beautifying some of the grimmest places in Manchester, we'd also be doing our bit to keep our demonised hooded youth out of trouble for a couple of hours, and giving them something long term to look after and be proud of.'

We agreed that the two of us would fix a date when I got back to the country. I had two dreams about wandering onto an estate in the north-west under the wary glare of the kind of kids who stand around with bikes. In one, we got such a huge amount of garden-ing done that it was featured on the national news and on waking up I believed, for a few seconds, that I was a folk hero. In the other dream, though, I was chased away by a gang. Either outcome would certainly give me something to talk about 'down the pub'.

But there was no time to go down to the pub. I was an activist, suddenly. Or at least, I was behaving a lot like one. I forged links with a group called Change Is Coming, whose aim was to inform the environmentally curious-but-naive, and also with a girl called Wendy who was engaged in a personal campaign to change 'one little thing' each week with the aim of arriving at a 'cruelty-free, ethical and considerate lifestyle'. I took advice from Anna Shepard whose Eco-Worrier feature, to be found in the 'Body and Soul' section of the four-kilo labyrinth that is *The Times* these days, anticipated the concerns of many people who'd started to post questions on my site in the mistaken belief I knew what the hell I was doing. I was finding, actually, that the principle of CATE – a watered-down version of environmentalism for people with other stuff to do – was far from being my innovation, as I'd perhaps imagined; people were doing it all over the place. This led to the following exchange on my MySpace blog:

> **Mark**: The longer this goes on, the more aware I become that there are a lot of people doing, or attempting, very similar things to CATE. This is both inspiring and somehow existentially depressing.
>
> **Sarah**: 'Existentially depressing' – haha, spoken like a true stand-up . . . surely the notion of a world full of people bumbling around to make things less doom-laden is a lovely thing? No matter how bumbling . . .
>
> **Mark**: Yep of course it's a lovely thing. It's just occasionally I get that panicky dread that everything I've ever done in my life could have been done, and indeed perhaps has been done, by someone else. Then I remember I'm going to die anyway. Then I normally have some tea.

Futile narcissism aside though, it was, indeed, very encouraging to see how many people had the same aims as me, and, moreover, were reassuringly incompetent at pursuing a lot of them. Incompetence, however, may be charming, but doesn't get you very far – this is one of the main lessons of *Mr Bean*, along with more specific life pointers like not picking up a kitchen knife when you have a turkey on your head – and it was quite late in the week when, while wading through a crammed inbox of green-themed emails, I realised I had not got round to doing any of the CATE Challenges myself. It was time to get cracking.

First, then, a newspaper pot. I had a newspaper, all right; indeed a copy of the *Adelaide Advertiser* with a favourable review of my show. This seemed like perfect material for my pot, as, with success in entertainment famously fickle, the spectacle of a complimentary article about oneself rotting and disappearing into the earth is a good metaphor for the likely trajectory of a comedian's career. I watched the video of Andy cutting and folding like a *Blue Peter* presenter of old. I gathered the other necessary materials. I looked at the newspaper. I watched the video. But after a short while I knew it wasn't going to happen.

I have to elaborate, at this point, upon a point which I've already treated in passing. It is important for you to grasp this theme, because it has a bearing on almost everything that has happened to me during the minor adventure described in these pages. The fact is that I'm not merely Crap At The Environment. This specialised crapness is in reality only an individual symptom of the pestilence of Overall Crapness which has dogged my days on this planet.

Oh, don't get me wrong, I'm good at a few things and luckily you can make money out of some of those. I am, however, crap at an overwhelming number of other things. I'm something of a person of extremes, in terms of attainment; I will either master something easily or never, ever get the hang of it in a million years. If you were to draw a Venn diagram – which I wouldn't do myself, as I never got the hang of them – of activities I have taken to well and things I've utterly failed in, you would hardly need that bit in the middle. It's one or the other. And as I am a person of feeble moral fibre and little powers of perseverance, it tends to be the case that if I can't do something, I'll simply find ways not to do it, even if the long-term consequence is a series of huge, embarrassing holes in my ability to deal with human life.

We've established that I can't ride a bike, and this is one of the most spectacular embarrassments in my CV of shame, but it's really only one among many can'ts. I can't open jars and bottles. I can't peel an orange. I can't play a musical instrument. In terms of operating electrical equipment I am like the teacher you had at school who used to put the educational video in the player and then sit there rubbing his hands together nervously and finally have to get a sweaty Mr Jarvis out of a PE lesson to press 'PLAY'. I can't carry more than one thing without dropping the lot or crashing into a child. I suppose I need hardly add that I cannot drive a car, and the one time in my life I've been at the wheel of a dodgem car, I panicked so much that the fairground attendant had to hop on the back and take the wheel from my hands. It was the most embarrassing incident since the previous week, when we went ice-skating at school and I was given a chair to push around so that I could keep upright.

In fact, even the above mention of *Blue Peter* makes me out to be more can-do than I am: the truth is I didn't watch it as a kid, because I knew I wouldn't be able to do any of the arts and crafts, and that really just left some nonsense with a dog.

I only mention this litany of humiliation so that you understand that, confronted with the challenge of greening up my act, I was not merely facing up to a lifetime of environmental negligence but to a long existence of inadequacy. Not just cycling, but a host of other simple green activities, adopted by others, filled me with fear. It's all very nice for other people to talk about reconnecting with nature by 'going for a walk without knowing where you're going, just for the fun of it', as more than one green website does, but my sense of direction is so poor that I can only find a place by walking there by the exact same route every time. It's a lovely idea to unscrew every light bulb in your house and replace them with low-energy ones, but not quite so attractive if, like me, it takes you the best part of a day to prise a bulb out of a fitting and the remainder of the day to screw the new one in, an all the more awkward process because you have a superstitious fear of being electrocuted and so more or less have to get the entire National Grid turned off before you will attempt the changeover, and even then you hold the bulb like a live hand-grenade. (Hence the old joke: 'Q. How many Mark Watsons does it take to change a light bulb? A. None, he can't do it; this isn't even a joke. Shut up.') As we've mentioned, some people are overjoyed at the prospect of grovelling around on an allotment, but those people can probably hold a spade the right way up. As for advanced greening like 'loft insulation' – it may well be, as www.diydata.com remarks, 'within the capability of the do-it-yourself householder', but it is so far beyond my own capabilities that, if I ever find myself in possession of a loft, I'm less likely to get it insulated on my own than I am to go up there and cry quietly to myself about the state of the world.

All this is to give you some idea of why, having hitherto bravely battled the odds and dared to believe I could make a difference, the simple video about making a newspaper pot set my environ-mental confidence back considerably. I can't hear someone saying 'and then you fold here . . . and then make a very gentle cut here . . .' without being filled with a panicky, almost nauseous anticipation of failure. It was this as much as anything that prevented me from ever being a contestant on *The Generation Game* and, in my heart of hearts, I fear my chance has gone now.

Very well then, I thought, we'll come back to the newspaper pot. Let's try something a bit more manageable. Not using a lift seemed like a realistic aspiration. I was staying on the third floor of the hotel in Adelaide and could quite easily use the stairs each time I left for my show (walking to the theatre of course, rather than getting a cab; more of that in a moment) and also on the way back if I were sufficiently sober to remember. I would save myself quite a lot of time waiting around for lifts, I would stay trim – not a major concern as I am so thin I sometimes put people off their food, but it couldn't hurt – and the electricity savings, according to Sam, were considerable. By not using the lift for a week, he estimated, I could save enough energy to power a 42-inch flat panel TV, fifteen energy-saving bulbs, a washing machine, two stereos and a bread maker *all at the same time* for one hour.

And so I gave the cold shoulder to the lift in my hotel. My week without artificial elevation, though, was thrown into jeopardy when I went to visit my friend Tim, bard of the canvas bag, in another, swankier hotel. Quite simply, I couldn't find any stairs. I asked the bloke at reception and was politely shown to the lift. I said that I would really rather use the stairs. The staff member said that this would be possible, but he'd need to get a key to open a fire door. I began to feel a bit of a dickhead putting people to trouble just for the sake of my silly little challenges, when, after all, the lift was going to run whether I used it or not; but on the other hand, this was the difference between a complete week of success and a blotted copybook. Amazingly, rather than tell this pleasant man (Kevin) that I was trying to conserve energy, I claimed to have serious claustrophobia and to be medically incapable of getting in a lift. He then became very solicitous, got the key straight away, and even said, 'You"ll be all right now, mate,' as I began to climb the ten flights, as you might to someone who had just collapsed on the street.

As I was making the ascent, it did occur to me that rather than me feeling sheepish about causing inconvenience, it was the hotel who should be apologising for not having readily available stairs. What kind of a building is so dependent on lifts that the stairs end up being treated like the best china, to be locked away and only got out in the event of a visit from a maverick pedestrian? What if they had a fire? (You should never use a lift in a fire; if you didn't know that, you weren't listening very hard when the firemen came to your school to speak in assembly.) All the same, I had a strong feeling I was going to be the one looking stupid when I left the hotel, with the staff giving each other funny looks behind my back. Unless of course there *was* a fire. But I couldn't really hope for that.

Still, stupid or not, with this obstacle hurdled, I got triumphantly through the week without a single lift use. I resisted the temptation to go out and buy a 42-inch television and watch it at full volume while making bread roll after bread roll and chewing on them rhythmically along with pumping beats from my two new stereos. It felt like a small green victory, even though it was – once again – somewhat easier to pull off a lift-less life in Adelaide than it would be back at home, as I observed in my blog:

I'm not sure what sort of reaction this will get in London, where doing everything as fast as possible tends to be the priority. In my experience, on the Underground, if you choose to take the staircase rather than an elevator, people look at you as if you had just got a live bird out of your case and started waving it about. Any sort of eccentric behaviour on public transport, in these terror-fixated days, gets you the kind of looks that would otherwise be reserved for whoever on the train looks most like the 7/7 bombers. Perhaps when I get home I'll begin playing up to this assumed eccentricity and start sauntering up and down stairs with a jaunty bit of whistling. Maybe even a song or a bit of juggling.

And yes, it may be a bit gruelling in some Tube stations, where the staircases go on so long you fear you will die of old age before you reach the summit, but overall, I think we can say elevators are best 'lift' alone. Actually, no, let's not say that. Let's delete that straight away.

The timing of my conversion against the elevator could hardly have been more apt, as, right around this time, I had written a one-off comedy for BBC4 in which four strangers got stuck in a lift and had a pretty bad time with one another. After its transmission, a number of people left messages on my website saying things like 'I'll never go in a lift again!' It made me wonder whether perhaps I should try writing a sitcom called 'The Selfish Idiots Who Hated The Environment'.

As I mentioned, I'd been making the fifteen-minute walk to my venue each night rather than jumping into a cab, as I would almost certainly have done in pre-CATE days. I decided to make this my Funrifice of the week. My limbs, already well and truly elasticated by all this lift-avoidance, now sang out in health as I trotted jauntily along. I took time to notice some of the charms of the everyday which might otherwise have eluded me: the weird cries of Australian birds in the trees, the pink-purple beauty of a sunset at the end of a long hot day, the assorted lunatics who flood into Adelaide at Fringe time and lurch out of doorways asking you for money or muttering about the Government.

This small daily carbon-saving jaunt did of course remind me that the time was coming when I was going to have to tell my producers that I wouldn't be able to fly from Adelaide to Melbourne next week – despite the fact it had been booked and arranged some time ago – because I was saving the planet. I continued to put this off for as long as I could, because I was probably going to look like an idiot; it joined the newspaper pot on the mental shelf of unacknowledged items.

Crap at the Environment

I did reasonably well with the other challenges of the week. Since I was living in a hotel room, flushing the toilet as infrequently as possible caused me less social difficulties than it might have done. It's yet another argument in favour of spending time on your own in hotels, the only real counter-argument being the ever-present threat of loneliness, insanity and complete mental breakdown. After a couple of days I got into the habit of leaving a 'DO NOT DISTURB' sign on the door when I went out, so that a housekeeper wouldn't come in and be met by a welcoming committee of wee. Fairly soon, as a result, my room was not just a solitary cell but a pretty squalid one at that. Nonetheless, it was helping the environment. What would have seemed a rather frivolous, and even sordid, challenge was lent a certain nobility by the fact that water conservation continued to be a big topic in Australia. Every non-flush of the toilet, I felt, was a trickle of hope for rural communities; and pissing on a bush on the way home late at night became an altruistic act almost akin to voluntary rationing in wartime.

When it came to making stickers, I was not so effective, partly because the amount of admin already generated by CATE made me lazy about photocopying and cutting up and so forth; partly because of the already discussed shortcomings of my life (making stickers comes dangerously close to art and craft).

And, to conclude my Week One challenge efforts, in the field of declining plastic bags I excelled, not surprisingly, having trained for this before I left my native land. Armed with a canvas bag, I went about saying 'I don't need a bag' left, right and centre (though normally to shopkeepers, to be accurate). I executed twelve IDNABs (the correct term for saying 'I don't need a bag') in the first day of the challenge alone. A lot of time I was really buying nothing more than a few apples or a bar of chocolate, and really – as I said to my audience one night – if we must kill wildlife by dumping these plastic parasites in areas of natural beauty, let's at least use the bags to carry something heavy first. A concerted campaign in Australia has meant that far more people there walk around with canvas bags than in the UK, so, once again, my independent receptacle use attracted no venomous looks from the equivalent of Kevin. Even in a climate where people are used to bringing their own bags, though, there were several occasions when I was called upon to rescue my shopping from the jaws of a plastic bag, and twice it meant actually taking things out of a bag to the bemusement of a shopkeeper.

On the second of these occasions, I received a significant morale boost in exchange for showing a little courage. After muttering, 'I don't need a bag' to no avail, I was forced to repeat it, quite loudly, and in my awfully English voice, which, in the flat-vowel territory of South Australia, sounds to the locals as posh as Stephen Fry doing an impression of Brian Sewell reading the poems of Tennyson. There was a pregnant silence and then a reproachful rustle as the clerk started to empty the would-be shopping bag of its contents. Then, on the next checkout along, a woman – who had been observing the exchange with a whimsical smile at my funny accent and ways – said, 'Yeah, y'know, I don't need a bag *either*,' and flashed me a conspiratorial grin. There was a real feeling of *esprit de corps* between us and other customers visibly began to consider saying no to bags when it came to their turn. I haven't been back to that shop in Adelaide but I'll very surprised if they have used a single plastic bag since that day.

So, no bags taken all week, and alongside my non-lift-usage this meant two of the challenges completed with total success. Some people regard the struggle against plastic bags as a rather petty focus for the environmental movement but, for me, the fact that plastic bags are produced and used in such astonishing numbers sums up a number of the core facts about my own Crapness At The Environment, and society's at large.

FACTLET: Plastic (Not) Fantastic

We all know plastic bags clog up landfills, make up 90 per cent of floating litter in the oceans, poison animal life (causing an estimated 100,000 deaths a year) . . . but also, they are made from ethylene, a by-product of fossil fuel production. So they're a menace even in the manufacture, before they start getting out and murdering turtles.

Although, as anyone knows, they are damaging in all sorts of ways, especially in the mind-blowing quantities demanded by the West, you may say: well, yes, but this is still bags we're talking about. It's not exactly a huge problem compared with forty trillion cars on the roads, is it? Plastic bags, though, are unusual in that they're, literally, absolutely unnecessary. There is no reason why a single plastic bag ever needs to be produced again. It is absolutely within the capability of everyone shopping in the known world to vow never to use a single plastic bag again.

Why don't we? In my case, and probably most other people's cases, sheer laziness is the answer; many's the time I have been on my way to the shop, realised I hadn't bothered to bring a bag with me, and narrowly failed to summon the energy to bother going back to get one. Really, it wouldn't kill me to put a little notice up or something reminding myself to take a bag out with me. But over the years, I realised as I looked back on this challenge, the habit of going to the shops and coming back with Stuff In Bags had become as surely ingrained as checkout staff's habit of Putting Stuff In Bags Whether Necessary Or Not. We had become a society which endlessly craved stuff we didn't really need, and then insisted on its being supplied in bags it didn't really need to be in. Of course, you are not going to destroy capitalism overnight by removing the stuff that we use to carry capitalism's products around in. It could well take longer than a week. But it did seem a start. That was it for me and plastic bags, I vowed, for ever.

So, a mixture of success, part-success and cowardly failure characterised my first week of Crap At The Environment challenges. It had been, as I admitted in the blog, 'a solid but not inspirational performance'. Not a stirring display of leadership, but I had, at least, dealt with what had at times been some rather awkward tasks. I attempted to use this to provide inspiration for the CATE community:

> Guess what? Doing things IS awkward sometimes. Life in fact is a thoroughly awkward affair. But we have pretty much no choice other than to have a good old crack at living it before we die and (probably) never exist again.

> This is a roundabout way of saying that I did not make a newspaper pot.

The blitz of blogging on MySpace revealed that dozens of people had joined in with the challenges. Actually, three dozen. Well, slightly less than that. There were in the region of thirty blogs, ranging from just a few words (the briefest, from someone called Kevin, said 'I didn't do any of this, but I might in the future') to lengthy accounts of almost coming to blows over plastic bags (Sian recorded a shopkeeper looking at her 'as if I'd just spat on her neck' after issuing an IDNAB). One hundred recycled stickers about mooncups had been stuck up on toilet walls. Thousands of steps had been mounted in Underground stations while lifts sat inactive. Not many people had made a newspaper pot. We'd all tried and failed together. Well, all right, I hadn't even tried when it came to the newspaper pot, and nor had most people, but we had all at least made, and sustained for a week, one or more minor lifestyle improvements. The first CATE challenges could be pronounced a qualified success, in a crap sort of way.

Caught up in everything as I now was, I had left it pretty late in the day to sort out cancelling the flight from Adelaide to Melbourne, where my show would open in a few days, and to sort out a passage by train across the vast flats of land between here and there. I thought it might save a bit of trouble and worry for everyone if, rather than bother my producers with this, I sorted it out myself and presented it to them as a *fait accompli* ('Oh, by the way, I'm saving the world, so I've redone my travel arrangements. Nothing for you to worry about.') In making this plan I had overlooked some fundamental truths of the entertainment industry:

Producers tend to be very alarmed if you try to do things yourself rather than asking them for help, because you are likely to make things worse.

For me, a comedian, to take on work which comes under the normal remit of a producer constitutes a potential professional insult as large as if I were to arrive at my venue and find the producer up on stage entertaining my audience with my material.

I am an idiot and can't do anything right.

Oblivious to these ominous truths, I went to Adelaide's central station to see about buying a train ticket to Melbourne for what was now the coming Sunday. I knew it was likely to be very expensive and I wasn't yet green enough to say things like, 'The question is, can your children afford for you *not* to do it?' to myself. However, I was prepared to take the hit in the interests of adding to my impressive catalogue of flights-that-had-become-overland-journeys.

Local residents warned me that the station was unpleasantly crowded and busy and I'd be better off doing it online, but at the moment I was so enthused by the whole 'walking everywhere' programme that I was actively seeking pedestrian opportunities even when I could have done everything sitting on my bony backside. I decided to walk there straight from playing beach volleyball. This wasn't the best idea. I'd only played once before – the previous week – and I was fairly bad, but put it down to being a beginner. This time I was fairly bad and could only put it down to being fairly bad at everything. Not far from the end of our match, with the scores poised at 17-17 in the fifth game, I dived for a crucial shot, whacked the ball uselessly into the net and fell face-first into the sand where I collected an eyeful of sand, a few grains of which, as I write this in December, I can still feel wedged in a tear duct.

Still, the walk to the station was pleasant; it was a beautiful day and I only got significantly lost twice, covering the quarter-mile in an impressive time of just under an hour including breaks to ask for directions. What Australians call busy is still pretty relaxed by the frenetic standards of the UK, and compared with the mayhem of the ticket office at King's Cross or Liverpool Street, Adelaide Station felt like a hot-air balloon ride. I explained to a big, flat-headed man called Rich that I wanted to go on the train to Melbourne on Sunday. He was a typical South Australian with vowels as tight as wire and a laconic manner. The conversation went like this:

Mark: *(Mumbles, self-consciously)* I'd like to go to Melbourne . . .
Rich: You'll have to speak up, mate.
Mark: *(A bit louder)* Is there a train that goes to Melbourne . . . ?

Rich: Yep. There's a train.

Mark: OK, I'd like . . . um . . . a ticket. For it.

Rich: You'll have to speak up, mate.

Mark: *(Finally, audibly)* I'd like a ticket to Melbourne.

Rich: OK. You can take the Overland. It leaves here at seven-forty and gets in to Melbourne Spencer Street exactly eleven hours later at 6.40pm.

Mark: Eleven hours.

Rich: Yep. *(Pause)* You realise it's possible to fly there?

Mark: Yes, I, um. *(Mumbles)* I'm trying to reduce my carbon footprint.

Rich: You'll have to speak up, mate.

Mark: *(Loudly)* I'm trying not to fly.

Rich: *(After a long look at Mark)* Yep, well, you'll manage that on the train all right.

Mark: *(Bracing himself inwardly)* How much for a single?

Rich: *(Consulting computer screen)* A hundred and thirty-nine dollars for first class. Or sixty-nine standard.

One of the pleasures of being British in Australia is realising everything's two and a bit times cheaper than it first seems. When I made the calculation into pounds, I thought I was going to have to sit down. Sixty-nine dollars is about thirty pounds. Thirty pounds for an eleven-hour journey across a massive swathe of Australia. I would have asked Rich to repeat himself, except that we'd already done quite a lot of that during the conversation.

Thirty pounds was about a sixth of what I'd imagined I was likely to pay; indeed I was so euphoric that I briefly thought about buying six, turning up to the airport and offering five tickets to all-comers, as an evangelical gesture. To put it into perspective for Australian readers – in spite of my enthusiastic blogging about what good value it is to scoot around the UK by train, the fact is that if you fail to book in advance, you can be hit very hard in the pocket. If you turned up at a London station two or three days before going to Edinburgh, which would be about the equivalent journey, it would probably cost you around thirty quid even to stand on the platform and watch the train leave.

Here, I was being offered the chance to travel around five hundred miles in comfort for less than the price of a single from London to Nottingham, with the added bonus of being much less likely to be hit in the face with a broken bottle when I arrived. It worked out at about two pounds fifty per hour on the rails. In fact, I could easily afford to go first class, were it not for an ingrained miserliness which, every time I'm booking a ticket for anything, causes a cautionary voice in my head to go 'Why give them more money? Nothing wrong with standard class,' even if the price difference is about a pound and first class has performing elephants and a snooker hall. Had I been a passenger on the *Titanic* I would certainly have been one of the rabble in steerage who trampled each other to death. (Although in reality I probably wouldn't even have qualified for steerage, because in a world before stand-up comedy, I would have been a penniless vagrant. I live in the first period of history when someone as dispensable to society as myself can make a decent living.)

Rich: . . . so did you want to book it?

I realised I had probably been performing mental cartwheels for some time, and the boulder-headed Aussie was looking at me with more irritation than amusement by now. I thought I had better go for it straight away before these fairytale prices changed: one pitfall train travel has in common with budget flying is that, because of prices that vary automatically according to minute-by-minute demand, it is quite often £50 more expensive to book at lunchtime than at breakfast time, and I've known a ticket rise in price by a tenner in the time it took to book it on the phone.

Mark: Yes please. For this Sunday.
Rich: That'll be difficult, mate. They don't run on Sundays.
Mark: At all . . . ?
Rich: If they do, mate, they haven't told me about it.

No matter how much he called me 'mate', the news was bad. My dreams of a great train adventure shattered in front of me. God's command to keep Sunday as a day of rest is still observed by a surprising number of people.

Luckily, as you'll be aware if you know your Bible, this commandment exempts bus drivers. There was a coach to Melbourne on Sunday. It left at a similar, dismal hour of the morning, cost about eleven pence, and arrived late at night. I didn't find any of this out myself, of course; I asked my producer, shamefacedly, to do it for me. She booked a ticket and was kind enough not to point out that I should have left the whole thing to her in the first place, nor to question my motives for travelling overland. So that was sorted. Another carbon saving made and a very long coach trip ahead of me. It would be like being a traditional British backpacker in Australia, except, hopefully, I wouldn't end up with my picture on the news.

I was now in a nice regime of switching lights off, saving water, walking everywhere possible, buying local produce, and so on, which I felt confident would translate into a decent reduction of my carbon footprint when I came to do the sums, but which I was, admittedly, struggling to balance with the work generated by being chairman, secretary and main spokesman for Crap At The Environment. The second set of challenges was set by the officers and I put them up on the site. Some of them involved saving water, re-using bags in creative ways, and other manage-able things; at the advanced end of the scale, however, were tasks which demanded recycling and growing your own pro-duce. I threw open the challenges and invited people to persuade their friends and associates to write blogs and post them on the site, all the time mindful of the fact that if there were many more blogs for me to read, I would need to apply for an extra hour to be added to the day. Plus, of course, the more participants there were in my online community, the more time I would have to spend online, the more electricity I would consume, and so, in a horrendous irony, the greatest possible ultimate success of the Crap At The Environment campaign (everyone in the world joining in) might lead single-handedly to a massive rise in sea levels.

There were quite a few things to think about as I prepared to leave for Melbourne, where, on top of all this, I would have to remember to concentrate on my actual career as well; I'd be doing some of my biggest shows so far, including the Gala night which is watched by about 2,000 people in the theatre and around a million on TV. The way my mind was, there was a distinct possibility I would go up on stage and only be able to say the word 'carbon' over and over again. Accommodating as Aussie audiences are, I wasn't sure that would be quite enough.

The night before my epic coach trip was humid and oppressive. Everything was ready to go, except that I hadn't packed any of my things; I had an outstanding balance with the hotel which I couldn't pay because my bank wouldn't let me take any money out, for their own reasons; I still had sand in my eye, rattling around like a pea in a jar; and my obsession with the CATE site, and with the other scientific websites I had started to frequent, had led to most aspects of my life at home dissolving into chaos. Still, everything was more or less ready to go.

Unfortunately, as I prepared to walk to the theatre for my final gig, completing my unblemished record of not having used a taxicab the whole time I was in Adelaide, God – or whoever it was who had tried to thwart my elevator-avoidance earlier in the month – threw another unexpected obstacle into my path, in the form of a thunderstorm. It was a lively one, with white flashes every five seconds, making everyone go 'ooh' like spectators at a firework display, and massive melodramatic cracks of thunder.

Naturally, the locals all regarded this as a blessing; it was the first rain to fall in South Australia since about 1961. In the courtyard of the hotel, and in the street below, I even saw a few people going so far as to run out and splash about in the puddles, cooing with delight as the sky lit up. Only a nutter, though, would contemplate walking to the gig in this sort of weather. Of course, I'm a comedian, so you might think nutty antics are exactly what I'm paid for. What fun it would be to hurry through the storm to my show, arriving all wet and rumpled like some sort of comedy emergency services battling through the elements to deliver my cargo of mirth! Ha ha! What doggedly amusing fellows comedians are!

The thing is that I have a paralysing phobia of thunderstorms. At the merest suggestion of thunder in the distance I have to hide under a bed, unplug electrical appliances, and lie shivering, waiting to die. I have in the past (in Malaysia) checked into a hotel for a night when I was meant to be staying with friends, because I couldn't bring myself to go through a storm to their house. One of the worst experiences of my life was performing during a full-blown storm at an outdoor festival, in a tent full of metal girders and spikes, my hand quivering on the microphone in pure terror, which was luckily mistaken by the audience for some kind of ingenious socially dysfunctional persona. (A mixed blessing of being a comedian is that you could go on stage, talk about how your life had fallen to pieces and shoot yourself in the face, and people would go, 'It's very funny, that persona.')

The chances of my walking to the gig through the storm, then, would normally be nil. But there were only forty-five minutes to go until I was actually due on stage, so unless the elements eased off very quickly, I was going to have to choose between facing up to my fears and saying goodbye to my dream of a taxi-free Adelaide Fringe fortnight. If only I could be one of those people cavorting around in the street in glee at the downpour, but this behaviour has always struck me as absolutely insane. What next? 'Ooh, I love a good storm! Let's go and run around and wave a golf club in the air!' Do these people not realise that lightning kills 5000 people a year? In Jack the Ripper's day would they have paraded around in petticoats in an attempt to tempt him? According to the text answering service AQA, of those 5000, around 85 per cent are male, because 'males tend to venture out in bad weather'. I didn't want to affect that percentage.

In a way, this moment summed up my CATE month. Clearly, in terms of saving the planet, my abstaining from a single taxi ride would make about as much difference to the global situation as if I took a bucket down to Brighton beach, filled it up from the ocean and said, 'Right, that should keep the sea levels in check for the time being.' But it had, of course, all been about the principle, and I was determined not to drop those principles now, even if nobody cared.

I raided the mini-bar for a bottle of wine, making sure, of course, that it was Australian-produced, drank half of it, and, filled with Dutch courage, took a breath and ran out into the street. There were twenty-five minutes till I was meant to be on stage. With stand-up, of course, you can get away with a lot more dicing-with-time than in other forms of entertainment; if I were performing in *Cats*, I thought to myself as I charged along Rundle Mall, I would be in all sorts of trouble. But then timekeeping would probably only be one of many problems if I were in that show.

The thunder cracked and lightning flared, at each flash I flinched as if I had actually been electrocuted. Nonetheless I was filled with exhilaration. I was putting my life on the line for the sake of the environment. This was the first time I could ever remember voluntarily going out in a storm and it was in a worthy cause. I felt like a sort of Crap At The Environment King Lear. Perhaps it would have been a suitable reward for my hubris if the powers of nature, whose place in the environment I was seeking to stabilise, thanked me by striking me down. But it wasn't to be; I won my tiny moral battle against myself and arrived, dripping and triumphant, in the theatre.

'How did you get so wet?' a member of staff asked me.

'Oh, it's a big storm out there,' I said, nodding sagely towards the window as if I were Captain Ahab. Actually, it was dying down a bit now but the threat of death was as real as ever.

'But where were you coming from? From the hotel?'

He drew me a map of Adelaide to show that if I'd walked the quickest possible route, I should barely have been able to get wet, never mind getting struck by lightning. The way I had been coming to the theatre for the past two weeks was about the fourth most efficient way of getting there from the hotel. My stash of carbon savings won by not taking taxis were somewhat cheapened by the knowledge that the journey was about a third as long as I'd believed it to be.

Still, no matter. I'd done my best. I finished my show and celebrated by drinking well into the night, in the full knowledge that, in just a few hours, while those flying to Melbourne slept the sleep of the hung-over, I would be getting up to get on a coach for thirteen hours.

*   *   *

One of the more interesting lessons I'd learned from the past few weeks, I thought blearily as I boarded the bus with a very small handful of other brave or weird people – time would tell which, was that, perhaps, the message of anti-capitalists that 'less is more' did actually have something going for it. As a result of watching virtually no TV, getting a lot more exercise, buying hardly anything, basically *doing less*, I had spent a good portion of the past two weeks in an excellent mood. It was true to say that I could probably make a contribution to the environmental cause simply by inactivity. This is so obvious that it barely seems worth setting it down here, but, if this book fails to strike a single other chord with anyone, there will at least be some people delighted to take away the message that they can help save the world by sitting on a park bench staring out into space.

In recognition of this, I decided to try an experiment. I remembered Damon Albarn of Blur saying, on this sort of subject, that he'd once gone through an entire day in Spain without speaking a word to anyone, and had experienced a lot of 'inner calm', or whatever it is that pop stars call it, as a result. I was quite impressed by this at the time; if only Liam Gallagher could be persuaded to do the same thing, and instead of a day, maybe the next thirty years.

I'd never tried anything quite like this myself: certainly there were days in my university career where I didn't speak to another human being all day, but that was less a lifestyle option than a lack of lifestyle options, a result of only having two friends at university, and one of them normally being in bed. Now, with the journey stretching interminably ahead of me, I decided to see if I could literally *do nothing* for thirteen hours. No listening to my iPod, no working on my laptop, not even any reading or writing in my notebook or anything. Thinking would be my only permitted defence against the nothingness rolling by outside and the slow, slow drip of time through the still afternoon.

You may say that this is stupid – using the laptop would only have run the battery down, the same with the iPod (and in any case, iPods can only go for three and a half minutes at a time without running out of power altogether) . . . and as for reading, well, that has never had any carbon cost whatsoever, unless you count the trees that made the paper, the electricity used to power the lights you read by, or the DVD player you used to watch the film version of *The Name of the Rose* because after spending half a year of your life on the book, you weren't totally sure you had got the point of it.

But for me, this was a symbolic task, a bit like in those shows where misbehaving kids are sent out into the desert. As you will have gathered, I fill my brain and consequently my life with all kinds of miscellaneous nonsense. When I look back on my life as a disappointed old man, the retrospective documentary will show that I attempted more than I could possibly accomplish, failed in most of it, and where I *did* succeed, neglected to enjoy it because I was too busy thinking about the next thing.

So, by spending an enormous amount of time not letting myself interact with anyone or even any*thing*, other than what was beyond my control (I would, for example, probably move out of the way of a snake if it slithered into the seat next to me), maybe, I thought, I would be getting close to the secret of making a difference both to the health of the planet and to my own psychological health, and the secret, simply, was less.

We were soon on a long, straight road, laughably free of traffic, trundling through nothing but parched fields and dry dirt for mile upon mile upon mile. Various people who'd done this trip had warned me that it was almost completely free of sightseeing opportunities, but, once again, as a Brit, I was delighted just to look out on the miles of empty space. There's so little of Britain left that isn't covered in people, buildings, or buildings with people in.

Of course, this has been pointed out many times over the past hundred years by everyone on the continuum of intelligence from John Betjeman to the *Daily Mail*. Personally I've always been inclined towards pragmatism: our island is just not very big and lots of people want to do stuff there; you can't have everything, and the trade-off is likely to be a bit of greenery. But then, as we've already seen, that standpoint was always based on the fact that I didn't care about nature because nature to me mostly meant Geography trips at school where you slipped over in the mud while trying to write the word 'estuary' on your clipboard; or a place you'd only really want to visit if you were the Famous Five getting cream from a farm, which, to look at it in the cold light of day, I never will be.

I had as a result of CATE begun to learn the lesson that 'the countryside', 'the environment', 'nature" and so on did not have to mean plants you learned the names of for a week in 1996 to pass a GSCE, or animals on collecting tins that you sort of felt sorry for, but not quite enough to pay 50p to save them. It could just mean the absence of Stuff and the opportunity to think and recover your senses. Unfortunately, it would take several more months and an encounter with a former Vice-President before this message seeped through the thick layers of self-absorption encircling the bit of my brain that makes policy changes. For now, I simply noticed that it was, as older relatives say while crawling along the motorway to Norfolk, 'nice to be out on the open road'.

You might be wondering, by the way, whether covering so much road on a half-empty coach really constituted any kind of carbon saving over a short plane ride. I'm not quite so crap that this hadn't occurred to me, but setting my mind at rest on the subject had not been all that easy. While it's easy enough to find websites (and indeed people) who will calculate your carbon footprint for a year (and in the case of the people, reprimand you on it), it is not so easy for the layman to assess the relative merits of different methods of making a single journey. I did remember, though, that the Act On CO_2 site that helped with my original carbon audit had recommended buses as being even better than trains, and that I'd seen George Monbiot quoted as advocating a massive programme of inter-city bus-lane building to cut down on car use. A cynic might say that also, having made such a fuss about cancelling the flight, I was too scared to look up how much of a difference it was going to make. So let's all just be grateful that such a cynic is not among us at the moment.

On and on we went, with me just staring out of the window, allowing the psychic shrapnel that accrues over the lunatic scramble of an international comedy festival to dissipate, just in time for a new load to build up over my time in Melbourne. Now and again I would catch fragments of the conversations of my fellow passengers, who had all bonded as lone travellers are meant to do, and were perhaps wondering why I didn't join in with their conversations. There was the obligatory British gap-year student who, after his time in Australia, was planning to fly back to the UK for a month to raise the money to fly out to Cambodia for an 'eco-holiday'. He would be working on 'sustainable development', whatever the hell that was: I was still a long way too Crap to pretend I knew. There were a couple of grizzled old Aussies who were evasive with the Englishman on the subject of what they were actually making this journey for, which led me to hope that they might be highwaymen or something, but was more likely to mean they were riding the coach because it was nicer than being on the street. All in all, it was fairly missable conversation and I blanked my brain out successfully for at least the first three hours of the trip.

Somewhere not too far from the South Australia/Victoria border, we made a stop at a tiny town which, rather aptly in view of my minimalist agenda, was called Nil. I ate a packed lunch, which I'd brought in my canvas bag. In truth, it was just a (Fairtrade) chocolate bar and a (locally grown) apple, so to call it a lunch is stretching a point, and it wasn't so much 'packed' as 'drunkenly thrown together', although there were certainly kids at my school whose mothers made no such distinction. I walked around Nil, not going very far because if I got lost in my usual fashion, I would certainly end up living out the rest of my days in this place. I was unable to resist turning on my phone and texting a couple of people to boast that I was on a twelve-hour journey, but I switched it straight back off again. I got back on the bus with something like tunnel vision beginning to develop, and it is no lie to say that as we finally began to approach our destination I felt almost disappointed that I had to return to a world where it would not normally be considered acceptable to sit in silence for whole days at a time.

From the twentieth floor of the Oaks Apartments in Melbourne, a stylish but clinical place which ranks among the five most depressing hotels I have ever stayed in, I looked out over my favourite city in the world, the buildings twinkling all through the night with their pointless lights, and reflected on the effect my 'less is more' journey had had on my brain. For years I had resisted all attempts to get me to do less. If someone argued that less was more, I would probably counter that actually, more tended to be more, and use simple mathematics to make my point. Anti-capitalists and anti-materialists had had very little impact on me, and once when a Hare Krishna bloke on Oxford Street engaged me in conversation and told me I'd be more relaxed if I owned less, I pointed out that the chief thing threatening my relaxation at the moment was the incessant din of their chanting and the rattle-rattle of their bloody tambourines.

Not for the first time during my Crap At The Environment mission, I was forced to accept that I might always have been missing something. Yet, in typically pig-headed fashion, I responded to this lesson by throwing myself into the busy aspects of CATE with twice as much energy as before. The second week of challenges was well underway by now and, with even more blogs than in Week One, I spent half of one day reading them all in order to compile the latest roundup of activity.

WEEK 2 CHALLENGES: Highlights

After the heady excitement of the first Challenges, this was a week of cautious introspection, with quite a number of bloggers recording failures or discouragement. 'I haven't set the environmental world alight this week,' concluded Janine sadly, after remarking that she had 'once again looked like a shoplifter' in the course of the bag challenge. 'I keep meaning to start growing things, seem to be incapable of getting to Homebase,' Laura reproached herself in one of the week's saddest admissions. Lily's 'yucky little heart sank a bit' after a muted response to crystal deodorant. Serendipity (one of last week's star challengers), already taxed by illness, saw CATE threaten her relationship as an argument pole-axed a romantic bath-share. 'I'm a monster . . . I know fuck-all, clearly,' lamented Sarah. 'I was awful, I hang my head in shame,' sobbed Steve as, distracted by a Sesame Street song, he found water-saving more difficult than expected. Immy's 'funrifice' turned out not to be much fun. And so it went on. Your correspondent meanwhile experienced around fourteen of the usual 'why did I begin this, I don't know what I'm doing, is everyone just going to get bored with it' misgivings.

Of course, emotions of this sort are precisely the impetus that started CATE on its way. And despite the general gloom it was in fact an impressive week for amateur, but devoted, enviro-bloggers all over the country, our tiny achievements far surpassing the first week's in several areas. Here are just a few highlights:

* Sian led the way in the 'Grow Your Own' challenge as she continued 'turning our relatively meagre flat into one big greenhouse'. But less naturally green-fingered sorts also reported growing cress, lettuce, spinach, even sweetcorn, which many of us imagined could only be cultivated in far-off places and shipped over to our shores at an awful price to Mr Ozone. In general the Pimp My Plant Pot-inspired vogue for gardening continued to be one of the most pleasing developments of CATE so far.

* All kinds of things were deployed as bags in Cathryn's challenge, among them magazine wrapping, shoeboxes and a sack fashioned from a scarf. Charlie (another one of the pessimists, who earlier in the week sadly said that 'everyone would be forced to live on the moon if I was in charge of the world') was highly commended for turning surreal theatre to her advantage. But the shining star here was Immy who, on top of a number of useful contributions to the pool of CATE knowledge, and good performances in other challenges, made a bag out of no less than a suit. Go to her page and see it for an example of what can be done with scissors and a bit of spirit.

* Howard asked people to reuse water. This caused a blazing row in the Dipity household after which 'no bath was had by anyone'. Mr Dips later redeemed himself by telling a shopkeeper he 'wasn't allowed carrier bags'. Quite a lot of people reported having done away with unnecessary showers, and, basically, washed a little bit less without seeming to

alienate friends and family. (Your correspondent endured his first bath-less week in many years, but more of that in a separate blog.)

* Axing The Aerosol elicited a favourable response from CATErs, with several people, encouragingly, reporting they actually felt better without them. Opinion was divided on the efficacy of the crystal deodorants advocated by Lily, with some choosing various roll-ons, or other routes to fragrance altogether. Lily herself continued to tough it out in the unfashionable role of minister for the disgusting. Let's all show her some support; probably better to discuss these things than to have major personal and environmental problems, eh?

* Recycling proved popular, and this is obviously something which most of us will try to sustain from now on (though hopefully the same can be said of every CATE challenge).

It's always nice to see pictures of CATE in action (hats off also to whoever photographed a 'don't flush' sign on a toilet seat).

* As for funrifices, there were a number, including giving up TV, cancelling a journey, and stopping eating foods or buying cut flowers that had travelled a stupidly long way.

So CATE this week has been a bit like Weight Watchers – despite everyone thinking they've not been very good, the cumulative effects are rather cheering. It's been unlike Weight Watchers in that it's not advertised by sinister, glossy women. Nice work everyone.

The ever-increasing involvement in challenges continued to give me a lot of satisfaction. Photos of home-grown vegetables, bags made out of things that oughtn't ever to have been bags, guerrilla-posted signs about recycling and, of course, more and more pimped plant pots were now all over the network of CATE-related sites, and so were stories of voluntary sacrifices, arguments over water conservation, anecdotes of hope or discouragement. I would never have expected there to be a chapter of my life when I influenced anybody to grow cress. The last time I remember coming across it was in an egg-and-cress sandwich at a party when I was six, and after that I imagined cress and I would be lifelong adversaries. Now, I had helped more of it into existence. You never stop changing.

It was also quietly heartening that so many people, rather than posting triumphant photos, reported episodes of crapness. Much as I wanted everyone to do well and make their own contribution to environmental wellness, I didn't want to be completely outperformed. For one thing it would be slightly embarrassing if my efforts were eclipsed by people I'd once been the leader of; plus, there was always the danger of a bloodless coup and a re-branding of the organisation by my usurpers into Not Quite So Crap At The Environment, Actually. So the current mixture of success and failure was about right.

My own Week Two challenges ended up following this pattern, too. In some areas I did spectacularly well. Most impressively, not content with the 'Funrifice' of the coach journey, I succeeded in giving up baths for a week in favour of showers. There'd been so much talk about drought in Australia that I didn't feel I could justify bathing any more, and I pledged that if I was successful in getting through the week without a bath, I would continue showering indefinitely (always taking showers when washing, that is, not getting in the shower and staying there for ever). Most Australians were already doing this; in fact the Government was recommending a limit of 'three-minute showers'. It struck me as one of the ironies of adulthood that so many of us who hated having to wash as kids, and would go to all sorts of lengths to avoid going in the shower, were now being threatened with legislation to prevent us from doing so.

It might have been all right to have a bath if I could re-use the water, say for tending to a garden, but as I was staying on a high level of a hotel, all I could really do with salvaged water was to pour it over my computer when the Internet connection refused to work, something which I've repeatedly been told creates more problems than it solves. So, a shower-only policy came into effect in my hotel room.

For a lot of people, this would have been no real problem or, as the young people say these days, 'no biggie'. For me, though, it represented a piece of self-denial so huge that it was perhaps surprising it didn't get more news coverage. As I explained on my blog, baths are one of the main reasons I would rather be alive than dead:

I like baths as much as normal people like sweets. I find there's virtually nowhere in the world as good as a bath for simultaneously relaxing and getting thoughts in order. I can understand the argument that lying in a bath is tantamount to wallowing in your own filth, but I'm unmoved by it, because (a) wallowing in your own filth is a good metaphor for the job I do and (b) try looking at someone who's just come out of a bath and is in a dressing-gown and all shiny and red and nice-smelling, and tell me they're not clean. Pffff.

Nope, I love a bath, me. At times of high intensity like, say, an international comedy festival, I'd have two baths a day if I could.

But no more.

There's nothing wrong with showers, of course; being in the shower is still better than being dry, on the whole. It's just that nothing quite compares with the womb-like immersion of a bathtub. It's like the difference between having sex with someone and just giving them a quick hug on a station platform. Plus, being useless (cf: most of the previous pages), I've never really mastered the delicate art of getting a shower to run at a temperature in that surprisingly small sweet spot between heart-stoppingly cold and hot enough to burn a hole in your flesh. I'm exactly the sort of person you might see in a sitcom scalding and immobilising themselves alternately, all the time letting out shrieks which the neighbours misinterpret, to the hilarity of the studio audience. (For those of you not in the entertainment business, I should explain that pain and misunderstandings are both scientifically proven to be very funny.) You can understand then why I favour a good soak in a bath. Most of the few decent ideas I've had in my life have come in a bath, while pretty much the best idea I've had in the shower was to get out of the shower.

The Oaks was, as I've mentioned, the kind of only-just-finished hotel where everything looks amazing and has been 'conceived' by an award-winning designer, but nothing actually works. I was never entirely confident I'd mastered the shower dials, which were sophisticated enough to suggest the control deck of a spaceship, so it wouldn't be true to say I ever managed to relax entirely, but I did do my best to enjoy the showering experience. I whistled and sang to keep my spirits up. I relished the excitement of not being 100 per cent sure I wasn't going to be stabbed, like in *Psycho* (baths don't really have the same potential for being taken by surprise by a psychologically disturbed landlord) – I just had to remember to leave the en-suite unlocked, or the deadly game of cat and mouse might have lost a bit of its intensity. And I had to admit I was saving time. Probably at least fifteen minutes per shower, I reckoned, which, over a week, was not far shy of two hours. Which of us hasn't dreamed of an extra couple of hours a week? Imagine the amount of extra admin *24*'s Jack Bauer could catch up on.

And like a farmer turning shit into fertiliser, I converted this by-product, extra time, into more environmental deeds. I wasn't going to be able to grow much in the way of my own food while I was in a hotel, but I did go to my first farmers' market, in St Kilda. It was very busy and not noticeably full of hippies. It was also, mercifully, much better organised than I had feared; for example, it wasn't the sort of market where you have to haggle. As a dyed-in-the-wool Western consumer, I like the prices of things to be fixed and certain. Partly it's just that I find haggling incredibly embarrassing; to me, looking at something that's labelled £12.50 and suggesting 'What about eight pounds' feels like saying 'That thing is about two-thirds as good as you think it is.' Plus, I don't really have the guts for the cut-and-thrust of negotiation with experienced hagglers and will as a result normally astound them by paying the marked price of £45 for an old Guess Who? set which we both know is worth less than a pound. I've also got this deep-set middle-class dread of talking too much during any kind of transaction in shops, restaurants and so on, so I dislike bartering over price for the same reason I find it toe-curling when someone in a restaurant tries to order something that's not on the menu ('Can you make me chilli con carne?' 'Yes they could,' I want to shout, 'but it's not on the *menu*. Otherwise what's the point of a menu!? Why not order walrus?')

I am digressing: don't get me onto restaurant etiquette again. The point was, my trip to the market went well. I picked up apples and oranges, bananas and cherries; almost a complete fruit machine. I also bought some locally prepared elderflower wine which I thought might make a nice chaser when it was too early in the day to start drinking other types of wine; and some locally-grown flowers to herald the arrival of Emily, who, for some arcane reasons of her own, is always a bit disappointed when she flies to the other side of the world to find me living in filth. Having forgotten to bring my canvas bag, I bought one there and, when I'd filled it up, stuffed the remaining fruit into my pockets like an old-time urchin from London town. I went home better stocked with fresh fruit than some supermarkets I've been in.

Things were stacking up all right as I continued to juggle my actual career and my phantom career as part-time world-saver. I got through the Gala show without disaster and even managed to mention climate change afterwards while recording a short piece of VT for Oxfam asking people to give money to charity if they thought I was funny. April wore on. There were more challenges, more ideas for future CATE events, more invitations to speak at environmental events where I really wasn't qualified to serve the tea. I was getting so many emails about it that any emails on other subjects, such as, for example, a last warning about my council tax, failed to make any impression on me. We were approaching the end of my second month as a declared Crap At The Environmentalist and I was pretty sure things were heading in the right direction. I was a fanatical amateur trying to keep control over something I didn't really understand. What could possibly go wrong?

END OF APRIL REPORT CARD

Credit: Outdoor pursuits replaced electricity-using activity in many cases; successful challenges included non-use of lifts and carrier bags; starting to take note of carbon cost of foods, etc, and eat local; generally enhanced awareness of environmental issues; tentative embracing of 'less is more' idea encapsulated by bus journey undertaken in place of flight.

Debit: Chickened out of tasks, inc. newspaper pot, showing persistent reluctance to do really difficult things. Still too much faffing and lack of focus.

Savings: Noticeable, thanks to sustained non-use of electricity.

Status: Still Pretty Crap At The Environment.

SARAH'S APRIL BLOG

I did quite well with a lot of the challenges. I filled an old pop bottle with water and stuffed it in my loo. Said no to carrier bags, something I've always been fairly good at doing anyway. On the few occasions I've been caught short without a bag, I've taken it home safe in the knowledge I can reuse it as a bin liner. I've always thought buying new bin liners was the height of ostentatious wastage of precious resources, worse than burning fivers in an orphan's face. But then I've never owned a fashionable, awkwardly shaped bin and maybe those posh people with a two-foot high stainless steel Brabantia with soft-touch lid deserve my pity, rather than ire. Part of the challenge, though, was to encourage other people to say no to carrier bags. While queueing in my local corner shop, I noticed on the counter they had a little dish with a damp sponge in for wetting the finger, in order to get the carrier bags off the roll quicker. While I admired its cute, post-office-y vibe, I couldn't help but think it accelerated the 'no bag thank you . . .' 'oh I've already put it in one now' process, and was therefore a tiny tool of evil. I resisted the urge to steal it, although it would have made a nice trophy for CATE HQ, should we ever get an HQ.

But it's not just CATE's members who are talking about carriers. Suddenly, it seems everyone has an opinion on the 'This Is Not

A Plastic Bag' bag, created by spendy handbag designer Anya Hindmarsh. With a limited number of these benign beige bags available for £5, there was a blip in time where they became the trendiest thing ever to own. As the hype reached breaking point, suddenly the papers were filled with rather gleeful reports that the bags, far from being eco-friendly, had been knocked up with non-eco-friendly cotton, in dubious factories in China, and air-freighted all around the world. Over March and April this one bag has generated more column inches than Diana.

Bags have been sold on for £175 on eBay, which got some columnists frothing at the mouth, even though rich trendy people will always spend £175 on stupid things given the chance. An Anya Hindmarsh spokesperson said they'd never claimed the bags were 'green' in themselves, saying: 'Our aim has been to use our influence to make it fashionable not to use plastic bags. [It] was designed to be a stylish, practical, reusable bag that would raise awareness of this issue and spark debate.' Which it certainly has, although not especially useful debate.

As far as I can tell, both sides, pro and anti, are a bit right, but for entirely the wrong reasons. The arguments basically come down to: 'They're good because they're really trendy and with-it,' versus 'They're crap because fashionable people like them.' No one seems to have pointed out that the whole saga means there has been a story, every single day in the papers, about replacing disposable plastic bags with a reusable cloth bag. Admittedly, a cloth bag that was about as green as a ripe tomato, but still greener than mountains of carrier bags. It seems to me like no one is asking more important questions – ones like, 'Is the awareness raised by something worth the immediate environmental and ethical impact of its production?'

MAY

Get up. Make sure the phone charger is turned off. Go for a walk. Buy Australian-only produce, root around for Fairtrade coffee. (NB: for Australians, 'root around' means 'hunt', or 'forage'; it has nothing to do with the meaning you have for 'rooting'.) Debate with yourself whether, if you supplied your own recycled toilet paper in your hotel room, you would be placed in a secure institution. Bring it home in the bag you brought, or, if you forgot the bag, wrap it in the folds of your shirt and waddle home looking either like a cast-iron lunatic or a supreme Luddite who frowns upon the idea of the bag as a new-fangled nonsense. Think about buying a bottle of water, then reprimand yourself – bottled water is a wasteful, unnecessary product and you really oughtn't even to have imagined buying it because that's exactly what *they*, the carbon producers, want. Return to your hotel. Walk up twenty flights of stairs – at the top of the eighteenth, in a seemingly prescient piece of graffiti, an unknown hand has written in pencil: 'TIRED YET?' When you get to your room, the plastic card you were given fails to open the door. Good, fine. Back down the twenty flights of stairs to negotiate with the reception staff, who are bright and helpful but outdone again and again by the teething problems of their establishment.

Up the twenty flights of stairs again, sorely tempted to use the lift this time, but imagine if Jesus had caved into the temptation and turned those rocks into bread. The graffiti isn't as funny the second time. Finally you're in your room. Turn off the air-conditioning, which you don't understand the workings of, but which you are fairly sure is a waste of energy. Try in vain to open the window instead; as in many hotels, though, especially ones where someone might commit suicide, they are fixed so you can only open them enough to let out a spider you might have caught, and a skinny spider at that. Put the computer on, wade into the sea of CATE-related virtual paperwork, with only the cheery graphic of the Microsoft paperclip to jolly you along: 'this does not seem to be a sentence!' Remember that you had a huge load of washing to do, and if you don't do it before this evening, you may have to take to the stage naked, which tends to be regarded by the theatre-going public as a poor second place to being clothed. Get your canvas bag of clothes and lug it out of the hotel foyer and four hundred yards down the road to a launderette which boasts that it uses special, low-energy washing machines, a claim that you of course have absolutely no way of verifying. Trudge back up the street feeling distinctly low-energy yourself. Return to your room to find you've left the computer on, for no reason, and not even in any sort of energy-saving mode. Feel dejected.

There are challenges to do. Unfortunately, though, you are doing one of your 24-hour shows in a couple of days and that takes quite a bit of organisation. In the 24-hour show you'll have computers on for the duration, lights, electricity blaring. You could try not to use some of this stuff, but the show probably won't be as good; as it is, it's going to be a bit of a stretch to entertain the audience for a whole day. Still in your diary is a trip to Japan as soon as you get home from this side of the world; you are starting to feel you ought to cancel the gigs if you're not going to negate everything you are doing, but you haven't got the guts, and, of course, the longer you leave it, the more difficulty you will cause if you do eventually do ask to cancel it – a similar fix to the one Hamlet experiences, but with a lot less poetry, a lot more pragmatism.

Immobilised by indecision, you sit for about an hour not doing anything at all. You put the TV on to try and jolt you out of this, but your electricity-saving regime doesn't really smile upon needless use of your TV set – especially this huge, energy-hungry one – and since it's Australian television, pretty much anything except sport must go down as 'needless use'. Sure enough, it's a 20-year-old episode of *Morse*. Enviously, you contrast Morse's impeccable grasp of the situation with your own addled state. Morse wouldn't let the planet down if he were in your position. He would find the people who were responsible and very, very slowly reveal who they were. What are you doing?

Eventually remember to collect your washing from the place down the road. When you have got it home, discover that 'low-energy' washing machines in this case simply mean ones that don't put much effort into washing your clothes. You pull on a soggy, dirty T-shirt, half the day is gone, and you are a waste of space.

Last thing that night, you return, tired and in a crumpled T-shirt, in a distinctly negative frame of mind, and after you've walked up those calf-torturing stairs for the fifth time that day, you find that the little plastic square again refuses to open the door. This is the final blow; the planet is melting down and you can't even get into your room to watch the last days from the window. You turn on a hapless member of staff who is making his beat along the corridors, collecting breakfast-in-bed orders people have left on their doors, and make an emotional appeal. 'Why don't these things work?' you ask, alcohol giving a voice to your pent-up grievances.

'Why can't we just have proper keys?' The helpful staff member takes a look at your card and points out that you are trying it in someone else's door.

This moving autobiographical sketch gives you an indication of the way my brain was by the end of April. Even in the midst of what had seemed like a series of green breakthroughs, I was committing a welter of sins commonly associated with 'eco-warriors': joyless self-satisfaction/self-deprivation, obsession with tiny ecological economies, and being shabbily dressed. I was in danger of not being able to see the wood for the trees I was trying to save.

You'll already have gleaned from the story so far that I tend to do things in an 'all or nothing' manner, with suitably death-or-glory results; and, after throwing myself headlong into my little environmental challenge, I experienced a sort of compression sickness as I came up again. There had been a collision between two things I took too seriously: my Crap At The Environment campaign, and everything else in my life. And the collision had resulted in quite a bit of mess, as with all collisions – except in the case of dodgems, or in my case, including in the case of dodgems.

The system of setting challenges was out of hand. In Week Three, there were challenges to put a brick in a cistern, get a microwave, find something outside you could re-use, recycle Tetra Paks, pass on a plastic bag you had lying around your house rather than throw it away, and quite a few more that other people had chipped in. What was I going to do – sternly tell newcomers that they weren't allowed to set challenges? This wasn't school, was it? Accordingly, the fourth week saw a still greater number of challenges set: go through a day without spending money, never leave a tap running for more than five seconds, do something to glamorise a disgusting area of the environment, make a musical instrument out of rubbish and put a song up on the new CATE music site, make a costume out of something that used to be something else, in preparation for the CATE disco we were meant to be having in June (and on that note, I realised, I'd agreed to a date I couldn't actually do, so that was going to have to be sorted out). There was a cycling challenge (and on that note, I realised, I hadn't learned to ride a sodding bike yet). There was a challenge about trying to be vegan for a day.

I tried my best with quite a few of these, and so did my increasingly bemused followers. I found a discarded pizza box outside and used it as an extra coffee table for my room while entertaining friends to watch the England-Australia cricket World Cup clash; I then stuck it in a recycling bin in time for Emily's arrival because, once again, when it comes to interior decoration she has a penchant for actual furniture over things we've found that used to contain cheese. (You may by now be thinking that she probably married the wrong man, and time may still prove you right, but I'm hoping not with all my heart.) I collected various things that looked like they'd be fun to hit, with the intention of bringing them to the 24-hour show and using them during musical interludes as bongos – which would have been an even better idea had I remembered to actually bring even one of these articles to the show. I restricted all my tap-running to five seconds (and of course, I was still not taking baths, even though there was at least one occasion when, returning from a strenuous show or waking up hung-over, I lamented this vow in the bitterest terms since the book of Lamentations itself).

But the task of keeping track of others' challenge efforts was now beyond me or anyone this side of Stephen Hawking, who, as ever, proved difficult to get hold of. The CATE website and the MySpace page became a confusing melange of blogs which no one who'd not been following the whole story, and hardly anyone who *had*, could hope to make sense of. Rather than joining in, newcomers to the site were actively deterred from doing challenges because there seemed to be about eight hundred of them. In other words, it looked like some sort of clique. Crap At The Environment was in danger of turning into the sort of thing it had been partly a reaction *against.* Like the French Revolution, or Johnny Rotten living in a really nice house. But at least the Revolution had managed to kill a few people and Johnny Rotten wasn't really doing any harm.

Feeling like a feeble, non-scientific version of Frankenstein, I posted a somewhat overwrought blog.

Obviously, when I started CATE I didn't know what I was doing. That was the whole point. It was a case of 'let's see what happens'. What happened was, lots of people got involved and started pitching in with ideas. Brilliant.

But in the short time this has been going on, it's already got rather out of my hands. Have you ever had a party and at one point or other during the night, looked around your house and just panicked? That's a bit what I feel like.

There is a paradox. I don't want people to be less involved. If anything I want ten times as many people blogging, 100 times as many people reading. I want this to be the biggest thing since, I don't know, at least since all that stuff Malcolm X did. I'm massively into this whole thing.

But I do need to get a grip on it.

A good example is challenges. When it began, it was great. But now there are too many challenges, and people just look at the page and think 'Shit. Nope. I don't know where to start.' That's one example. It sums up the problem, which is, things are going too well.

So. I'd like a few people to help me organise the site, in an
active way. And I'd like a bit of time to work out how to
restructure things so that more people can join in, without
feeling like CATE is becoming exactly the sort of
environmentalists' club we set out to challenge.

Please chip in with your suggestions and remarks. I don't mean
to criticise anything anyone has done. It's been amazing, the
way people have thrown themselves into this. And I feel like
we're on the verge of this being a quite spectacular example of
co-operation and people power and everything, exactly like I
dreamed. I just want to make sure it heads in the right
direction.

Tell me if this makes sense.

Looking back, the pompous tone of this, as if I were Frankenstein watching his monster weep over the lack of love rather
than a comedian not sure how to proceed with his online
community, is very embarrassing. I'm only including it for
the sake of veracity, and also I suppose because if I start
censoring things which look embarrassing with hindsight, my
memoirs, when I come to publish them, will be flimsier than
Kerry Katona's. (In case this itself seems pompous, I will quickly
reassure you that I will never publish 'memoirs', and anyone
who can announce such a plan with a straight face should take
a long look at themselves.) (Of course, quoting that sentence
would be a pretty funny way to begin my memoirs, if I *did* ever
write them.) (But I won't.) All you can really learn from all the
rhetoric is that I was feeling rather out of control of what I'd
begun, and, I suppose, I am something of a control freak, which
is an unfortunate combination of traits with not being very good
at controlling things.

There was a sympathetic response to my snivelling. People quickly set about redesigning the site so it was easier to follow. On the subject of challenges, the consensus, not surprisingly, was that we should probably just do one thing a week, but try to make sure we all did bother to do it. Then, it would be much easier to monitor each other's progress and our progress as a team. Various correspondents were also kind enough to suggest that I was getting a bit too caught up in things. The eventual publishers of this very book wrote in an email: 'You know, you can also contribute by just not doing so much' – echoing the lesson I'd almost learned, then relinquished, during my coach marathon. I thanked all these people while reassuring them that I was quite all right, and then mentally sidelined their opinions. Luckily, arriving any day was Emily, the one person with a decent chance of talking some sense into me.

Before that, there was the small matter of my 24-hour show. It testifies to the psychological instability I was in, what with the comedy festival, being away from home, and the rigours of Crap At The Environment, that I regarded the prospect of talking to strangers for an entire day, while sleep-deprived, as something of a pleasant break.

The show took place in the Umbrella Revolution, a sort of big top next to the Yarra River, beginning at midnight and going through to the next midnight. It would be a lie to say that I succeeded in dwelling for long on environmental matters – that was to come, I hoped, in the Edinburgh version of the show – but as a concession to my attempts at harmony with the planet, I resolved that the audience and I would at least go outside a few times. This we did: once, at the seven-hour mark, to serenade the first early-morning rowers with a chorus of 'Row, Row, Row Your Boat' (at this point this audience was about twenty-five); then at the halfway point when we all went on a Ferris Wheel (by now there were around sixty); and then, an hour from the end, an audience that was by now two-hundred-strong went back out to watch, on the same Wheel, a kiss between two audience members who had been match-made as part of the show. The lady, Amanda, claimed never to have had a boyfriend; the young man, Jono, impressed her (and the audience) with a dance to win her heart. We then sent them on a wineries tour and followed their progress as one of the show's little narratives. By the time they kissed, it was the payoff to a storyline more than twenty hours in the making. Out in the night air by the river, I felt, once again, a flicker of that total joy in the great outdoors which proper nature people talk about, even though there was a lot of noise and commotion, and even though, to be perfectly honest, my mental state in this thirty-second consecutive hour of wakefulness was not all it could have been.

According to my friend Bec, I kept my no-cab vow and walked home at the end, but I don't remember it particularly well.

Luckily, by the start of May, Emily had flown out to join me. Her arrival, as well as dispelling the clouds of my rather self-indulgent pessimism, imposed a certain common sense. Emily is impulsive, energetic and fun-loving, where I am cautious, slow and don't mind fun, but would rather just watch *Soccer Saturday*. Despite this ability to milk every conceivable droplet of enjoyment from life, though, Emily is very good on common sense and has been, since 2001, the main thing standing between me and that thing called the Darwin Awards where people die from sheer idiocy. Emily pointed out, gently but firmly, what was obvious to more or less everyone – that my website had become an ungovernable mess, I had about as much chance of being able to juggle all the things I was taking on as I had of being able to juggle in real life, and (a harsher truth than either of these) I was letting Crap At The

Environment overwhelm my own environmental efforts and hence becoming Crapper At The Environment, or at least No Better At The Environment Despite All This Talk (a state of affairs so demoralising that there is no shorthand for it, but if it did correspond to a name, it would be something much more ominous than CATE: perhaps GARTH).

We were off to Sydney, where I'd be performing in the Opera House, in a couple of days. Emily suggested that I took this change of scene as a watershed and boiled things right down to a single challenge a week, and made damn sure that I accomplished it myself before paying too much attention to what other people were doing.

But what about the CATE Disco, I protested? What about our plan to Pimp A Patch? What about involving celebrities, doing some sort of tie-in with the forthcoming Live Earth concert, and with the BBC's forthcoming Planet Relief show, which promised to do for the environment what Comic Relief had done for the Third World, i.e. torture television viewers for a whole night but raise a lot of money? What about the idea someone had had of trying to release our Crap At The Environment song as a single by putting it on iTunes? What about the other hare-brained schemes which I had in the pipeline, a pipeline now as long and damaging as the ones sunk into Alaska to drain it of its natural resources? What, in short, about my aim of becoming the planet's comic saviour and, you know, achieving great things? And what about learning to ride a bike?

None of this nonsense, Emily ruled, concentrate on the small stuff. As usual when saying something that irritated me, she was right. We flew to Sydney – that's right, we flew, because it was impossible this time to fit in a train journey. I felt chastened, but also encouraged, by the new perspective my wife had supplied. (Other examples of times when my wife has given me perspective:

when I had to cancel my first ever paid gig because of a lung problem, and predicted, 'Well, I'll never be offered £25 to do comedy again'; the time I believed I had broken my iPod and threatened to throw it out of the window, which would have been a bit of a shame, as it wasn't broken, I'd just not managed to turn it on; and in general during thunderstorms.)

So, a new wave of one-at-a-time challenges began in the week of May Day, to the relief of many on the CATE site, including someone called Jonatan from Norway who wrote in an email: 'It's a good idea to simplify the operation because I was trying to do six things at the once, what a stupid joke!' A stupid joke indeed, delighted as I was that we now officially had a Norwegian participating, as well as people from North Wales to Western Australia. (By that, I mean we had people in North Wales and Western Australia; we couldn't in all honesty have drawn a line between them and gone through CATE people all the way. Uzbekistan was proving a difficult recruiting ground.)

The first challenge, set originally by Andy and Dave in the bad old days a couple of weeks ago and consequently buried in the landfill of my ambition, was an attempt to keep alive the revelation that not doing very much was, all things being equal, better than doing lots of things, in environmental terms. Quite simply, the challenge was to Spend No Money For A Day. 'This challenge could be considered quite easy!' wrote the twins, jauntily, on the site. Indeed it could, I supposed, for people who could find fun in foraging and knew how to make things. For me, trying to show my wife a good time in one of the world's flashiest cities and make her forget that she had married a man who was never at home, it might be a different proposition.

I had already done the spend-no-money day when it was originally set as a challenge near the end of April. I achieved it by the fairly simple expedient of getting up late (having got drunk the previous night, purely in the interests in easing the logistics of the operation), going for a run around Melbourne's Botanic Gardens on a chilly autumn afternoon, in other words about 22 degrees, then staying in my room worrying, watching the cricket, and – after my show – combining the two previous endeavours by worrying about the cricket: as it turned out, rightly. When midnight beeped its arrival on my mobile, I had not spent a single dollar, and despite the modest energy expenditure involving in watching England's feeble exit from the World Cup, I felt it had gone pretty well. You may object that by staying in a hotel, I was technically spending money, but I would retort that the Comedy Festival was covering my costs. You might then argue that they paid for it out of the profits of my show, so if you looked at the balance sheet, I was still technically 'paying', but I would clinch the argument by parroting the word 'if' mockingly, and maybe adding the Italian proverb 'if my grandmother had bollocks, she'd be my grandfather', which I have never known fail to end a conversation.

Anyway, I planned to repeat this success in Sydney for the first week of the new, do-able CATE challenges, but chose the wrong day: Saturday, 5 May. At first it looked a pretty savvy choice. The forecast was very good, so it should be possible to spend a lot of time outside not doing very much at all. Also, two momentous events were scheduled for the evening, which should obviate the need to spend money on making excitement happen. My football team Bristol City were involved in a death-or-glory game back at home, the biggest match for nine years; it kicked off at midnight Sydney time, which meant from about 9 p.m. I would be too nervous to eat anything and so wouldn't have to buy food. And on top of this, a man called Anil, who'd approached me by email, was planning on proposing to his girlfriend during my show that night, and was counting on me to 'work it into the show' somehow.

People have asked me to 'work' all kinds of things into shows before. These requests range in ambition from the perfunctory ('Hey, are you the comedian? Can you mention my mate – he's called Kev and it's his birthday') to the more specific ('Hey, are you the comedian? Can you take the piss out of the bloke with the sideburns? He's getting married') to the man in Loughborough once who said 'Listen, mate, all of us work for a carpet company, we'd fucking love it if you did some jokes about lino'). No one, though, has ever before decided to place in my hands the most important question he will ever ask in his life. You might think that this man Anil was obviously a huge fan of mine; on the contrary, though, he'd never even seen my act before. He just wanted to propose at the Opera House and saw that my show was on at about the right time. For all he knew, I might have been planning an avalanche of jokes about what a disaster my marriage had been, or, for that matter, be peddling an act based on that of live autopsy specialist Gunther von Hagens. In any case, I was meant to meet the would-be groom before the show and have coffee with him. I was pretty confident he would pay for the coffee, since I was about to make myself responsible for the smooth running of the rest of his life. So, all in all, it was certainly theoretically possible to go through the day without spending a thing.

It went well for a while; I went for a long run on Bondi Beach with Minchin, yet again having cause to be thankful for the upsurge in my interest in outdoor pursuits since the planet and I became friends. Bondi is very spectacular and, at the time of year, not even particularly full of other British people. We ran for about an hour. Minchin was full of nostalgia for the time he used to be, in his own account, 'really fat and stupid-looking', and spent a summer doing this run over and over again, a period he now referred to as 'my summer of not being chubby any more'. I hoped by the end of this year I would regard moments like this as part of a halcyon period when I too lost, as it were, some flab from my carbon footprint. There was talk of having a cup of tea in a café with our wives, but I managed to downgrade the venue to Tim's flat. He drove us back and finally dropped us off at the Opera House, saving us the paltry fare it would cost to board a ferry to the show. The no-money plan was coming together beautifully. Again, none of this was actively helping the planet, but for someone so used to buying this and that piece of rubbish, and to hell with the consequences, it is a salutary experience to try avoiding commerce altogether, and one which gives you faith in your ability to cut carbon emissions simply by opting out. There have been lots of times when opting out would have been a great idea. Where was the 'Spend No Money' challenge back in March when I needed it to save me from going to the cinema and squandering two hours of my life on *Becoming Jane*?

I met Anil, who had prepared a poem to advance his proposal, and we agreed that I would contrive some way of getting him onto the stage near the end. He paid for the coffee. Sucker. I was nearly there.

It wasn't till I was up on stage that Fate dashed the cup from my lips in bizarre fashion. Halfway through a joke, I gazed out into the audience to see none other than my mother sitting with some friends. This could only be an optical illusion because my mother lives in Bristol and had not announced any intention of visiting Australia, let alone coming over specially to see me. After two or three looks, though, there could be no denying it any more; whatever my shortcomings as a person, I have a good track record of recognising my mother. What the hell was she doing there? There was no option but to ask her straight out, on stage. She said she was sorry I'd noticed her as she was hoping not to disrupt the show. Emily, listening to events from backstage, poked her head through a gap in the curtains and asked, within earshot of the audience, 'Is your mum here!?' It was now like a scene from a family get-together, being played out before an increasingly bemused audience in the Sydney Opera House.

Manfully overcoming my amazement, I tried to take control of the situation, assuring those members of the crowd not related to me that it was not some sort of bizarre set-up and that the rest of the show would be as normal as could be. Unfortunately, I still had the proposal to oversee. As Anil got down on one knee and began to recite a long, emotional discourse in which he likened his intended to a ray of sunshine in his life, punning on her Swahili name in a manner unlikely to raise much of a chuckle with anyone outside their family, I could see audience members looking at me much as you would look at someone who had charged you ten pounds for fish and chips, and then, rather than serving food, done a Morris dance for you. So far was it from being a regular performance of the show, in fact, that I could see the 'Spend No Money' pledge being undermined by having to give refunds at the door.

That didn't happen – and the proposal went off without, no pun intended, a hitch – but there was still the puzzle of my mother. She was apologetic afterwards in the foyer. 'I wanted it to be a surprise.' Yes, but why was she there in the first place? 'Well, I was just talking on Tuesday about how much I'd like to see you in Sydney, and someone at work said "Why don't you just get a week off and go!" So here I am!'

This was highly uncharacteristic behaviour for my family; normally we're the sort of people to plan ahead pretty thoroughly. Every year my parents get one of those calendars you find in stationery shops, with no pictures of animals or landscapes or anything, just stern blank squares to write appointments in. My dad took a dim view of my brother's impulsiveness once when he went to Leicester to watch a rugby match. And we're a middle-class family with no history of whimsical, extravagant journey-making. Normally my parents would no more 'pop down' to Sydney to watch me than they would have 'popped up' to the Mir space station just because they fancied a look through the telescopes.

Of course, I was delighted. How many people have a mum who is so proud of them – especially after entering a profession which many parents rightly consider a slightly advanced form of busking, but without a guitar? Nonetheless, after all my small gestures, it was disconcerting to consider that my mother had taken a flight emitting more CO_2 than I could save in a decade of 'not buying anything' or 'growing your own'-type challenges. Hell, maybe even making a newspaper pot wouldn't be enough. Given that my mother lives in Bristol and I perform there on a fairly regular basis, her flying to Sydney to see me there instead made, in terms of energy efficiency, as much sense as if the Eurovision Song Contest were held in the Sahara (although that might be a good idea for other reasons).

But what was I meant to say? 'Lovely as it is to see you, your visit is an ecological disaster.' This is a big problem for people advocating a proper ban on long-haul flights, or a carbon rationing system. Some of the loveliest moments in life come from individuals making absurd, unexpected long journeys to see loved ones. It's hard to imagine there would be anything other than uproar if this luxury was forcibly taken away from people, or made into a restricted commodity in pursuit of which they were forced to sacrifice other things like cars or heating. So flattered was I by my mum's gesture, in fact, that I didn't even have the heart to make her watch *An Inconvenient Truth* back at my hotel and then send her home on a paddle steamer, which might have been the hardcore eco-warrior's response. I pushed the whole topic to the back of my mind, which was, by now, quite crowded.

We went to a restaurant in Circular Quay which my mother, with typical parental logic, was worried would be a bit 'pricey'. Arguably, an air ticket is also 'pricey', a London-Sydney fare could even be considered 'a fair whack', but I didn't pursue this point. After the usual reverse haggling that goes on when two people are trying not to let each other pay the bill, we went halves. Just two hours from the finish line, I had gone back on my promise not to spend anything. There was still the chance that the restaurant owners had heard of my courageous attempt and would waive the bill to allow the dream of a no-money day to live on, but despite a lot of raised eyebrows meant to communicate 'perhaps you have heard of Crap At The Environment?', no such offer was forthcoming. So I'd failed the challenge and, when Bristol City pulled off a 3-1 victory to clinch promotion, I hammered a nail into the coffin of my now-dead resolution by buying a round of beers. Australian beers, at least (Victoria Bitter, not Foster's, which, despite the advertising, real Aussies do not drink, for much the same reason they don't drink urine), but still. A bittersweet end to my 24 hours of non-consumerism. I made a promise straight away to observe the next 'Buy Nothing Day' in November.

But the next day, when the remarkable events of the previous night had faded, I was forced to ask myself whether it was time to be more ambitious with my CATE tasks. For all the small good I had done and cajoled other people to do, the fact was that I was still going to fly back to the UK soon; I would be flying to Japan right after that; it was looking increasingly likely I would return to Australia later in the year; and now to cap it all my mum had flown out just to see me. What was the point of making small carbon savings when my life was so dominated by international travel that I might as well just package up a load of greenhouse gas in a nice parcel and send it first-class to the atmosphere? Looking at the bigger picture, it felt as if I'd helped an elderly woman across the street only to kick her crutches from under her. You wouldn't do that in real life and it didn't seem right to do it in a metaphor, either.

It was at this point that I decided to look properly into carbon offsetting, something I had done in a disorganised manner up to now, but with little idea what I was actually paying for or why. It was July before I finally raised the energy to do this. I also finally decided to grasp the nettle of this proposed trip to Japan. I was flying there for just three gigs. I really wanted to go for the fun of it, as well. And, of course, if I didn't go, someone else would take my place – it wasn't as if they would have one fewer comedian on the bill and get the MC to say 'at this point, we would be welcoming Mark Watson, but he decided it was bad for the planet if he flew, so let's have a clap for those carbon savings!' And of course even if *that* unlikely scenario took place, my seat on the plane would most likely still be filled by someone else; British Airways would probably not suspend services to Japan, and take steps to greening up its fleet, because of the withdrawal of my custom. All the same, I felt that if I continued to travel with my current regularity, anything else I could do would seem more or less meaningless.

It was with a heavy heart, therefore, that I asked my agents to see if I could withdraw from the trip to Japan without being executed by the promoters. Naturally, I didn't mention the word 'carbon' in my explanation. I cited extreme tiredness, the logistical misery of coming home only to go halfway back around the world again, the likelihood that one more long flight would disorient me so much that I'd end up like Bill Murray's character in *Lost In Translation*, staring bemusedly out of the hotel room window at the bright lights, and possibly having a frustrated romance with a philosophy graduate. All of these were genuine factors in the decision, but the destructiveness of my continual flying was the main clincher. It would have been a much braver decision if I'd explained this, since then it might have inspired some other people to take an interest in the subject and maybe scrap their own unnecessary flights. But I didn't have the guts and so it goes down as a well-intentioned act and a wasted opportunity all in one.

Still, it would be a shame to lose faith in the smaller stuff. A survey of the CATE site showed that an encouraging number of people had responded to the simplification of the challenges by taking part in non-spending alongside me, some with better results. It was time for another cheering blog. The only problem was that I didn't have time to do it; I was committed to a TV appearance – specifically, on JTV's regular segment *Boast About Your Toast*. In this feature, viewers send in their favourite toasted sandwich recipe, and the guest (in this case, me) makes it and rates it out of five. You can perhaps see why I sometimes don't feel my life adds up to very much. In any case, Emily bailed me out by guest-writing the round-up of the first new-style CATE challenge.

Hello. This is Emily, Mark's wife. Mark is currently taking part in the Australian TV show *Boast About Your Toast*. This leaves me to summarise the week of blogs as all sorts of people record their efforts at trying to be better. I must say that reading the blogs was continually surprising and marvellous, and gave me a very exhilarating sense of how many interesting people there are in the world, and the complex fun of their lives running concurrently. Which is the opposite of how I usually feel.

On that note, this particular challenge seemed to unleash a wave of philanthropy in those who tried it, or at least make them do good things when they might have otherwise watched an episode of *Friends* and bought an unpleasant, over-packaged tuna melt. Ben spent the day at his grandparents doing their DIY and gardening, and in exchange ate all their food, and Laura made a birthday card instead of buying one, thereby making a friend feel worth more than £1.20. McPinky does philanthropic things all the time and had to spend money on breakfast for strangers' children, so that's probably fine. Other people were the beneficiaries of other people's goodwill – Cecilia, for example, only made it because of a kindly neighbour who wouldn't take any money for lettuce plants.

Not spending any money was an easier challenge for people who didn't have any money to spend. As Hannah put it, 'Today I've not spent any money. Yesterday I didn't spend any money. The day before yesterday I didn't spend any money, and the day before that I didn't spend any money.' Not so much a challenge as a lifestyle.

Other people were helped or hindered by Acts of God. Serendipity wrote, 'I found it incredibly easy not to spend money while in bed with an infection from hell due to sideways wisdom teeth.' In fact, most bloggers had some bleak moments. Eating called for extreme resourcefulness, especially for those particularly rigorous participants who refused to stock up on food beforehand. B-gurrl wrote, 'Lunch was pasta found in the back of cupboard, and the ends of cheeses . . . for dinner I found a can of spaghetti shapes . . . I think they were Bob the Builder.' Sarah wrote at 1 p.m., 'There's nothing in my fridge but cheese and booze. Can't face more bread. Eat some cheese, half a party bag of stale Doritos, and the chocolate out of the chocolate Deal Or No Deal I got for Christmas.'

Things got worse for Sarah though. Seconds later she wrote 'OH MOTHER FUCKER I JUST SLICED THE END OF MY PINKIE OFF

SLICING SOME HALLOUMI.' Which is pretty awful. She went on to write, after getting butterfly stitches in A&E, that she blamed Mark. And she was quite right to. Without CATE it would never have happened.

Finally, the Icarus of Crap At The Environment, Andy and Dave Self-Sufficientish (who oddly write about themselves as one person) had quite a few problems after trying to cook with the ground. 'I picked some nettles, sorrel, ransoms and garlic mustard from the surrounding area to have for my lunch,' he wrote. But while 'cooking up a nice bannock loaf from barley flour' he realised he might have poisoned himself. 'I quickly put my fingers down my throat and made myself sick.' Extraordinary.

These acts of heroism for CATE are really quite uplifting in a gross sort of way. Congratulations to everyone for enduring considerable hardship to make a tiny bit of difference.

I was pleased that a number of people were so committed to this project that they were prepared to be ill for it. It was now time to use this as a springboard for a more wholesale tampering with the diets of others, not to mention my own. It was time to contemplate flirting with something as inimical to my instincts and character as bike-riding or, for that matter, grave-robbing: in a word, vegetarianism.

Searching the Internet for inspiration for challenges, I had come to the unwelcome conclusion that it might not be a bad idea to do something about my meat intake. Even before I was interested in environmental causes, I had been uneasily aware that there were some powerful arguments against eating red meat. A vegetarian told me years ago that if I were ever to set foot in a slaughterhouse, or whatever they're called in these equivocal times – an abattoir, a 'bovine anatomy re-alignment facility', I would never eat a sausage or a steak again. 'Blimey,' I thought, 'I'd better not go in one of those, then.' This probably wasn't the outcome the vegetarian was angling for (not that veggies approve of angling, of course), but I did once walk past an abattoir while doing a gig somewhere in the North of England. The cries of animals could be heard faintly on the wind; not being Doctor Doolittle I couldn't be certain what they were trying to communicate, but it didn't sound like 'Well, this is a lark.' A man came out with a cigarette, exhausted, with animal blood all over his hands and clothes and the stench of death following him home, looking as depressed as anyone I've ever seen, including the crew of *Boast About Your Toast*. And in the hierarchy of the abattoir, he was one of the winners; compared with the cows he had had a pretty good day at the office. This small taste of the reality of the meat industry left me with a distaste for burgers so profound that I didn't eat one for a good hour after that.

Also, of late, there'd been more and more stories in the press about how eating too much meat could give you, among other things, bowel cancer and heart trouble. Of course, many of us feel the same way about health scares as we do about politicians: there are too many of them and you don't know which ones will be discredited in a few years. At the same time I don't want to be one of these people who scorn all such stories in the press as the workings of a 'nanny state' – 'Honestly, next they'll be telling us that jamming pokers in our eyes is bad for us!' And anyway, these days I was quite into scares, now I'd decided that the environmental scare was a genuine one. So this was a compelling argument. If I was unmoved by the idea that poor innocent animals would die for my spaghetti bolognaise, surely the idea that *I* might die for it would pack some sort of punch.

Now, with my CATE colours nailed to the mast, I was brought face to face with another major argument against meat: its production adds an enormous amount of greenhouse gas to the atmosphere, both because of the energy involved in killing, slicing up and transporting cows and making them into the shape of hamburgers, and also because of the methane emitted by the cows themselves while padding about in a field waiting for death. A study commissioned by the United Nations, with the title *Livestock's Long Shadow*, as well as evoking a frightening image of super-sized farm animals waiting in a dark alley to take revenge on carnivores, found that meat and dairy production was 'one of the most significant contributors to today's serious environmental problems'. Emissions from animal agriculture apparently contribute more greenhouse gas to the atmosphere than all the cars and trucks on the planet combined.

Could my responsibility to the planet succeed where my basic sense of right and wrong had failed, and convince me to cut down on my meat-eating?

The trouble is that, if climate change is an emotive issue, vegetarianism is doubly so, and when you put them together the result is often unpalatably bitter rhetoric. Though my research into the subject had begun to convince me that it might be better for the planet if I turned my back on animal products, or at least had slightly less of a love-affair with them, the facts to support this were normally overlooked. A lady named Naomi emailed me shortly after I began CATE to say that, really, I ought to set an example by giving up meat and milk altogether because, 'We are the only species that drinks the milk of another species. How can it be natural?' The fact is, we are also the 'only species' that drinks alcohol, dips marshmallows in chocolate, or, for that matter, forms community groups to play 'Good King Wenceslas' on the handbells at Christmas. We are a bit more advanced than, say, corn snakes, so it's not surprising we do a lot of stuff they haven't yet thought of. And who can say what is 'natural'? We only have potatoes or aubergines because we plant them in carefully mon-itored patterns at calculated times of the year, just as we rear animals. If you really want to rely on what is 'natural', we should all just stand with our mouths open hoping for tasty things to fly in.

But I can't honestly claim that the corrosive nature of anti-carnivore literature was what had made me put off meat-related sacrifices thus far. It was much less principled than that. The simple truth is that, as with baths, as with trips abroad, there is a major point in the defence of meat, which is that (in my opinion) it is really, really nice. Most of us will have had the experience of coming across a protestors' stall in the city centre festooned in heart-rending pictures of cute animals doomed to die horribly, and thinking 'I suppose they do have a point', only to be irresist-ibly tempted by the smell of flesh wafting from a shop whose daily specials are Traumatised Sheep Pie and Rissoles of Inhumanity with a Ducks' Tears Dip.

I've always loved meat. It's not just my major source of protein but one of my major sources of joy in life. Asked to order my last meal on Death Row – assuming that I wouldn't be allowed some-thing like parfait of eleventh-hour reprieve – I would have sau-sages and mash (real mash, of course, made with butter and mustard ideally; I certainly wouldn't go willingly to an electric chair with Smash or some other packet product inside me). Yes, I know there are vegetarian sausages and soya burgers and what-have-you, but to me that is like saying there's no point in going to Ireland because there's an Irish theme pub down the road. A meat-free sausage doesn't seem like a sausage to me at all, more like a sausage-themed attraction. The concept makes as little sense to me as other products with their chief selling points removed: decaffeinated coffee, sugar-free Coke, going to the hairdresser and leaving with all your hair.

Still, the website www.wannaveg.com suggested a way of making a CATE-sized gesture towards vegetarianism. This site advocates that all meat-eaters abstain from animal matter for just a single day a week. There are some alarming statistics to show that if we all did this for a year, we would, for example, save 7700 square feet of rain forest – which sounds like plenty to be going on with – as well as 84,000 gallons of water, and this, of course, is not to mention the carbon savings and the animals not being killed. A good challenge, therefore, would be Go Without Meat For A Day. Those who were already vegetarians, I challenged to try being vegan for a day; for the few who were already vegan I could only imagine what the next stage of abstinence would be, perhaps tearing pictures of food out of books and eating those. I wrote my blog full of trepidation at the non-meat-feast I was about to unleash.

This is difficult. I love meat. There's scarcely anything I would rather do than eat something that was once an animal. Even as I type this I am muttering 'oh, bloody hell' to myself.

But, as with the previous, spend-no-money week,
this challenge is aimed precisely at people like myself who need to consider whether our enthusiasm for perhaps not entirely necessary things, like laboriously imported steaks, is a contributor towards the global culture of waste and pollution which CATE is quietly agitating against. As you'll see if you go to the Wannaveg site, one meatless day a week by every carnivore would make a substantial difference. So here we go.

Many of you, especially those of you who are students, or fans of things like cheese, will sail through this challenge. I am expecting it to be an ordeal.

That 'fans of things like cheese' comment, which strikes a rather odd note, can be explained if you understand that I hate cheese and am therefore not able to munch on a nice bit of Cheddar or something to take away the craving for meat, because for me a nice bit of Cheddar is as hard to envisage as a nice bit of measles. I can tolerate a thin layer of cheese on a pizza, or a lasagne; I acknowledge its usefulness as a binding agent, but the idea of shoving it in a sandwich or putting it with grapes or something for a snack – no, I'm afraid not, no thank you, sir. I have never got the taste of it; when people talk about how much they like Brie or feta, it's like listening to an account of a country I know I will never visit. This, along with a fairly mainstream attitude to vegetables (I like parsnips and carrots and so on, but I'm hardly going to get involved with a butternut squash; what am I, Hugh Fearnley-Whittingstall?), meant I was never going to find it easy to replace one of the big plus points of meat: its chunkiness, that feeling of having a big mouthful of *stuff*. I'm a traditional Englishman in that I like meals to be composed of two or three different types of stuff, fairly well demarcated from one another (e.g. here is your meat, here are your potatoes) and presented in nice satisfying chunks. When I look at sophisticated food like a risotto or a mushroom stroganoff, my first misgiving is 'but where's the actual . . . *stuff*?'

Still, for the sake of my vow, it was time to try and serve just 24 hours as a vegetarian. Once again it may have looked like something of a half-measure, but by now I was well into my half-measures; it was better than no measure at all.

A precedent for this dabbling in vegetarianism had been set by my beloved – not specifically because of CATE, but, as she wrote on the site, 'as a general protest against the meat industry with its grim ways, including of course carbon emissions and environment-shafting'. Emily had decided in about March to experiment with becoming a pescetarian, in other words, someone who'll eat fish but not meat. This is one of quite a number of semi-veggie movements which have caught on recently, and which can found all over the Internet by doing a Google search for something like 'semi-vegetarian': people who'll eat anything except cow, people who won't eat anything that once had a face, people who continue to eat meat as normal, but mutter 'Sorry cow, sorry sheep, sorry planet' as they are doing it.

Emily's fish-but-no-meat experiment carried an even more lenient clause, which was quite simply that, if at any point she felt like having meat, she was allowed to. If a restaurant didn't offer much option to the vegetarian (for example, if we were in a Little Chef, or in France), or if the fish in the fridge looked as if it might have gone off, or if she simply thought 'Oh to hell with this, what I need now is to feast on a slaughtered calf' – in any of these eventualities she would permit herself a holiday from pescetarianism. So it was not so much of a commitment to a meat-free diet as an undertaking to try it where circumstances allowed. The idea was that this freedom would inspire her to keep trying, where a more regimented approach would only provoke rebellion. It may sound like a pretty weak resolution compared with www.fruitarian.com ('we eat raw fruit only . . . and we feel GREAT!!!), but, as we shall see, the results were – as they say on shopping channels – surprising.

As for me, I chose to attempt a meat-free 24 hours on a day when we'd planned a trip to the Aquarium. I hoped that having had congress with at least some forms of living creature would lessen my inner indignation at not being able to consume other ones. The example of my wife by my side would also, in theory, strengthen my resolve. As the day's blog shows, though, it was every bit as hard as I had originally feared.

For breakfast I had pancakes with banana and watched jealously as some businessman, obviously one of the many people in the world still not taking part in CATE, tucked into a rasher of bacon which I might have had myself in different circumstances. The pancakes were very nice though, and caused me to reflect that it is often a good idea to choose something you weren't expecting to eat. Good.

Lunchtime, however, saw my frail vegetarianism lurching all over the place. I was fatally tempted by a 'tandoori chicken pizza' on a menu. I like pizza, I like tandoori chicken, I could only see their union being as successful as Simon and Garfunkel's in the good old days. If I avoided this dish I would have to eat a vegetarian alternative largely composed of spinach and good intentions. All right, I thought, I'll just have to do the meat challenge another day.

But CATE-fate intervened as, totally uncharacteristically for Sydney, the restaurant turned out not to be very good at cooking (it's a café called Wild World or something attached to the Aquarium; don't ever go there). The pizza turned up looking very pessimistic about its own chances, and after a single, chickenless bite into a blanket of processed cheese as thick and cloying as a tourniquet over an open wound, I was nauseous. Less than three bites in, it was clear there was no future for me and this pizza. Dramatically, the non-meat day was back on.

After that, it was quite easy, because for some time after this dismal experience, I didn't feel much like eating anything for the rest of my life. During this pizza-imposed lacuna I reflected that I could probably benefit from seeing my near-poisoning as a sign. Maybe humans aren't meant to eat chopped-up birds; or at least, maybe they shouldn't do it as often as I do. It's been suggested that we should have a CATE official list of vegetarian treat recipes. That would help people like me. Maybe I could manage to nourish myself without plundering the birds and beasts of the earth.

Maybe not, though. By the evening I was famished and temptation popped up again, this time in the shape of fish and chips. My wife's recent conversion to pescetarianism allows me to see meat- and fish-eating as two different matters, though a lot of people would assert that they're two different sides of a rather bloody coin. The clincher though was that the fish under offer here had pretty much been caught in the harbour we were looking at with our own eyes, so, all in all, I believed I could do practically no harm to the environment by eating it.

Well, to cut a long story short, I ate the fish. It was fantastic.

Technically, I'd succeeded in not eating meat, but in the most inglorious way: by ordering meat so foul that my ambition to live beyond my twenties obliged me to stop eating it, and then by dining on something which, although not capable of the sort of heartrending noises and big-eyed expressions that stir up compassion, most likely did not think 'good, this is working out nicely' as it was hoiked out of the water. My point about the relative environmental effects of eating locally caught fish and imported meat probably stood, so as a low-carbon day it had sort of worked, but it was going to be very difficult for me to achieve this on a weekly basis. Nonetheless I would have to try, I supposed.

Some of the CATE bloggers shared my struggles: one, Jools, began her blog by recording, 'This week I've had haggis, chicken biryani, chicken curry, fish, chicken drumsticks, chicken pasties and mince,' which, as a record of a week meant to kick-start an attempt at a form of vegetarianism, is pretty unpromising. Others had done very well and some reported chalking up a meatless day almost without noticing it. This, though, flagged up a possible problem with the one-challenge-a-week programme we'd been pursuing: quite simply, where before the range of tasks had been unmanageably broad, now it was almost no challenge at all for some people. A good of number of CATE's active participants were students, and students, as everyone knows, routinely eat very little, spend almost no money and in some cases don't get out of bed until it's too late to do anything that day. For such people with their feeble empty larders and indifferent nutritional habits, 'eat no meat for a day' was no more of a gauntlet to pick up than 'make sure you don't go mountain-climbing for a day'. For the next week's challenge, I felt, we needed to make at least a bit more of a demand. Once again it was Andy and Dave who gave me the idea. For the final week of May, CATE participants would be dared to avoid buying any plastic.

That's right. It was all very well trying to shun plastic bags – and by now I estimated I'd issued more than two hundred IDNABs – but this was only a tiny part of the overall struggle against plastic. Plastic packaging wastes a colossal amount of energy, produces all manner of toxic pollutants, and takes so long to decompose that, for example, the 'protective case' shielding your Peter Kay DVD from harm will still be knocking around somewhere even when the terrible day comes when Kay can't make us laugh any more.

So, for a week, no yoghurt pots. No multi-packs of beer with those little bits of plastic holding the cans together. Any CATErs who owned a football club would not be allowed to rip up its pitch and install a plastic playing surface this week. If Michael Jackson was taking part in CATE, and I had no hard-and-fast evidence that he wasn't, he would be prohibited from having cosmetic work done for seven days.

This stringent challenge drew online gasps from the Crap At The Environment community. Even Andy and Dave admitted that it was 'likely to be pretty tough'. I was determined to mark my final

week in the Antipodes by succeeding in this exacting last challenge of the month. By this point I was shacked up in a hotel in
Auckland and Emily had gone home, which was a mixed blessing
as far as the challenge was concerned: on the plus side, it meant I
would revert to a monkish lifestyle with my consumerist impulses
largely kept in check by apathy; on the minus side, there was a
danger that I would also revert to loneliness and gloom, and be
forced to go out and buy myself something to cheer me up which
would turn out to be harbouring plastic somewhere.

Throughout the week, a record number of blogs – getting on for
seventy – testified to the extraordinary difficulty of avoiding
plastic. It is everywhere. I imagine if you buy sheets of plastic
wholesale, they come wrapped in more plastic. Of course, sometimes it is the most appropriate medium, especially for fragile or
precious goods which need a bit of insulation from the world; you
would think it a bit remiss of PC World if they handed you your
new MacBook wrapped up in newspaper. But a casual browse of
the shelves reveals an awful lot of goods that are being over-
protected. During 'No Plastic Week' I tried to buy a new toothbrush and was forced to visit an actual dental surgery because all
the brushes I could find in Auckland's chemists came suffocated
in little plastic packs which were themselves mounted on cardboard. It's hard to understand the need to segregate a toothbrush
quite this thoroughly from its surroundings. Admittedly, one I saw
claimed to have '360-degree micro-sonic power for the most
thorough coverage', so perhaps it had to be quarantined in plastic
for the protection of anyone who might accidentally set it off and
find themselves assaulted by its awesome bristles. And the trip to
the dentist's was just one of the odd measures I had to take to
avoid coming into contact with the enemy.

I couldn't buy newspapers without checking whether they
contained plastic-wrapped supplements (which tripped up some

CATErs, as you can see below); I had to make sure my milk came in cardboard cartons; had I seen a Frisbee on special offer, I would have been powerless to purchase it. I was frustrated in my late-night craving for meat pies, because they all seemed to come in fiddly, rustly little wrappers. The only time I did manage to find, as it were, a naked pie, it was my non-meat day and I couldn't allow myself to eat it and ruin the gesture after I'd made a point of eating pasta and soup and potatoes all day.

It wasn't till the final night of the challenge that, suffering from acute pie-withdrawal symptoms of the kind only known to those like myself who stay up very late and eat rubbish food, I walked about a mile from my hotel to find a 24-hour shop where I could whisk a pie straight out of the oven. Admittedly, it was so hot that it removed most of the skin from the inside of my mouth, but it was a small price to pay. If there's one thing nicer than a beef pie, it's a condiment of pure self-satisfaction. I had survived a week without buying plastic; the planet was pleased with me.

Not everyone was so lucky.

There were many times this week when, confronted by the pitiful spectacle of two bananas wrapped in plastic for a 'healthy fruit pack', CATE people wondered: would it really be so dangerous to put this stuff on the shelves without a protective case as thick as a suit of armour? Supermarket trips ended in misery as challengers found plastic lurking where they least expected it. Captain Cat found a seemingly innocuous box of tissues contained a 'little plastic thing to keep the tissues in. I was angry and ripped this out.' Cat, a new and determined blogger, was also distressed that a cardboard box of spaghetti had a little plastic window so consumers could see inside and satisfy themselves of the contents: 'Whatever happened to pictures, people?' Jools had a similar problem with a loaf of bread whose packaging contained a needless plastic strip: 'was it in case I wanted to peer inside and admire its crust?'

Milk in general was a problem. Many bloggers lamented the decline of the old-style milkman with his glass bottles and – in Enid Blyton books at least – his cry of 'Milko! Milko!'. There was some talk about why you can't seem to get organic milk in bottles, though WildGarlic, who does still have a milkman, found out that if there's enough demand, they might start doing it. Andy and Dave, as often, led the CATE hardcore backlash by making their own soya milk: www.selfsufficientish.com/soyamilk.htm. Ace. And you thought only cows could make milk.

Even if you did get home from the supermarket safely, plastic, as Andy and Dave observed, is often 'lurking to catch you out'. Occasionally there's nothing you can do. Dipity had already decided to forgive herself for her kid's plastic juice cartons, since she bought them before the challenge started, and 'I didn't want to start every day feeling a failure, though I believe this is a standard emotion for parents everywhere'. But she was driven to distraction when her husband and offspring's magazines arrived housed in plastic wrappers, which were themselves only there to seal in an enormous number of pointless bits of paper advertising subscriptions to fishing magazines, or Princess Di 10th anniversary commemorative toilet roll holders and God knows what. I'm heartily in agreement with Dipity on this, magazines and newspapers are so often crammed with bits of paper which 98 per cent of readers instantly discard. There should be legislation forcing them to replace all this crap with a single strip of recycled card saying, 'If you're interested in buying a load of utter shit, go here,' and then a web address.

But the efforts to battle the plasticocracy of modern Britain were heartening. Where they couldn't avoid buying things in plastic, people simply gave certain products up, including: peanut butter and Maltesers (Cat, who watched a film without the latter product for 'the first time in about six years'); meat and cheese (the hard-as-nails Andy and Dave); Oreo biscuits (me, at 2 a.m., on my own, in New Zealand, displaying true heroism for the first time in my life); lentils and ice-cream (Knox); bottled water (Trip Hazard); even the Sunday paper (Cathryn), and the list goes on and on.

And, displaying the resourcefulness which is one of CATE's best weapons against its own crapness, plenty of people found ways around plastic-buying. Sometimes it was just going to local grocers and loading up a rucksack with fruit and veg, rather than going to the supermarket. Sometimes it was bulk-buying, to get a better ratio of produce to packaging. When forced to play the plastic game, people reused bags and bottles to at least cut down on the amount they used.

Me: for once I did pretty well with this. While long-term hotel residency has made certain things difficult, it played into my hands for plastic avoidance. A single, plastic-free supermarket shop – largely loose fruit and veg, which I carried back in a canvas bag, fresh bread etc. – kept me going for snacks, and by eating a hearty breakfast in a café opposite most mornings, and basically being a hermit most of the week, I succeeded. I was desperately tempted at times, but I managed it. So despite numerous setbacks and disappointments, this was probably the best week yet for the CATE challenge.

And, by a fortunate coincidence, this was also the week that Innocent – purveyors of smoothies so packed with fruit and goodness that drinking one is almost as good as getting your teeth into a lovely great chunk of animal flesh – received an award for using recycled plastic in their drinks bottles. It would be wrong to say outright that CATE sparked a sea-change in attitudes to plastic which led to Innocent's prize, but we certainly didn't stand in the way.

It was some days later, re-reading my blog, I realised that in my courageous quest to find a toothbrush not wrapped in plastic, I had overlooked the obvious fact that toothbrushes are themselves made of plastic. I had, after all, failed the task. It was an odd sensation to feel betrayed by one's own teeth. Teeth are strange customers; like football referees, if you don't notice them, they're doing all right.

But even with this dental disappointment behind me, I prepared to travel back to the Northern Hemisphere in reasonably good spirits. After the chaos of my early attempts at motivating people to action, things had settled down into something like a proper organisation. As for my own efforts, well, hardly inspirational perhaps, but I was getting there. A month of relative asceticism had seen my personal carbon emissions plateau at an acceptable level. It was a bittersweet feeling – after a trip Down Under characterised by sincere if not always very efficacious attempts to clean up my personal act – having to board a plane and chug a load more greenhouse gases into that crowded area where they all congregate. But I was trying, and now, I was trying in something like a structured manner.

END OF MAY REPORT CARD

Credit: Successful boycott of plastic; slight decrease in meat-eating; evasion of trip to Japan.

Debit: Still eating a lot of meat, despite efforts; another long-haul flight plus a couple of short ones, where travel planning failed.

Savings: Big, thanks to cancelled Tokyo gig. Would have been larger still with more commitment to dietary changes, however.

Status: Largely Crap At The Environment, But Light At End Of Tunnel.

SARAH'S MAY BLOG

My first attempt at Spend No Money day started enthusiastically and ended with a trip to casualty.

I deliberately didn't stock up on food and stuff in preparation for the challenge because that would be a bit of a cop-out, so I made a big pot of tea and tried not to worry about my near-empty fridge. I wasn't sure if using electricity counts as spending money. It costs money ultimately, obviously, but I was really going to need to use my computer so I reasoned that it's a grey area and only to be used 'essentially'. With that in mind I resisted a traditional Saturday morning ritual of staring blankly at T4 – missing two episodes of *Friends* I've seen eleven times (a genuine hardship) and a Natasha Bedingfield special (not a hardship). Instead I practised my ukulele for a couple of hours and mastered 'She's Like The Wind' by Patrick Swayze. One day when all the oil runs out we may be sitting in bunkers with nothing but ukuleles to amuse ourselves – someone needs to know how to play the *Dirty Dancing* soundtrack.

Taking sympathy on my self-imposed poverty, a journalist friend gave me a present to amuse myself – a pair of old-fashioned blue and red Roller Girl type roller-boots and legwarmers. This was a 'press gift' to my fashionable pal from a legwarmer manufacturer. That is, someone who makes legwarmers decided a good way to get a journalist to talk about their legwarmers in their magazine would be to send them some old roller-skates. This works more often than you'd think. The boots are two sizes too small, but beggars can't be choosers. I took them to the park (leaving my wallet at home so I couldn't be tempted to spend anything) and wobbled about for an hour or so trying to remember how roller-boots work (the key is not to push off with the stoppers on the front but kind of slalom with the sides of your feet). Got a bit sunburnt and rather happy. Afterwards I wobbled back home past the Bethnal Green Buddhist centre, which was having some sort of open day. The charity shop bit had a clothes rail outside and a blackboard saying 'these items are free, with our love'. Those Buddhists! I nabbed a perfectly serviceable cheesecloth shirt. The Buddhists' vegetarian café had a sign in the window saying 'come in – please pay what you can afford' which was tempting, but I reasoned that I'd look a bit heartless just stuffing my face and then roller-booting out with my hands in my pockets, whistling. And it would probably be bad karma.

The thing that niggled me most though was not being able to buy a newspaper, but then I remembered that they're all online these days. I forget about that constantly. Saved a good percentage of tree by doing the crossword online. There is something ergonomically satisfying about a paper though, which I miss. Doing a lap of honour of my lounge, I caught my skate wheel in a Cornetto wrapper that had fallen out of my handbag and landed on my face. Slick. I decided to take off the skates to prevent any more accidents.

By teatime, I was having a bit of a sulk about not being able to go out anywhere, or buy any nice food. I ended up eating everything edible in my flat, including a stale 'party bag' of Doritos. Mainly, I was annoyed with myself for not having organised some kind of fun free activity – living in the UK's capital it should have been easy to find a museum or walk or something to perk myself up, and here I was, alone, sulking, and breaking my no-telly rule to watch the 'talent show' *Grease Is the Word*, which is kind of like breaking a vow of chastity to sleep with your sister. It was then, in huffy mood, that I jabbed a knife into an innocent bit of Halloumi rescued from the back of the fridge, and managed to slice the end of my little finger off. This produced an amazing torrent of blood and even better swearing. Spending no money, I walked, hunched over my injuries like Mr Orange in *Reservoir Dogs*, to Whitechapel A&E. After a fun wait, a nurse declared that I only needed 'butterfly stitches', which is such a weedy name for a treatment that it just added insult to (in my mind) life-threatening injury. As it was, I was just unable to play an F minor for a couple of weeks. On the plus side, good old NHS, it was an entirely free procedure.

What I learned from all this is that as soon as you start thinking about 'spending no money' in terms of a sacrifice, you're doomed. You may even end up slicing off bits of your body. Maybe. So with my bandaged pinkie cocked in the manner of a posh lady drinking tea, I typed a list of things that were both free and life-enhancing.

1) Join a library. They even do DVD now.

2) Sign up to The Church of Stop Shopping.

3) Visit a city farm. If you live in a city, that is. If, like me, you fear the bucolic and get freaked out when a traffic island is a bit too grassy, it's easy to forget about nature. On a whim, I visited Hackney City Farm, and realised that it's a great way to remind children (and grown-ups) how the environment works – food

grows from the ground, bacon comes from pigs and all the stuff that's so blindingly obvious we're capable of utterly forgetting it. Watching a child slack-jawed with excitement as they realised the eggs under the chicken were the same ones in the supermarket was astonishing. Showing a kid just how delicate and clever nature's cycles operate, I realised, can have a massive impact on how kids think about the world. Also, a cow licked me, and cows are awesome. Find your local city farm here: www.farmgarden.org.uk.

4) Sign up to www.tvrecordings.co.uk – watch telly programmes being taped for free.

5) Go to church. Even if you're not religious, it's calming, the architecture is usually fabulous and you get free wine.

6) Go to court. The public are allowed to sit in the gallery at most trials, so pop down your local Magistrates' Court and witness real human drama. Could be a council tax evasion, could be a grizzly murder case!

7) Poke round posh people's houses. Under the Conditionally Exempt Buildings code, there are hundreds of buildings and art collections that are tax exempt on the condition the public is allowed access. Visit the HM Revenue and Customs site (www.hmrc.gov.uk/heritage/rights.htm) and find your local Lord, then go and bother him for a look at his Monet.

8) – 10) (it counts thrice as it's a long one) Sign up to Freecycle. But that is a story for another chapter . . .

JUNE

By the time I returned, the environment had well and truly established itself as the topic of 2007, and more and more people were addressing society's general CATEness and trying to combat it. As World Environment Day approached, posters all over London urged people to recycle (which I was just starting to do), enjoy walking around more (which I was quite well advanced with), and ride a bike (hmm). Plans were announced for Live Earth, a massive simultaneous chain of awareness-raising concerts across the globe. The BBC ploughed on with its preparations for a climate-change version of Comic Relief. The plot of the long-awaited *Simpsons* movie hinged on Homer's irresponsible dumping of waste in the Springfield River. It would be wrong to claim that I caused these things to happen – the Red Hot Chili Peppers got the nod ahead of me for Live Earth, and I was too busy to help with the film – but it certainly felt as if CATE was part of a growing awareness that we all had to change a little bit together.

Smaller news items backed up the impression that Joe Bloggs, as the average Briton used to be nicknamed despite no one in this country being called Bloggs, was getting interested in the environment. In the *Daily Telegraph* a man called Henry Wallop wrote a report claiming that sales of clothes pegs had gone up by 1200 per cent over the past year, because more and more of the nation's launderers were trying to keep costs down by pinning their smalls on the line rather than feeding them through energy-guzzling machines. After three months of staying in hotels, I celebrated this news by putting my own washing out to dry in the garden – another example of a Funrifice, as the sight of clothes billowing in the breeze is much nicer than the buzzing and rumbling of an electrical appliance. Washer-dryers have always annoyed me, as they always seem to leave clothes damp, as if they were basically washing machines who just added drying to their CV in the hope no one would call their bluff. Admittedly, with Britain suffering one of its wettest and most miserable Junes in living memory, the clothes on the line have still not fully dried at the time of going to press, but at least it's been an energy-efficient process, and anyway, I've got other pants. Wallop concluded his article with the warning that dozens of people are admitted to hospital each year with 'clothes-peg-related injuries', a reminder that sometimes, sacrifices for the planet involve a degree of danger.

This was going to be the month that CATE increased its 'profile', as they say in advertising; we were going to 'create a buzz'. We were getting close to the official launch party, Green Feet, at which people (some of them wearing recycled costumes) would make pledges in writing to reform one or more areas of their eco-regimes – if, that is, they were able to write anything at all, because there was a danger everyone would be having too much fun to function as normal humans, but that's a risk I run every time I host a party. I would also be speaking at the British Library's corporate bonding day on the subject of the 'greener workplace', bucking an old tradition whereby guest speakers are expected to have some knowledge of their subject. I was going to be interviewed by *Friends of the Earth* magazine; I was appearing on a green radio station called Passion for the Planet; we made plans to unveil a

Crap At The Environment banner at the Glastonbury Festival; and Nicola promoted Pimp My Plant Pot at the Chelsea Flower Show – largely to septagenarians who were alarmed by the word 'pimp', because they probably weren't sufficiently phat to be down with her, but it all helps. A CATE participant, Emma, had volunteered to start up a CATE shop online with themed merchandise to raise funds for projects like Pimp My Patch, the scheme to transform a corner of Manchester into a modern Eden, which I was still working on organising. You could really have mistaken me, at this point, for someone who had a history of knowing and caring about the environment.

Having said this, my individual performance continued to leave something to be desired. I bought energy-efficient light bulbs from IKEA, but couldn't install them because, as previously mentioned, most of our flat is lit by weird bar-shaped lights or minute spotlights sunk into the ceiling and, as we don't own the flat, there wasn't a lot I could do about the wiring situation. I hadn't manage to impose the day-a-week of vegetarianism introduced by the earlier challenge. I was still merrily eating methane-producers at every opportunity, even as Emily, operating under her flexible pescetarian regime, found herself eating less and less meat. I was starting to look into buying more local produce, at least to the extent that I made an effort to look out for the little Union Jack stickers on fruit and veg, but then I would quite often find myself drinking Californian wine without noticing (without noticing it had come across the Atlantic, that is; my alcoholism hadn't quite reached the point where I didn't notice I was drinking at all). When we managed to squeeze a barbecue into the 25 minutes of June where no rain fell, I missed the opportunity to set an example by getting everything from a farmers' market. I was making sure I switched off phone chargers and didn't leave things on standby, and so on, but there were quite a few lapses. In short, while I was less Crap At The Environment than I had been, there was a long way to go before you could call me GATE.

What I should have done to tackle this was to keep concentrating on small improvements to my own routine. What I did, in keeping with the hubristic nature of this whole exercise, was to keep trying to organise bigger and bigger initiatives to draw attention to the environmental cause. I committed myself to doing what I'd been vaguely promising to do, and announced that I would be doing a 24-hour-long show with the general theme of the environment in Edinburgh, in August. As a first step towards a nature-appreciation strand in the show, I further announced that the show would not all take place in the one room as usual, but would begin in the great outdoors at midnight, and proceed on a tour of different venues over the twenty-four hours.

I didn't know what any of these venues would be, and I was pretty confident that anyone who stuck it out for the full 24 hours, in what would most likely be Edinburgh's customary summer weather of bitter rain and why-don't-you-just-kill-yourself fog, would either be spiritually enriched by the experience and feel empowered to do their best for this earth of ours, or be so crushed and exhausted that they would never want to do anything again, which is pretty carbon-efficient.

I needed the best producer money could buy. Unfortunately I didn't have a budget for the show, as I was planning to charge the usual feeble ticket price, to make up for the fact that at least sixteen hours of the show could be tedious crap – so instead, I thought, I was going to have to get the best producer that pleading and emotional blackmail could buy. Fortunately, within the ranks of CATE was the ideal candidate: a lady named Corry who was both a superb producer and a stupid masochist. I approached her with the proposition that I would pay her pretty much no money, in return for which she would do an unthinkable amount of work, including finding venues, getting green companies to donate various goods and services, organising an environmentally friendly publicity campaign, and arranging medical care in the event that my body did the sensible thing and caved in during the day-long performance. She had no objections to this at all.

Then it was time to launch what I hoped would be the biggest and best CATE challenge yet. The temporary vegetarianism, non-purchasing and plastic-boycotting had gone well enough to make me think that, as a group, we could push ourselves a bit harder. World Environment Day was just around the corner, on 5 June. Of course, it's the kind of event that is rather cheapened by excessive hype: we all get that sinking feeling when World Environment Day decorations start going up in the middle of May, adverts all jump on the bandwagon, the shops start playing nothing but environmental music and so on. Nonetheless, by the first of June you can feel that tingle of festive anticipation starting to grow, and you know kids will find it hard to sleep on the night of the 4th. In the spirit of the season, I decided to set a big task to the online community. Someone had sent me a link (www.unep.org/wed/2007/english/Information_Material/Alphabet.asp – there, now you know how I felt) to a website on which was published an 'Alphabet of World Environment Day', with an A-Z of ways Joe Bloggs, or in this case Blogs, could take part in the event. As with all A-Zs since the first children's illustrator thought 'fuck it . . . it's going to have to be "xylophone",' some of the alphabetical suggestions had a clutching-at-straws feel – it seemed unlikely anyone among us was going to manage a 'rickshaw rally' or a 'symposium', or even 'chair an environmental debate' – and there was a certain amount of repetition. But it seemed to me that between us, we could have a good go at achieving all seventy-seven of the suggestions. I named this the MegaChallenge, a word I invented by conflating the words 'mega' and 'challenge', though a magician doesn't normally reveal his secrets like that.

In the middle of June I proudly announced that we now had an online shop selling T-shirts, mugs and so forth with the Crap At The Environment logo. Emma had set this up on the website www.cafepress.com, with the idea that any money raised would go towards charities researching renewable energy sources. She was forced to call the company 'CATE UK', because someone was already selling memorabilia for another CATE: a group called Chicks Are The Enemy, who, from all I could gather, had rather different aims from ours.

When Emma told me about this initiative, I not only didn't stop to ponder whether it was a good idea to promote a commercial venture with CATE's name on it, I even went so far as to break the news on the website with the words, 'This is obviously a really good idea, so please support it.' Rather quickly, people started pointing out that it might not be such a good idea after all. Weren't we meant to be focusing on a 'less is more' policy and buying less crap which had to be transported over long distances? Wasn't it a bit counter-productive to try to raise money, for however good a cause, by adding to the culture of mindless online purchasing which already caused planes and boats and trucks to traverse the globe endlessly, whisking a set of Harry Potter key-rings from Alaska to a collector in Chesterfield who bought them on eBay? Didn't it also strike an uneasily commercial note, contrary to the agreeably amateurish atmosphere of the campaign as a whole? If we had to sell stuff, shouldn't we peddle handmade goods, like at the CATE summer fete which we hadn't, in fact, got around to organising yet, like quite a few of Spring's bright ideas? And was it not a final, rather damning irony that Café Press's mugs, T-shirts and miscellaneous knick-knacks arrived buffered by layer upon layer of the packaging I'd been so busily railing against?

To all this, of course, I could only answer, respectively: yes; um, yes; yes, you have a point; yes, you're probably right; and yes, I am an idiot.

After consultation with Emma, I came to the decision to perform what ITV news might call a 'humiliating climbdown' and refine the plan a little bit from having an online CATE shop to not having one. Of course, it was a lot less effort than shutting a real shop, but it was slightly worrying that I'd failed to give even a moment's thought to the consequences of this scheme. Admittedly, the objections of the website's readers, and the spate of emails the whole thing provoked, more or less constituted an 'environmental debate', so you could at least claim I'd made a contribution to the MegaChallenge, but that was a bit like the Met Police saying that by shooting an innocent man they'd raised the public's interest in anti-terror legislation. I had to do better.

Even as I was reflecting on the way that, in my eagerness, I'd forgotten the whole point of what we were trying to do, there came further discouragement. A vegan gentleman called Ben Green, who'd been monitoring my efforts, set up a website called Pretty Hardcore About Things (PHAT), intended as the 'scarier big sister' of CATE. He was goaded into doing this by the one-day vegetarianism challenge. While he acknowledged the theoretical value of what I'd been trying to do, he wrote:

> No matter what small or large, crap or hardcore, steps you take down the verdant green trail, you cannot, just can not, call yourself keen on environmental issues whilst consuming animal products. None of them.

What, not at all? Not even a bit of sausage-meat at Christmas?

Methane is twenty-five times a more potent greenhouse gas than CO_2. You can heat a house with a cow. Just keep it in the basement and the amount of energy it gives off will keep you toasty all through the winter. This is the original central heating.

The vegan society says that a cow needs to eat 10 kilos of grass to produce a kilo of meat, so without the moo-ers, there would be ten times as much food. I think this is a bit silly. Grass is a tiny cropper. I'm willing to bet that if you grew something nice and heavy cropping – some nice protein-rich bean or other – you would get ten times the yield that you would from grass. Or in other words, it is entirely possible that you would get 100 times more food from the same area of ground that it took to grow a cow.

That sounds to me like a far better use of the world's arable land in every respect.

He went on to say that this was not meant to discourage anyone from dabbling in vegetarianism, anything was better than nothing, and so on; overall it was hardly a poison-pen letter, more a bit of a jab with a biro. Nonetheless, I was slightly shaken by this correspondence. Was it true that methane was twenty-five times as potent as CO_2? Was it true that without our reliance on animals for food, we would not only burn less fuel and pump less methane into the atmosphere, but also have more food to go around? Can you really 'heat a house with a cow', and did any well-known energy suppliers offer this service?

The point was that I didn't know enough about the subject to counter these claims, or to do anything other than, once again, mutter 'um . . . yes. You might have a point' and so forth. For all the enthusiasm I had brought to my battle against crapness, I was still hamstrung by not really knowing what I was doing.

And this was becoming increasingly clear as I continued to be seen more and more, and wrongly, as some sort of ambassador for the green cause rather than the keen beginner I still was. My speech to the staff of the British Library was imminent. I was going to do an interview on Passion for the Planet, the Internet radio station, even though at this stage I still only really had a Sort of Interest in the Planet. I'd publicised the fact that I was going to force the audience of my 24-hour show to walk around in the rain because these days I was so keen on the environment. People were continuing to ask me questions about the subject – some of them cynical, some merely interested, but most of them capable of making me quite flustered.

Cynic: Did you see in the papers that article called 'Ten Global Warming Myths'? It said that some car journeys were better for the planet than going by bus, that 'local produce' was a meaningless term, and that everyone in Britain ought to kill a polar bear because we can power one-third of the country for a year from its screams.

Mark: No, I . . . I didn't read it. But it sounds, er, well, I'll have to check the facts.

Well-intentioned watcher of *Channel 4 News*:   It seems to me that China's fast-growing, coal-based economy – which I saw a very interesting feature about on *Channel 4 News* – is producing greenhouse gases at such a rate that individual economies are absolutely pointless. Do you see what I mean?

Mark: Er. Well, yes. But hopefully, er, that's wrong.

Hardcore environmentalist: I don't agree that our actions are pointless . . .

Mark: I didn't say they were.

Hardcore environmentalist: I know, I was arguing with the well-intentioned watcher of *Channel 4 News*.

Mark: Oh. OK.

Hardcore environmentalist: I don't agree that our actions are pointless, but it's about channelling them in the right direction. Although changing our light bulbs and switching our TVs off standby and recycling our bottles are all nice useful things to do, there is no chance of slowing down the world's dangerous carbon emissions without political action.

Mark: So are you saying that rather than doing small, conscientious things in the household, or even slightly bigger campaigns in the community, we really ought all to be lobbying parliament to set much lower emission targets, going on marches, donating to green charities who petition world leaders, and so on, otherwise we might as well start writing letters to our grandchildren which read, 'Dear Victor, here is why I ruined the once-resplendent planet you live on?'

Hardcore environmentalist: I suppose I am sort of saying that, yes. But Victor was your choice.

I still didn't have an answer to anyone who took the time to question me properly about the environment – not by a long way: I couldn't counter the sniping of cynics, reassure the concerned-but-pretty-sure-it-was-hopeless contingent, or defend myself against the politically active ecologists I met who understandably felt I was just playing at being green.

This latter feeling was continuing to bug me even when I encountered very nice environmentalists who had no intention of making me feel like a chancer. I was humbled by my visit to Passion for the Planet, the DAB radio station; the very long trip down to South-West London on public transport (I couldn't get a green cab company to take me there) left me in such a bad mood that I was amazed anyone could maintain such a passion while operating out of a pig-ugly building on a horrible, isolated industrial estate. On the walk from the Tube to the radio offices, without even thinking about it, I ate a sandwich from a packet and threw it in a bin and then sloped along thinking helplessly about the continued wastefulness of my instincts, however many pretty challenges I might try to take on. I got to the radio station, said my piece about trying to change my attitude to the environment and walked back to the station in pouring rain, a part of me wishing I could just get in a big fat truck and drive back home and turn my hand to something I was a bit better at.

Not that the MegaChallenge wasn't having some positive results. I myself had taken on 'keep your neighbourhood clean', 'organise a special event', and 'bicycle races'. For the first one, I had taken to picking up litter discarded by people among the estimated 53 million in Britain not yet participating in the Mega-Challenge. I scurried around after crisp packets, drink cartons, and boxes of Dairylea slices that people had got halfway through before thinking 'Hang on, this isn't really food.' I salvaged anything that didn't look as if I might get a disease from touching it. If possible, I would find a recycling facility to deposit my rescued treasures; if I had to bin them, at least I would feel I'd kept the neighbourhood a bit cleaner and tidier. Organising a special event – that, of course, was covered by the preparations for the 24-hour show. Bicycle races: I pledged that as part of the enviro-show, I would finally do what I'd been half-promising to do all year and learn to ride a bike in time for the marathon show. And I stepped up my I-don't-need-a-bag efforts in my local supermarket by taking the fight to Kevin when he tried to wrap a single peach for me. After our traditional 'I don't need a bag'/'Well, I've already put it in a bag now' exchange, I made my point by taking the peach out of the bag, eating it with gusto in front of him, and tossing the remains nonchalantly into the bin beneath the checkout. Looking back, a grander gesture would have been to plant the stone outside the supermarket where it would sprout into a magnificent tree, but there was no way of knowing if Kevin would still be employed there by the time it grew.

And plenty of the other seventy-seven special World Environment Day challenges were also being taken up by CATE participants. Amy walked several miles rather than using a car, all to see me doing the first preview of my new show, which is a bit like watching someone perform a song before they've worked out the tune or most of the words. Andy, from Andy and Dave, undertook a zero-carbon journey, and taught everyone how to construct a straw urinal, a tip they'd got from TV's Adam Hart-Davis, who, as well as making absolutely sure we all know what people throughout history did for us, reportedly likes nothing better than to wee outdoors. On the same lavatorial note, three people had switched to using recycled toilet paper, something I also decided to do. (The singer Sheryl Crow had recently made a public plea for people only to use one square per toilet visit, which seemed reasonable, if hard to police.) Recycled paper quickly becomes such a self-evidently good idea that, as with Fairtrade tea, I found it hard not to become smug within minutes of converting to it, and had to prevent myself from falling into the old eco-warrior trap of looking at people with non-recycled toilet paper as if they were absolute barbarians who by rights ought not to have a bathroom at all.

Then there were people harvesting rainwater, taking over disused allotments, planting trees, doing workshops with kids, and cycling around on bikes they got from websites, like the aptly named Freecycle (www.freecycle.org), which promotes the free redistribution of unwanted stuff. There was all manner of small good being done in the CATE name. But the smallness was bugging me a bit.

The final Friday of June was the day I'd been booked to give the morning speech at the British Library staff's green-themed team-building day, and also the day of Green Feet, the CATE fundraising event. Some analysts went so far as to call it the biggest day of CATE's four-month history. I tried to avoid being drawn into this sort of hysteria and concentrated on the task in hand. As I have previously mentioned, I am not very good at the environment, and the prospect of speaking on the subject at this still-early stage of my mutation into Al Gore was daunting indeed. My strategy was simply to talk about how fun the environment could be, and how un-frightening the whole subject was, and go pretty easy on the actual detail, as – beyond the obvious stuff – I had very little idea how to 'make the workplace greener'. If there was any detailed questioning, I would be in trouble, not least because it fairly quickly came out that I was lucky enough not to have what's called a workplace.

When I got there, though, this very fact turned out to be a point in my favour; I'd forgotten that 'company fun days' tend to instil a sense of dread in employees, just as at school, when 'swimming' and 'fun' were put together, I knew there was extra-special aquatic humiliation in store. As a result, the mere sight of a comedian lifted the mood of people who had previously been put into groups and forced to spend about ten minutes constructing a 'mascot' for the day out of discarded paper and other materials, and giving it a name. (I was one of the panel given the respon- sibility of judging the winning mascot; the quality of entries was impressive given the demeaning nature of the activity.) I got through my speech, as planned, by cracking some jokes about how poor I'd always been at dealing with environmental issues, and how very gradually I was making some improvements. Every- one seemed very satisfied with this companions-in-crapness mes- sage and I was reminded once again of the double-edged sword of my position: on the one hand, by saying 'Well, we're *all* crap' I was allowing people to feel comfortable with a subject they'd otherwise have run, or driven in an SUV, a mile from; on the other hand perhaps I was allowing them to feel that making an honest but rather feeble attempt was more than enough, when in fact, I was beginning to feel uneasily that actually it wasn't.

In the afternoon, there was an activity based on the popular TV show *Dragons' Den*, in which would-be entrepreneurs try to pitch money-making ideas to a bunch of people who already have money and sit there with sceptical expressions and bark spoilsport objections like 'The thing with this is, no one will want to buy it in a million years.' The idea was that the different groups would each come up with one way to make the British Library greener in its operations. The panel of 'dragons', including me, would quiz them on their schemes, and give a rating to each presentation. Of course, no actual money would change hands, so I wouldn't get to say, 'I'm not investing in this' in a belligerent Scottish accent, but it would still be a bit like being a TV tycoon, and as with the earlier activities I was simply thankful that I didn't have to do it myself.

When I met the other dragons, though, I knew that the shoddiness of my credentials was finally going to be shown up. One of them, Alexis Rowell, was a Liberal Democrat councillor with a 'strong environmental track record' according to the organisers; another, Arthur Potts Dawson, owned a restaurant, Acorn House in King's Cross, which was the 'greenest in the country', and which did things like making menus out of scraps of old menus, feeding food leftovers into a wormery, and by the sound of it everything up to – if not including – powering the whole premises with nothing but the anticipation of hungry diners. Both these green men looked as intent on their judging duties as if this were really on the television. I muttered something about being a comedian and hoped for the best.

Sure enough, what I had imagined would be an amiable exercise in mutual back-slapping turned into a gauntlet for the hapless employees who came forward to present their hastily thought-up schemes. The first, for example, was a plan for a 'virtual library', whereby a lot of paperwork would be scrapped in favour of a scheme in which all staff were given a USB stick; recycling bins would be placed all over the library; recycling monitors would do the rounds collecting discarded plastic cups, and so on. After this, they concluded, we'd be a bit closer to saving the polar bears from drowning for a bit. This all sounded reasonably sensible to me, and I started saying some nice positive things and preparing to give them about seven or eight out of ten in each category. Then the two proper dragons piped up. The USB stick idea was a waste of resources of a different kind, one of them pointed out, as they are inefficiently produced from plastic. Also, recycling plants all over the country were already at capacity for paper, said the other – the restaurant owner – so there was no point in sending them any more. Instead, we had to look at reusing what we already had, as his restaurant did with their menus-from-other-menus shenanigans. Also, talk of 'polar bears' was irrelevant; it was us that had to bear the brunt of the consequences of global warming. By now the presenting group had each shrunk half a foot and you could see other groups frantically consulting and scribbling things out, learning from the mistakes of the fallen, as – with my W surname – I did time and time again at school at the expense of people called things like Alan Awkwardson. I changed the seven or eight to a five.

But almost all groups fared the same, with Alexis and Arthur pointing out how their supposed savings would in many cases make things worse. 'I can't believe no one's talked about energy conservation yet,' Arthur fumed. 'This is all too small-scale,' Alexis lamented. 'This just wouldn't work,' they both said simultaneously at one point. Meanwhile Alexis was getting more and more irate at the constant mentions of polar bears. 'I really hate this emphasis on bears!' he said venomously at one point, something I never thought I'd hear – not realising that the well-meaning but ill-advised organiser had, for a bit of 'fun', dared each group to mention polar bears at some point, and there was even a penalties system for those who failed to do so.

It all ended amiably, with the two dragons saying that everyone had done really well and we'd all learned a lot, while I kept up my role as banal encourager by chipping in with remarks like, 'I thought it was well presented.' But my head was spinning. A few months ago I would have regarded Alexis and Arthur's rather aggressive insistence on bigger, bolder environmental schemes as the talk of fanatics, competing to out-green one another. Now, I was forced to ask myself: But haven't they got a point? What *is* the use of taking tiny steps forward if the situation is as parlous as everyone says it is? Shouldn't we be concentrating on forcing businesses to convert to green energy rather than fiddling about putting recycling trays in offices in the hope of saving three paper cups a day? Is it true that recycling plants already have all the paper they can possibly handle and, if so, why haven't we all been told this so we can get on with other stuff?

The organiser thanked me as I left, for having contributed to an educational experience for the staff; I said that it had been educational for me as well. It came out sounding like a bit of a platitude, but actually, it was all too true.

I was still thinking about this at the CATE disco, Green Feet, which took place that night at Clockwork, an atmospheric club in Islington with a name encouragingly suggestive of alternative sources of power. While a range of top comedians cracked jokes up on the stage, the publishers of this book (who stamped the hands of patrons with a specially issued green stamp, as per the MegaChallenge) manned a stand at which revellers could take time out from having the time of their lives and answer some

FACTLET: The recycle cycle

Is it true, as the expert claimed, that paper recycling plants are at saturation point? I asked several people in the industry and received conflicting answers. What did emerge was that paper recycling alone is not good enough to make a proper impression on global damage. We need to be thinking about actually 're-using' things, e.g. restaurants making coasters out of bits of old menus, rather than carting everything off to recycling plants as soon as we're done. For inspiration, see later bits about Freecycle. I suppose this has been less a Factlet, more a Tentative Muse-let.

questions to assess the precise level of their crapness. If you've been reading this book with half an eye on getting involved, you can play along with this specially adapted version of the Green Feet Quiz.

HOW CRAP AT THE ENVIRONMENT ARE YOU?

1. You're on a plane waiting to take off. Which of these is closest to summarising your emotions?

a. 'Gosh, I'm blasé about this – I mean, I fly so often. I even flew to my son's school sports day though it's less than two minutes' walk away.'

b. 'This is probably the only flight I'll take this year. Apart from the return leg, of course.'

c. 'I don't fly that often but, in the airport, I saw Monarch Airlines are flying to Sharm El Sheikh for 79p or two tokens from cereal packets, so I'm tempted to nip over there for a jolly with some of the lads from work who are into Egyptology.'

d. 'Reluctantly, I have climbed aboard this plane because my grandmother in West Virginia is critically ill, I am being presented with a Pulitzer tomorrow, and a part of the Golden Gate Bridge is being renamed after me in a ceremony on Thursday next. I am still only on this plane because I tried to swim across the Atlantic but ran out of lipids.'

(a) 1 point   (b) 3 points   (c) 2 points   (d) 4 points

2. How big is your car?
   a. 'I don't have a car, and if I did, I would attack it with an axe.'
   b. 'Like other people with insecurities, I have a massive car. There she is over there. I tell you what, she goes like shit off a shovel. Nought to ninety like that: whoof!'
   c. 'It's a bit bigger than I need, to be honest. There's only the two of us but it's nice to have the space in the back.'
   d. 'It's a little hatchback. Nice word, hatchback, isn't it? Satisfying to say. Like spatchcock.'

(a) 4 points   (b) 1 point   (c) 2 points   (d) 3 points

3. Do you use non-A-rated electrical appliances?
   a. 'I don't have a clue what you are talking about, but I hope you will stop soon.'
   b. 'I've had an efficiency check done on all my appliances, and I reduced a man in Argos almost to tears by badgering him for a certificate.'
   c. 'Um, our oven is efficient, I think. I remember Pamela saying something about how efficient it is. She might just have been talking about how well it cooks flans and stuff. You should talk to Pamela, I guess. She does most of the stuff with appliances.'

d. 'If I'm honest, I'm not sure whether A-rated is the best or worst, but I'm not shy about asking, and I'm about to move into a new place so I will kit it out with the most efficient gear I can.'

(a) 1 point   (b) 4 points   (c) 2 points   (d) 3 points

4. Do you leave your mobile phone charger plugged in, your TV on standby, all that kind of thing, overnight, or when you're out?

a. 'No, and I threw my son out on the street for a 48-hour probation period after he repeatedly over-charged his Nokia.'

b. 'I have been known to, yes. I like the comforting sight of those little red lights when I'm trying to sleep. It's not been an easy couple of years.'

c. 'Of course I do. This is 2008, mate. I suppose you'd rather we all listened to the radio and did cave paintings?'

d. 'I used to, but I'm reforming. It's a nice feeling to put the phone charger off. You can sort of imagine it's having a little sleep of its own.'

(a) 4 points   (b) 2 points   (c) 1 point   (d) 3 points

5. How much a part of your diet is red meat?

a. 'We have it most days, I suppose. Well, three or four times a week. Hang on, is chicken red meat? OK, good.'

b. 'I am a vegan, and I wash my hands every time I meet someone who isn't.'

c. 'Mmmmnnnn . . . sorry, I can't answer that, my mouth's full of Argentine steak garnished with New Zealand parsley.'

d. 'These days I mostly have a bit of fish or chicken. Maybe one bit of red meat a week. Or two smaller bits. Or four really rather small bits.'

(a) 2 points   (b) 4 points   (c) 1 point   (d) 3 points

So, how crap are you?

16-20 points   You are actually very good. You shouldn't be reading this book. Go and do something else.

10-15 points   You aren't doing badly. You could easily improve in some areas, though.

5-9 points   You're about at Mark's level. Your efforts so far have been lacklustre to say the least. You could do a lot better.

1-4 points   You are a scourge upon the planet. May Mother Nature weed you out soon.

Having undergone this harrowing confessional, participants could then sign up on a list with a pledge to change some aspect of their lifestyle which had just been exposed as inadequate. I pledged to eat and drink locally sourced produce, using farmers' markets where possible, and never to leave electrical items on standby or otherwise waste electricity. These were things I was meant to be doing anyway, and had indeed done intermittently, but I hoped the gravitas of this public pledge would stiffen my commitment a bit.

The headline act of the evening was Andy Zaltzman, who encouraged everyone – 'A sea change has begun, but seas are very big and tend to stick with what they know, so it will take a while yet.' He went on to caution us against indiscriminate acts of misguided world-saving: 'I do worry that the whole environment will be tarred with the same apocalyptic brush, and there will be vigilante attacks on entirely unpolluted bits of the environment. In fact, the other day, I saw a man beating up a lake, shouting: "Why do you hate the West so much, you ecological piece of shit?" ' I hosted the whole extravaganza in the 'shambolic' style which has become my trademark, i.e. not really finishing any sentences and missing every possible opportunity to talk about the environment. When all was said and done, we had raised £500 for CATE projects, made about fifty people promise to make a little change, and got everyone to ponder the environment, briefly. It was a successful event and an organisational triumph for Miriam. But I couldn't help imagining the Camden councillor and the eco-restaurant guru standing there muttering: 'This is all much too small-scale.'

It didn't help that, despite the reasonably impressive response to the MegaChallenge, a lot of the seventy-seven challenges were still left undone, and although this acid test of the whole challenge system had hardly been a failure, I had to admit to myself that the growth of the CATE site had nowhere near matched the level I'd been hoping for when there was the initial surge of interest. We had well over a thousand people signed up now, plus another couple of hundred on Facebook, the rival to MySpace that was spreading like a virtual forest fire; but from what I could tell, only about sixty or seventy were participating in challenges, and fewer than half of those were doing a blog about it so we could track some sort of improvement in their routines. (Also, oddly, practically all of these were female: the decline of the earth as a viable habitation for our race continued to be seen, seemingly, as a girly thing.) Lots of people had expressed interest in the whole idea, participated in one or two challenges, only to have their eye taken by one of the eighty billion other web communities out there – Crap At The Single Currency perhaps, or Not Sure What To Do About All The Genocide You Hear About – and vanish. It was clear that I had overestimated the ability of websites like MySpace to unite people behind a cause. Our MySpace page was really only ever going to bind together a small number of dogged types. To have a greater reach than that, I was going to have to be much bolder.

Plus, even the more modest ambitions of the CATE site were not all being achieved. We'd still not managed to organise a CATE fete, and the summer would be over soon, if, indeed, there was going to be one. We had still not managed to 'Pimp a Patch' in Manchester. I still hadn't learned to ride a sodding bike. As August, and the Edinburgh Fringe, approached, and my schedule of preview shows took me up and down the country faster than a politician before an election, the amount of time I had to devote to the organisational side of CATE shrank from hardly any to about half of that.

Right at the end of June, on the Underground – after a walk down a hundred and forty-five steps – I encountered Johann, my journalist friend and Good At The Environment contact. 'ALL HAIL, MARK!' he boomed at me over someone's shoulder. He started telling me that scientists were working on a new way of feeding something to cows which made them fart less; there was optimism that it would substantially reduce methane levels in the atmosphere. He then told me that in August he was going to a 'climate camp' at Heathrow, where activists would spend a week protesting against the proposed expansion of the airport, and being glared at by police who wished they'd been sent to the football instead. One of his friends, Joss, was the leader of an organisation that agitated to stop planes taking off. 'This is the sort of thing that moves the environmental lobby forward,' said Johann, enthusiastically, 'visible action on a major scale.'

It was at this point I remembered that, last time Johann and I had met, he'd left me with a cliff-hanger by saying there were two types of amateur environmentalism, one of which he loathed – and then we'd been separated. What was it he meant to say, I asked.

'Oh,' Johann said, 'I think I was going to say that so much effort is wasted by people doing small, narcissistic things, you know – *composting* . . .' (he said it as if were something shameful, almost revolting) '. . . growing their own vegetables, re-using plastic bags . . .'

'But surely it's worth doing that sort of stuff . . .' I said hopefully.

'It is, but it's so small-scale,' said Johann. There was that damning word again. 'If everyone in the world stopped using plastic bags today, for ever, it wouldn't make a blind bit of difference to the fact that the world is on course to heat up by two degrees unless we have laws to force every country to reduce their carbon emissions.'

You'll have gathered by now that Johann is somewhat similar, politically, to the 'hardcore environmentalist' who has made a couple of cameos in Q and A sessions. But he wasn't 'hardcore' as in the slightly unhinged, I'm-sitting-in-the-middle-of-the-road stereotype. He was a normal bloke with a big hearty voice who worked for a newspaper and lived in a city and had a grasp of the issues.

'So you think', I said, 'someone like me should be concentrating on trying to bring about changes to society quickly, rather than raising my own awareness bit by bit . . . ?' I didn't mention any of the specific things we'd been doing, as I was pretty sure they would come under the umbrella of things that 'wouldn't make a blind bit of difference'.

'It's like with any big change,' Johann said, 'it has to be carried through forcibly. Like homophobia. Say you want to try to stop everyone in the world from ATTACKING GAYS,' he said rather loudly. A party of American tourists listened in to us, with the dad clearly torn between paying attention and trying to shield his kids from this tirade. 'You can either go round everyone in the world and ask them INDIVIDUALLY to NOT BEAT UP GAY PEOPLE,'

Johann continued, 'or you can simply pass laws punishing people for doing it. Only the second approach is actually going to get you anywhere, because such a large number of people will only ever do things if they're compelled to by law.'

We went our separate ways. I walked past a billboard for Monbiot's book *Heat*, which I still hadn't got round to reading, though a copy had been sitting next to my bed for some months. I thought about what Johann had said. It summarised what quite a number of people had been saying or implying, in different ways, sometimes by drawing parallels with attacking homosexuals and sometimes not.

If I didn't step up both my individual efforts and the scope of Crap At The Environment, then it was just going to be a pleasant hobby which would result in minor changes to my life, which in turn would result in very little on a global scale. Of course, I'd known this all along, but that had always seemed enough. Talking to people who really cared about climate change was making me think that, perhaps, it was not going to be enough.

I wrote a pensive blog announcing my unfocused, but definite, aim to try and use the next period of my CATE year to do something bigger and better.

> CATE is unique in being spearheaded by someone who's more shit at achieving its key objectives than most other participants. Admittedly, there are precedents for this: the Labour Party has been led for ten years by someone who doesn't agree with a lot of what Labour means; the England manager is about the tenth best football manager in England. But even so. I'm worried that I could be doing more harm than good, by organising everyone into a taskforce that gets obsessed over trivial do-gooding rather than getting anywhere near grappling with the reality of environmental problems.

On a personal level I'm going to hone my efforts by taking on more stretching initiatives. I don't know exactly what, or how, yet. But watch this space.

None of this is to criticise the efforts of anyone who's been involved in the past challenges, or who is still keeping up the no-meat and spending-no-money days every week; indeed, without you, there would be no point in CATE at all. I'm just constantly trying to refine my approach. I know a bit how Blair must have felt over the past few years. He did have quite a complicated job, to be fair.

The past three months had seen significant improvements in my habits and in my awareness of green living. But I had to separate mere ethical living – which should be a minimum requirement, really – from the more urgent race against the clock which global warming seemed to imply. And somehow I had to make my contribution to that race.

Or, it could still be that climate change was a hugely exaggerated, even completely fabricated, phenomenon, or that it was already well beyond the control of humankind, and I would be better off just growing some carrots in the garden. But to move on to a stage where I could truly say I was Good At The Environment, I needed to find out either way.

END OF JUNE REPORT CARD

Credit: Through MegaChallenge, incited various green acts; publicised cause; made pledge to save energy long term.

Debit: Discovering extent of ignorance; efforts shown up as small-scale; not a vegan nor likely to become one; general sense of discouragement.

Savings: Negligible.

Status: Disappointingly Still Crap At The Environment.

SARAH'S JUNE BLOG

Doing my bit to promote green style, I attended the Green Feet disco wearing my favourite new thing in the world – a 1970s polyester maxi dress in a Yellow Submarine type psychedelic print, purchased for pennies on a market stall. Not only did it generate a number of admiring comments, it also generated an enormous amount of static electricity. Polyester and frenzied dancing don't mix, and I was thrown unceremoniously across the room whenever I came into contact with something metal. Totally worth it.

It was all well and good boycotting unethical clothes companies, but I had the nagging feeling that maybe they weren't taking enough notice of my one-girl crusade. It was then that I signed up to The Nag (www.thenag.net), which is an excellent site for lazy activists. Once a month, they send you a gentle email asking you to do something to reduce your impact on the planet: maybe switching to a green energy provider, maybe ordering an organic veg delivery. What interested me most, though, was their suggestion to Nag your favourite clothes shops. As the site said: 'Between us we spend £38.4 billion a year on clothes. Should give us some bargaining power . . .' This was a tremendously exciting notion to me. The idea that the consumer is the one with the power should be obvious, but most of the time . . . just isn't. Shops NEED you to buy their stuff – without shoppers, Oxford Street would be a wasteland populated by a few Hare Krishnas and a man holding a Golf Sale sign. Cutting out unethically produced goods wasn't just making me feel less ooky inside, it was sending a message that I was taking my money elsewhere.

Rather than making a sacrifice, I was making a stand.

What The Nag made me realise, though, was that boycotting a company without telling them is the equivalent of giving your lover the silent treatment and then saying 'if you don't know what's wrong, I'm certainly not going to tell you.' So I wrote letters, using their incredibly easy-to-use template, and told every High Street clothes shop I'd previously frequented that I was SPURNING them until they promised to shape up a bit.

And recently I've started reading the phrase 'voting with your money' all over the place. With each purchase, or lack of one, you tell the people who make stuff that you're prepared to go elsewhere for stuff that's a bit less fe-fi-fo-fum than their stuff. Every time you buy recycled toilet paper, bam! Take that, Andrex. When you don't buy a Kinder Bueno because of the astonishing amount of packaging they use, ha! In your face, Kinder.

The downside to 'voting with your money' is that it still on the surface encourages you to spend in the first place. Spend No Money day, which I was still trying to keep up one day a week, pointed out the flaws in trying to consume our way to a greener future. As a society we need to consume less, no matter how many green stickers you put on the box. But some things, like toilet roll, or tea, or knickers, are pretty much essential (to polite society anyway), and the people who make them will do anything for your money, even go greener and nicer if that's what you demand. Cor.

Part Three
July, August, September:
Heat

JULY

Over the course of the first couple of weeks of July, I read an enormous amount of material about climate change. Throughout this process, a line kept coming back to haunt me from Monbiot's book *Heat*, which, six months after first having it recommended to me by a score of GATE acquaintances, I finally managed to read. Monbiot remarks at the end of the Introduction that, even if his recommendations aren't taken on board, his back-up plan is that the book will make everyone so depressed about the state of the planet that they'll never leave the house again. This sounded similar to my plan to wear everyone out over my 24-hour show, and moreover it was a good joke, which I still hope to steal at some point in the future. But as jokes go, it was fairly close to the knuckle. After even a small amount of proper, grown-up reading on the subject, I remembered why I'd always been so scared of the whole business in the first place.

The gist of *Heat*, without wanting to spoil the plot for anyone who might read it, is that we need to slash our carbon emissions by an astonishing 90 per cent over the next twenty years or so. I'm not a mathematician, but having done some sums, 90 per cent equates to nearly all of it. This is obviously a huge amount more than any government plans to commit to, because it would involve not just making factories greener and stuff, but actually restricting the rights of individuals in ways which would probably spark off riots if they ever came to pass, or if not riots, certainly some pretty disapproving *Daily Mail* front covers. Among other things, he suggests a carbon rationing system, limiting the freedom of the individual to, for example, drive a nice car; a massive reform of the transport network; a re-think of the ways houses and buildings are powered; a move towards getting everything delivered so we don't have to have supermarkets; and, of course, a huge cut in the amount of flying we're allowed to do – flying, in his view, being akin to killing other human beings. He ends the book by repeating his main argument that in order to make a proper difference to the environment, we need to get out of the modern Western habit of thinking that, because we are so far advanced technologically, we can have anything and go anywhere and do whatever we want. His conclusion is that the campaign to save the planet is ultimately a campaign against ourselves.

I could see the good sense of a lot of the book, and was prepared to take his word for some of the rest (for example, a fairly long comparison of different types of cement). As someone who loathes shopping centres, and would happily sign a contract never to set foot in any kind of retail outlet for the rest of my life (with a possible clause allowing me to wander around second-hand bookshops), the prospect of getting everything delivered from local sources is a very attractive one indeed. The privilege of being able to squeeze the hell out of each piece of individual fruit until you happen upon the perfect lemon is well worth sacrificing for the joy of never again having to wheel a trolley or being forced to listen to the greatest hits of Mariah Carey. Beefing up the national coach network, and making coach travel enjoyable, seems pretty sensible to anyone who's saved a few pounds going by MegaBus and then spent eight hours wondering when exactly the 'mega' part is going to materialise. Carbon rationing could just about work and in theory I'd be prepared to save up 'credits' to be allowed to go to the other side of the world, because, as Monbiot points out, it's only in recent generations we've become accustomed to being able to do this at will anyway.

But these were all extreme measures and, if a world-renowned environmentalist deemed them absolutely necessary to stave off ruination, what the hell was the point of me pottering away finding out the location of farmers' markets, or walking to a gig rather than taking a taxi, when I could be spending all my time campaigning for changes to the law?

Of course, Monbiot is regarded by quite a few people, even people with an interest in the environment, as being 'a bit much' – apparently his detractors call him 'Moonbat', meaning a crazily left-wing person, because the two words are quite similar: which just shows you how dangerously witty satire can be. But this kind of summarised the problem for me. Not just in Monbiot's book, but in several other books, many politically neutral blogs, and various conversations with people I trusted, the message was coming out again and again that if it was worth engaging with all this at all, it was worth doing it wholesale. Where did this leave the whole idea of CATE and the sort of environmentalism-lite I'd been experimenting with all the time?

Near the end of Monbiot's book was a bit which gave me even more specific reason to doubt myself. Introducing an Appendix, the author exhorts us all to join one of the environmental groups listed therein – Campaign Against Climate Change, Greenpeace, and so on – and says it is only worth starting a movement of your own if you're absolutely sure those ones are going nowhere; a multiplicity of tiny little groups can do more harm than good, by getting in each other's way and fragmenting what support there is for the cause. I was fairly sure that, in a fight between Greenpeace and Crap At The Environment, they would win quite comfortably: didn't they once take down a boat? At the very least, they probably had an office, so that already made them more of an organisation than me.

It began to feel more and more as if my idea of encouraging people to join me in doing little things for the common good was a naive one at best and, at worst, an absurd waste of time I could have spent lending my support to people who could actually help the situation.

You might say that the whole point originally was to combat this very train of thought. Well, yes, but what if the train of thought had been right all along, and rather than combatting it, I should ride it to the conclusion that my efforts didn't mean anything on their own?

Of course, it was stupid to measure my efforts against those of a proper, tough-guy environmentalist like Monbiot and in any case, by his own admission, not even he had really got it nailed: he lived in an energy-inefficient house, he travelled to the USA and Canada to promote his book, and it was reported in the press that he'd bought a car for unavoidable necessities. He even says in his book's Introduction that he knows a prominent environmentalist who goes snorkelling in the Pacific on her holidays. I could have taken comfort from these, and other revelations about the fallibility of even the greenest folk about, but in the fatalistic frame of mind I'd got myself into since I began to read up on the subject, it only cranked up the sense of futility. Hearing that Monbiot, who said flying destroyed people's lives, had got on a plane to the Americas (which are easily accessible by sea) to tell people so, and – at about the same time – that Al Gore was being criticised in the American press for the high energy bills generated by his own home, I felt, rather than freedom to fail, the disillusion of a Christian meeting God and having him say, 'Well, yeah, obviously you're going to commit *some* adultery. I know I do.' If even these top dogs of the fight against climate change were prone to environmental sins, then, really, what hope was there that anyone like me was going to be able to do this stuff? Weren't we all doomed for sure, if the people urging the most dramatic cutbacks in our consumption of unclean fuel were gobbling it up themselves?

Oddly, I was jolted out of this pessimism by an online encounter with some idiots. Emma, a CATE member, had recently set up a Facebook group calling for a ban on domestic flights. Obviously, as always, it was rather unlikely this alone would force the new Prime Minister into rushing a bill through Parliament, but it did bring attention to the lunacy of the short-haul aviation industry and stimulate debate on the subject. Unfortunately, the trouble with democratic debate is the problem with democracy in general: a lot of people are morons. Fairly early in July, a handful of the nation's enormous moron contingent began to post comments on Emma's page:

Moron 1: (Uni. Sheffield) wrote at 1:54am on 10 July, 2007

HA ha ha! Unbelievable group everyone! Obviously going to make a massive difference! Here's something funny, my dad flew from Heathrow to Gatwick last week! Hahahaha!

Moron 2: (Uni. Sheffield) wrote at 2:30am on 10 July, 2007

Moron 1, you're a hero. Because of this group I"ve just decided to never use the train again. It's fly time for me. I'll go on that 787, that's nice and eco friendly.

Moron 3: (University of Leeds) wrote at 2:14am on 11 July, 2007

Wank wank wank to this wank group hahahaha. My mate just flew from London to Manchester on business haha. And he is set to do it next month too. Haha. How funny is that.

Of course, this could easily be dismissed as a bit of undergraduate larking, like running through the town centre in one's pyjamas, forcing a friend to drink until he vomits, or draining the country's resources while masturbating in front of daytime TV. But it was a bit alarming for a couple of reasons. Firstly, these were students at reputable universities, not middle-aged reactionaries; secondly, at almost exactly this time, freak flooding had caused large stretches of Yorkshire, where these gentlemen lived, to disappear. Whether or not global warming had anything to do with the continued bizarre weather we were experiencing, it would take a truly obtuse individual to laugh at the future rising of sea levels after a reminder (one of many) that our little island was ill cut-out to deal with even the slightest climatic changes.

But it was that remark 'obviously going to make a massive difference!', and the tone of adolescent sneering, that sparked me into life. No matter how hopeless your actions may feel, nothing makes you defend them more vigorously than being told they're hopeless – especially by a dickhead. I might be crap, but at least I wasn't proud of being crap and actively looking for ways to be more crap. It occurred to me that not so very long ago, I might have sympathised with the sizeable number of people who lampooned the whole saving-the-planet project. Now, I was reacting to them. Weird as it may be to gain inspiration from such a negative example, I felt that there was a certain automatic nobility conferred by doing the opposite of whatever people like this were doing. It was the 'WWJCD' principle in action; not, as the abbreviation usually means, 'What Would Jesus Christ Do?' but 'What Wouldn't Jeremy Clarkson Do?'

And the more I thought about it, the more it seemed to me that, in fact, there were lots of examples of small actions combining to wreak considerable change. Consumer pressure had recently forced Mars to abandon the use of rennet, which is from an animal source, in their chocolate. What 'consumer pressure' actually means is 6000 people – not very many – writing or emailing or calling Mars. That was all it took to make an enormous corporation change their stance. (As another confectionery example, Cadbury's this year brought back the Wispa bar as a reaction to the ninety Facebook groups set up to campaign for it. This sounds like a joke, but look it up. Again, a lot of people at home, seemingly messing about online, goaded a huge company into a large decision.)

This led me on to thinking about those people I heard on the flight in Adelaide, chuckling about the immense amount of travelling they'd done. It seemed to me now that if someone asked me, 'Don't you realise those planes will take off, whether you get on them or not?' I would say: 'Well, yes and no.' Of course Ryanair flight staff aren't going to greet the news of my absence by taking off their caps and going to work on a ferry instead. But it's hard to deny that, in the long and even medium term, any public transport service, like any business, owes its existence to custom. Last year Emily's grandmother flew from Norwich to Bristol for Christmas; this year the service has been discontinued because most people do not want to fly from Norwich to Bristol. Of course, economics is a bit more complicated than that, but not *that* much more complicated. It only takes a small drop-off in passengers before airlines start to ask themselves whether it's worth running a route at all. That small drop is people like me thinking, 'Actually, let's not fly on this occasion, it's stupid.'

And as my faith in small actions began to rise again, I was given a reminder that there could be scope for me to make a difference on a grander scale – once again, from a slightly strange source. Just over a month before my 24-hour show was scheduled to take place, Live Earth, the Al Gore-inspired series of simultaneous concerts meant to 'raise awareness', hit the nation's screens. Even before it began, there was criticism of it. Foul-mouthed egalitarian Bob Geldof questioned the need for it, claiming that we are 'all fucking conscious of global warming'. This was a remarkable statement, given that people of my generation, almost without exception, know more about Third World poverty than they do about climate change, but there were much more serious accusations to come.

The problems with Live Earth (you see? like Live Aid, but . . . with Earth) have been well documented, so I'll give a brief summary of my experiences as an armchair viewer. Part of the problem was certainly with the BBC, who had no real idea how to cover it and ended up cutting the best bits, showing dreadful pre-recorded performances by dreadful artists, and interspersing the action with longish periods of Jonathan Ross nervously asking guests: 'So, er . . . should we . . . switch off our light bulbs and so on?'

But the BBC could hardly be blamed for the fact that many of the acts were of dubious quality, and some were desperately ill-suited to 'awareness-raising'. Sometimes this was amusingly bathetic – the idea of the Pussycat Dolls being the final bulwark between apocalypse and the ignorant public was the sort of thing you had to laugh at to avoid crying – but in other instances, it verged on the sinister. The spectacle of Geri Halliwell touting the impending reunion of the Spice Girls, a group that has arguably given rise to more landfill-choking merchandise than any other in pop history, as well of course as some of the most heartlessly engineered music, was enough to make one yearn for a five-degree temperature rise and an end to civilisation as soon as possible. As Sarah tartly observed in her blog, 'It was the first time I've wanted the informative videos to start and the acts to fuck off'. I couldn't help being reminded of how easily someone trying to use their 'clout' for good (admittedly, in my case in a rather smaller way, and without a mini-skirt on) could seem, not just self-regarding – which is something of an entertainment industry standard – but risible to an extent that actually harms the cause.

The main problem with the event, though, as has been pointed out in many quarters, was how breathtakingly Crap At The Environment it was. In spite of the buoyancy of the British music circuit, average American acts were flown across the Atlantic, and the combined distance travelled by participating musicians was apparently a bit over 222,000 miles, creating a carbon footprint which, if it were a real footprint, would have to belong to a mammoth. Even among British acts, not-very-bright poseurs Razorlight flew straight from the gig to Scotland by private jet, muttering something about planting trees to make up for it. On top of this, the whole shebang left the familiar post-festival residue of a field full of thousands of plastic cups. This sort of spectacle at Glastonbury or Reading has often made me think 'Stop banging on about how in touch with nature you feel and pick that burger wrapper off the ground, you novelty-hat-wearing prick' before turning my attention back to Beck; but here it looked like a sick joke.

Surveying the morass of rubbish over the shoulder of a news reporter while a slogan about loft insulation scrolled over the heads of the Beastie Boys, it was easy to feel that the sub-standard execution of Live Earth had made the whole climate change lobby look rather ridiculous. 'It wasn't as good as the Diana concert,' said a member of the public at the end of the news report, wistfully referring to the memorial event that had happened only the week before. That was what all the effort had come down to: the second-best themed concert of the month so far.

And, yes, of course the idea was that the pollution and waste caused by Live Earth would be a mere drop of petrol in the ocean compared with the awareness it would raise. But, according to the organisers, what they were trying to raise awareness *of* was that 'we all need to change our everyday lives'. How were people meant to get out of the wasteful, irresponsible electricity-squandering mindset of the Western world if they were confronted by an event which seemed to reinforce the notion that you had to have bands flying across the Atlantic before it was a proper event? It was as if the organisers of Live Aid had stipulated you could only attend if you had stolen your admission money from someone poor.

But despite all this, as I wrote in my blog,

I felt a certain sympathy with the event's organisers. The thing with environmentalism is that it's so full of contradictions, organising an event that dodges all possible criticisms is nearly impossible. Even if you look at Green Feet, we used more electricity than we needed to, they served drinks in non-recycled plastic glasses, a number of people probably used carbon-emitting transport to get there. Does this mean Green Feet shouldn't have happened? No, probably not. I think it is better to embrace some of the contradictions than to be cynical to the point where you don't do anything at all. The *Independent* is the leading newspaper on climate change, yet still carries adverts for Ryanair and Easyjet. Does this mean they should just hold their hands up and give up pushing the environmental agenda altogether? No. We just all have to admit we're Crap At The Environment and keep trying.

I think flawed activism is still better than complete apathy. Which is why even though I'd have been pretty miserable watching Snow Patrol 'do their bit for the planet' on Saturday night, I can't find it in myself to say that Live Earth was a bad idea. Let's just hope we can do a slightly better job in August.

Reading between the lines, you can see I was kind of relieved that an event of such magnitude had shown how easy it was to do a bad job of being Good At The Environment yourself while preaching to others. But in addition I drew motivation from what seemed the ill-judged grandiosity of the whole project, and the resulting backlash. Clearly, there was room for people to spread the word about green living in a somewhat more apologetic way. That was what I was planning to do in the 24-hour show I jauntily referred to at the end of the blog, and in general. Perhaps there was room for it after all.

So I'd recovered my faith that both teeny little individual acts, and whatever bigger things I could muster, were worth doing, or at least, maybe nothing anyone did in this area was worth doing – either way I was relaxed for the time being. I began to plan, for my next steps, a few ways I could combine the personal and the public sides of CATE.

One of the legacies of Green Feet was, as you have heard, a long list of pledges made by attendees. Though there were one or two 'comedy ones', such as 'I will try not to kill any more cheese farmers' (at least, I took this as a joke; if it was serious, it was a remarkably low-key way to turn over a new leaf), but the majority entailed some quite impressive commitments. Various people had promised to change their buying, dietary and transportation habits; one (Jo) even promised to sell her car. Among my favourite promises was Sian (Good At The Environment)'s, to eat less beef. It gave me heart that someone else was struggling with the lure of red meat: it was really all I could do to get through the single non-meat day of the week without running straight into a field the next morning and tearing a rabbit to pieces.

Checking up a few weeks later, it did seem that quite a few people had persisted with their pledges, which was refreshing news as the word 'pledge' is normally used to describe something a politician has hastily promised in the event of his re-election, and tends to be followed by the sentence 'but this, like the Government's other pledges, was broken'. Participants had changed their mobile-charging strategies, paid weekly visits to farmers' markets and promised to eat no chocolate that wasn't Fairtrade. As Andy Zaltzman has pointed out, it's something of an indictment of our world that 'fair trade' is seen as a commendably ethical consumer choice, rather than simply the least one would expect: 'Really, all NON-Fairtrade goods should carry a logo of a businessman pissing on an African.'

Cathryn, one of CATE's longest-serving ambassadors, introduced a system of legislation whereby, if she failed to keep one of her promises, she would walk some of the way to work, the distance to be covered on foot to be determined by the extent of her failures. This was a win-win arrangement, resulting in green activity one way or another. All in all, these pledges seemed a more sensible and – to use a green buzz-word – 'sustainable' measure than the frantic week-by-week challenges we'd been doing earlier in the year. If everyone stuck to at least one lifestyle change, there was a chance that CATE would make more of a lasting difference to our collective habits than if it was a sort of enviro-hobby. But could we be sure people would stick to them?

Inspired by Cathryn's self-policing system, I decided to literally put my money where my mouth was and introduce a system of voluntary fines, like an eco-swear jar. Whereas a swear jar tends to result in a nice collection of 10p coins, but the exact same amount of swearing, I was hoping that the threat of having to part with money would make me a lot more circumspect about my various eco-sins.

The initial tariff of fines I put in place was as follows:

Leaving charger on unnecessarily	£5
Buying non-recycled toilet paper, etc	£5
Any wastage of water	£5
Using car for journey which could reasonably have been made by public transport	£5
Buying non-Fairtrade products where Fairtrade available	£5
Using plastic bag	£5
Careless use of lighting, electricity not covered by above promise	£10
Taking any flight	Must 'offset' carbon cost*
Failing to learn to ride bike by agreed point, 24-hour Jamboree	£100

At the end of each month, as I explained in the blog, I would make a donation to Greenpeace, the proper environmentalists, thereby converting my own shortcomings into money to power bona fide green activities, like some clean fuel harnessing the renewable source of my disappointment and self-reproach.

Through my contributions, I hope I've found another way of linking the small (CATE) to the big (Planet Earth) – as well as being reminded to keep my promises, I know that, in the event of failure, I'm feeding into a much greater community of people trying to achieve much the same goals.

The more I've read on the subject of climate change, environmental heating, ethical living, etc, the more I run up against the obvious truth that, no matter how hard individuals like us try, governments and industry need to make large changes to stave off the prospect of global chaos. I think it's important that we fit into a bigger picture of environmental action, in which organisations like Greenpeace lobby for actual changes to the law, to compel people to do the sorts of things we're trying to set an example of.

And in the same way as I'm increasingly convinced that the country should be bound by 'green laws', even if that means what seem harsh fines and taxes and legislation, I'm pretty sure that making myself cough up real money for forgetting to do things will make me a lot more efficient. A tiny example of how the real world needs to work.

If all this sounds a bit serious, don't worry, I am still Crap at it, just trying to square that Crapness with the less Crap efforts of others.

There was an asterisk next to the clause about 'offsetting', because this was one of many areas I was still struggling to wrap my little mind around, as I continued my slow metamorphosis into the next level, Crap At The Environment Because Everyone Kind Of Is, But At Least Well-Read On The Subject. Since, for the time being – as we've seen – flying was a more or less indispensable part of my routine, purchasing carbon offsets was the best way I could counter the damage, and I'd already done this in February, and would do it again if I found myself going back to Australia. I'd also 'offset' my flight to Ireland in June. I had done my best to ensure that the offsetting companies I chose were ones that funded verifiable and probably useful schemes like researching alternative energy, since there's been quite a lot of press talk about dodgy offsetting websites where you're basically assuaging your guilt by paying £30 to someone who stuffs it in his pocket and says, 'Uh, yeah, we'll probably, er, plant some trees at some point' like the guy out of Razorlight and then drives off in a lorry with an engine constructed from the organs of endangered species. The company

I chose, Carbon Neutral (www.carbonneutral.com), was one of the best-known ones, had received a favourable write-up in a paper I'd read, and came up first on a Google search, so it was hard to see how anything could be wrong with them. They put their money into, among other things, 'renewable energy, energy efficiency and methane capture'. By ensuring I offset every flight I took from now on, I would, therefore, be doing something to make up for my CO_2 output.

Except maybe I wouldn't, because the slight snag with carbon offsetting was that it might actually be a load of crap. As was pointed out to me several times by CATE correspondents, the gas your flight put into the atmosphere couldn't be taken away by offsets; it wasn't as if, once you clicked 'accept' and the online transaction went through, God gave a cartoon wink and put a fan on, saying, 'All right, I'll overlook that one.' What it did do was allow people to feel they could fly as much as they wanted, as long as they could pay for it. (Monbiot compares it to when mendicant priests used to sell 'pardons', and the wealthy were therefore not too worried about stabbing their neighbour over a stolen pig, because they'd be able to buy their way out of the fires of Hell.) Even my return flight to Australia only cost around £50 to offset; you could probably do a flight to Dublin for about seven quid. Once a system like that is in place, what's to stop a certain type of person from flying over there on a Friday for a stag do, coming home on Wednesday, then nipping back over for the weekend for someone else's twenty-first; and then, when someone says the world is heating up, producing a receipt for thirty pounds and saying, 'Not on *my* watch it isn't'?

Yet if flights were unavoidable, wasn't it at least better to put a bit of money into something green than do nothing at all? I thought so, but it was hard to be confident. For this reason, and with an eye to maintaining the small-stuff approach of CATE,

I started something called CATE Community Questions, in which people could throw open these dilemmas to the floor. I hoped this would help some of the many who, even now after a few months of CATE-ing, were always being confounded by, for example, buying ethically traded chocolate only to find it was made from beans excavated from the stomach of a baby seal.

Again, though, features like *The Times'* Eco Worrier were more than capable of seeing to people's green quandaries much more authoritatively than I could. If I really wanted to make a difference to people's attitudes as well as reforming my own, I was going to have to be a lot bolder. I'd just thought this when along came an opportunity to do it, and, with it, take the Crap At The Environment story into a new and surreal territory.

END OF JULY REPORT CARD

Credit: Finally read number of books on subject; introduced voluntary taxing scheme; purchased offsets; rallied to defence of anti-flight campaign in the face of attacks by big-haired morons on Facebook.

Debit: Left copy of global warming manual on radiator.

Savings: Noticeable, thanks to increased vigilance as a result of self-taxing.

Status: Improving, Tiny Bit By Tiny Bit, At The Environment.

SARAH'S JULY BLOG

This month I read an article about a woman who'd decided to set up a company that would make ethical-as-possible T-shirts for children. It actually made me tired reading it. She sourced organic farmers, and soya inks and factories that weren't sweatshops and in the end made a nice small T-shirt that retailed for £24. I don't know what it was about this article that got under my skin, but my first reaction was 'Bloody hell, who spends £24 on a T-shirt the little angel will grow out of in six months? If I had £24 to spend on a child's top I'd spend it on gin. And I hate gin. But it's the principle of the thing.'

I think the thing that freaked me out was this sort of article was symbolic of the reaction everyone seemed to have when faced with the news of our planet's imminent demise: let's make more stuff. On the other hand, my internal monologue reasoned, the cotton farmers who had switched to organic methods, and the soy ink makers and the machinists in Third World factories were now reliant on the posh mothers of the UK for their income – without demand for tiny, fashionable T-shirts, they were out of a job.

More confusion, and still no real answers. I was no better than anyone else; when faced with conflicting facts, I give up, and go shopping.

For my mini-pledge at Green Feet, I made a promise that I would no longer fall asleep with the telly on. It's a terrible habit, borne of insomnia, and though I only produce a teeny 2.73 tons of carbon a year, a lot of that comes from the telly, in front of which I am mainly unconscious. So I bought lots of second-hand tapes from eBay, some *Jeeves and Wooster*, *I'm Sorry I Haven't a Clue*, and fell asleep to those instead. I have an old fashioned tape player, one that just switches off completely when it gets to the end of the tape (with a satisfying 'clunngg' sound) so there's minimal environmental impact.

But what of the MegaChallenge, I hear you ask? Well, I did my best. I got very excited to see the National Maritime Museum were looking for volunteers to clean up the Thames. How romantic, I thought, to be thigh deep in brown soupy water, cleaning otters and rescuing pigeons from those plastic can-holder things. I eagerly sent off an email offering my services, and you know what? Nothing. Zilch. I was furious. Bloody Maritime Museum. Your gift shop is mediocre. Also, I'm GLAD the Cutty Sark burned down. It was probably a couple of disgruntled do-gooders turned bad from your lack of even a polite 'no thanks' response.

A little downcast, I was buoyed when I saw that also on the Action Earth site, a local school was looking for people to help clean up their nature garden. I fired off an excited email and got a reply from a nice lady called Sandra. Sandra, as it turned out, was my key to taking my attempts to be GATE beyond the tiny and personal and into the wider world.

A 'lefty '60s hippy' (her words), Sandra has been tirelessly campaigning to build a conservation garden at the school where she teaches. We discussed, via email, how vital it was for inner-city kids to learn about the environment, and how a nature garden would help. I told her about my City Farm adventure, and she reinforced my realisation that it's not just this generation who need to up their game, environment-wise, but we should also be making sure the next lot don't repeat our mistakes. As Whitney Houston put it, the children are our future, although I didn't say that in my email.

AUGUST

The annual amusement orgy of the Edinburgh Fringe was now looming like a great monster: one of those monsters that are friendly, but result in performers having to re-mortgage their homes. The one hundred available tickets for my 24-hour vaguely-green-themed comedy banquet had gone; quite a lot more people had announced their intention to come and see if they could get in when others left for bed, or stormed out in disgust. Corry, my dedicated, slightly exploited producer, had been astonishingly busy putting everything in place for the one-off show, which I had called Mark Watson's 24-Hour Jamboree To Save The Planet. I chose the word 'jamboree' because of its dictionary definition: 'a large, noisy assembly; a festivity'. Only when it was too late to change the title did I discover another definition: 'a gathering, often of Boy Scouts'. Still, they would certainly be welcome if they did show up.

Corry had got hold of a bus, and a driver, which we could have for a portion of the show. We'd use the bus to drive to a nature-y place just outside Edinburgh, where my audience and I would plant trees. She had persuaded various people to donate ethical products which we could use as prizes during the show. She gained permission for me to begin the show outdoors –

specifically, on Edinburgh's High Street, in the middle of the night – and drew up a walking route to force the audience to spend at least some of the show outside as we went from place to place. She found a man who would not only teach me to ride a bike while I was up there, but mark out a temporary velodrome in the Meadows where we could do cycling-based activities. We were also planning a clothes swap, a competition to see who could travel to the show in the most original and environmentally friendly way possible, renditions of songs using instruments made out of rubbish, a mass litter clear-up, and – to demonstrate the joy of low power consumption – a stunt whereby the whole audience, or whatever was left of it by eight in the morning, would sing a song live on breakfast radio. None of these measures was going to set the world on fire, but then, that was the opposite of what we were trying to do.

In addition to assembling the nuts and bolts of the show itself, Corry ensured we would not contribute to the festival's astounding waste of paper by sourcing a green printer who would do a very small run of flyers on 100 per cent recycled paper.

FACTLET:
By 'sourcing' in the last sentence, incidentally, I simply meant 'finding'; like 'sustainable' a bit earlier, this is a word you can drop in now and again to make it sound like you know something about the environment. I shall be sneaking in more of these shortcuts, or shortCATEs, to apparent expertise in the remainder of the book.

This was important as I didn't want to seem like a hypocrite; not only had I spoken repeatedly in interviews about the need to stop printing millions of flyers just so that passers-by could take them from dead-eyed street distributors, glance at them and say 'No, thank you, I *don't* want to see a daring re-imagining of *Lady Windermere's Fan* set in a Japanese Prisoner of War camp,' but I'd even made my point by doing a press photo-shoot to publicise the council's Fringe recycling scheme.

In practice, this meant getting up at half past eight in the morning and going to the Royal Mile to sit awkwardly on a bin with a sort of thumbs-up gesture. It was another of the moments when I wondered how I'd ended up being seen as a spokesman for a cause that meant discussing rubbish with council officials first thing in the morning while everyone I knew was asleep. There was a bit of light relief, though, when the over-keen photographer got into the bin to take an experimental litter's-eye view shot, and a passing Scot helped him get into character by dumping some actual rubbish on him.

So, everything was more or less ready to go for the long show. There were just a few ingredients missing: I couldn't yet ride a bike; I hadn't yet seen the venue where I was going to be spending a long, long chunk of the night; I didn't know how the ticketing was going to work, if lots more people turned up than we could manage, or how to avoid complete embarrassment if far *fewer* turned up. Oh, also, I didn't know how I was going to do 24 hours of comedy.

Most of these issues would be cleared up in due course, but there was no putting off the most pressing of them all. After a period of procrastination and some adroit hiding behind the responsibilities of the festival, I finally admitted to myself, with barely a fortnight left before the show, that it was time I learned to ride a bike.

But no sooner had I begun to address this necessity, at long last, than something very odd happened. I was contacted by a friend who works for the Melbourne Comedy Festival. She told me that

Al Gore – as in, actual Al Gore – was doing a training course in Melbourne in September. About one hundred and fifty people, chosen from a couple of thousand applicants, would be coached to give Al Gore's lecture course; in other words, trained up like disciples. By Gore himself. The actual one. The people who were organising this had seen me do comedy and Gore's advisers wondered if I would be interested in applying for the course. And by Gore, I mean – Al Gore. The one who's famous.

As things were, there was a tentative plan for me to go back to Australia in October anyway, as part of my 'work'; if I cancelled four West End shows, I could fly earlier and attend the course, and I wouldn't be causing any extra pollution. Anyway, I probably wouldn't get on the course, so the question was academic. Just in case, though, I downloaded the form. The course was being jointly facilitated by the Australian Conservation Foundation and Al Gore's Climate Project, two bodies I have had limited contact with. I had to demonstrate that I had some experience of public speaking, that I could operate PowerPoint, and that I was passionately committed to raising public awareness of climate change. The public speaking wasn't a problem, I could get through Power-Point with a bit of swearing and muttering, and, yes, I had to admit I was into the whole global warming thing these days. I tidied these answers up a bit and sent the form off to Al's people. If they were really expecting two thousand applicants, I suspected there would be people ahead of me in the queue to lecture Australians on the environment – for example, people who lived in Australia and had been interested in the environment for more than a few months. But it couldn't hurt to apply, I told myself, though of course, it's that sort of thinking that lands people in the Army.

After that little distraction, it was back to the 'cycling project'. Despite having pledged £100 to the 'swear jar' in the event that I failed to transform myself into a little Lance Armstrong, I still felt fairly sure, deep down, that the closest I would ever get to cycling would be not cycling. I realise this is a contentious point, but I would go so far as to say that I was not one hundred per cent convinced that anyone could really cycle. I had never been conclusively shown that it's possible within the laws of physics. Oh, it's all very well putting one of your feet on the pedals, and you can just about balance your other foot on the other one if you stay where you are. But to do this while staying in motion defies good sense. And yes, I know that it's 'just a question of getting your confidence up' and 'finding your balance by instinct' and 'wiggling left, right, left, right quickly till you build up a rhythm' and all this other nonsense, but – really – it has always seemed extremely far-fetched to me.

Yes, I had seen people riding bikes, I was aware some people do it quite a lot, and even as I explained my still-unfashionable Cycling Is Impossible Theory to an audience in Edinburgh, plans were afoot in London for a mass cycle. I concede that the evidence against me was huge. All I'm saying is that, going into August 2007, I was fairly certain that this evidence belied a well-known but seldom-acknowledged fact – that cycling could not really be achieved, and everyone who claimed otherwise was either locked into an Emperor's New Clothes-style delusion, or engaged in an enormous conspiracy against me for reasons unknown.

Nonetheless, for the time being, I had to put everything I had into a renewed assault on the probably mythical art of cycling. I owed it to myself, to the planet we call home, to the many people who had helped me along the way, and, more to the point, there was a hundred quid at stake. I contacted a man called Darren, who was recommended to me because he claimed to be able to teach anyone to ride, absolutely from scratch. 'The first thing we'll do,' he said confidently on the phone, 'is take the pedals off.' Since I was unable to ride a bike with all its parts intact, I wasn't sure I would find it any easier if I mounted one that had basically had its feet ripped off. (I was experimenting with thinking of bikes as people, in the hope of becoming more comfortable in their company, though I don't always get on that well with people either.) Still, Darren had taught idiots to ride before – he didn't use this exact terminology, but it was implied by his manner of bright patience – and must know what he was doing.

For our first session, he found a piece of secluded land where it would only be fairly, rather than entirely, humiliating for me to wobble about like a pre-schooler. Sure enough, the bike he gave me had no pedals at all; I simply sat astride it, as if on a hobby-horse, and dragged it along using my feet to inch forward. Even before this, we'd done ten minutes on the art of simply walking the bike around. This was reassuringly basic stuff: I was almost surprised there wasn't a little tutorial on the stages even before this – getting the bike out of your garage, saying 'it's too nice a day to be indoors', etc. I quite enjoyed wheeling the bike around, it was a bit like walking arm-in-arm with a friend (a friend with wheels), and I couldn't help wishing that this was as far as the sport of cycling had developed: it was when some flash Harry started sitting on the thing that it went sour.

By the end of the session, the pedals were on again, and I was tentatively weaving the bike between patterns of cones, and learning to use the brake – still, I have to add, with my feet dragging along the floor pretty much the whole time, but at least I had spent some time 'in the saddle' as cyclists say, and – to use another piece of jargon, had a 'sore bum' as a result. The psychological wall of tyres between me and successful cycling was starting to wobble a little. Darren said that I was a quick learner – a finding seemingly contradicted by the fact that it had so far taken me twenty-seven years to pick this up – and said that with another three or four sessions, I would be riding around like a good 'un. There was no way that I was going to find time for that many sessions before the long show, but there was hope that I could still shift this monkey off my back and, who knew, maybe even save that hundred-pound donation to Greenpeace. I was only disappointed to learn, when I looked it up, that the application date for the Tour de France had already passed for this year.

The first month of my self-imposed fines had resulted in a donation of £30 to Greenpeace. I racked up this debt by making two trips by cab when I could have used public transport, leaving a phone charger in the wall on two occasions for no reason, and – my unfinest hour – leaving my copy of Monbiot's *Heat* half-open on a radiator which, in the middle of July, was cranked up almost to full temperature and left like that while I went out. As Emily wryly pointed out, it doesn't get much more Crap At The Environment than over-heating your house while distracted reading a book about the disastrous consequences of over-heating our houses. I made my donation to Greenpeace anonymously. I hoped they appreciated that my un-green lapses were funding their expeditions.

Shortly before the 24-hour show, I got an email from Australia. They were offering me a place on the Al Gore course. My initial reaction was one of panic. It was all very well on an application form saying that I 'would take the message to a young, motivated audience' and 'allow the Climate Project to reach a new demographic', but what I was going to do now that my bluff had been called? It's a lot easier to write the word 'demographic' than to make it mean something. I'd always been better at filling out application forms than actually doing things. Many times in my life I'd failed to deliver on the promises of my eloquence, ever since as a 16-year-old I got my checkout job at Waitrose by writing 'This is a top-class supermarket which deserves the highest calibre of checkout assistant. In other words, it deserves Mark Watson.'

Was it not hubris to think that I could preach about global warming when I'd barely begun trying to act against it myself?

I had other misgivings as well. Although a second trip to Australia had been on the cards anyway, it would still feel pretty odd to fly all the way across the world in order to be trained to persuade people that they should stop flying across the world. Obviously, you had to be pragmatic – Gore himself presumably wasn't attending the course by hot-air-balloon – but even so. Even as I was weighing this offer up, the news was full of protestors camped at Heathrow, making known their objection to expansion plans: I could imagine what some of those people would say to the spectacle of me toddling off a jumbo jet with my little bag of books about climate change: 'So, where's this course on the environment then? Should I just get in a cab?'

But it seemed like too good an opportunity to miss. I'd always started out saying that I had no knowledge, expertise, or even ability to stick to principles, but I did have energy and enthusiasm and the ability to convince people. Why, I'd even been called 'charming' in a review once. If I could do nothing else to do my bit for the environment, if I was destined always to fail to plant vegetables and forget to switch things off, and occasionally wake up sweating and shaking in the night with the phrase 'newspaper pot' running through my brain over and over again like the word 'umbrella' in the awful song that was 2007's biggest hit . . . well, at least I could talk about what I *should* have done and what I would try to do.

Taking up this place meant cancelling several West End shows, it meant telling Emily I was going to be away for rather longer than I'd envisaged, and, of course, it was going to mean making a commitment larger and more daunting than I'd ever dreamed when I first hatched my little caring-about-the-planet hobby. Also, I was going to have to spend three days with people who in all likelihood could recite the Kyoto Protocol word for word in four languages. And if I had to actually meet Al Gore himself, I was pretty sure he would be able to tell that I was crap, that I was a chancer, just by looking at me – like a wine connoisseur correctly identifying the crap wine with a blindfold on.

Such faint-heartedness had no place, though, in the death-or-glory scenario of our planet's future. If my Crap At The Environment project was ever going to go beyond my own household – and you might still be thinking it was pure egoism to want that, but I did want it – then this was the moment. I composed an email saying, 'It is a huge honour to be offered this chance and I accept it with the greatest gratitude and excitement.' After reviewing what I'd written, I remembered that the people organising the course were mostly Australians, and added 'mate'.

The week leading up to the 24-hour show was wet, frenetic and worrisome as expected. I could fit in only one more cycling training session before the big event, and even then, it would only work if I combined it with my publicity schedule by conducting a phone interview with a radio station while on the bike. (This sounds like one of my little jokes, but it's true, and gives a sample of the insane schedule of multi-tasking which ran underneath the whole of 2007, and which, I hope, mitigates some of my more pathetic failures.) One evening I snatched a bite to eat with Emily and TV personality Simon Amstell, who is a friend of ours. Amstell, with his scrawny 'geek-chic' figure, is a vegetarian and, remarkably, Emily was now not far off being one herself. Her easy-does-it approach to cutting out meat had resulted in her losing her taste for it slowly but surely. 'I used to crave chunks of meat so much,' she reminisced, 'but when you haven't had it for a few weeks, you just don't think about it.'

'I never really fancy it,' agreed Amstell, scourge of the jumped-up celebrity but not, it seemed, of the farm animal.

'I'm just as happy having a bit of fish,' Emily added.

'Oh yes, I like fish,' trilled Amstell. The two of them studied each other with the mutual respect of people who live off the many bounties of Mother Earth, rather than by carving limbs off fellow creatures. I was beginning to feel like a brute by comparison. When the waiter confided that he was 'a great fan of Amstell's work', I couldn't help hearing the subtext 'and he's also an ethical eater, unlike you, you murderer'. The point that meat-eating was just another habit, an addiction, rather than some indispensable component of a healthy life, had been put to me many times over the course of this year – as you've read – but seeing Emily eliminate it from her diet, really just by stealth, was more convincing to me than any number of demonstrators with pictures of carcasses. I resolved I would at least halve my red-meat eating and at home I would do away with it altogether, and join in with the increasing repertoire of non-dead meals she cooked up. Of course, I'd made weak versions of this resolution all the way through this little adventure, but maybe this one would stick: after all, I'd made it in front of someone who was noted for taking people down a peg on the telly. Imagine what his dry wit could do to me if he got wind of me gorging myself on a leg of lamb.

The day of my second and, regrettably, final cycle lesson before the 24-hour show was windy and cold. With the mobile tucked under my chin, I exasperatedly explained, 'I'm sitting stationary on a bike . . . yes, that's right a bike, ha ha! . . . yes, 24 hours *is* a long time to perform, ha ha! . . . yes, I probably *should* be resting rather than talking to you and trying to ride a bike, ha ha! . . . what's that, you're going to have a bit more of a chat with me after this from the Eagles? OK, but I really should get off . . .', while the genial radio announcer on the other end chuckled and tutted at my eccentricity. Darren helped me to build on the baby steps we had taken before, dragged me through the arse-aching cone circuits, and eventually started making me freewheel down gentle slopes, giving me the experience of actual cycling (if we concede that such a thing exists). This was now very, very close to proper bike-riding.

But the forces that had kept me at arm's length from a life in the saddle were massing quietly to dash the cup from my lips once more. Or to put it less grandly, it all went 'a bit pear'. The rain, which had been gentle and almost refreshing, had begun to fall rather heavily, in the unsentimental, businesslike way it does in Edinburgh, as if to say, 'You knew I was coming, and sure enough here I am'. In spite of this turn for the worse in the elements, and in contrast to our last outing, quite a few passers-by were now stopping to watch my display of incompetence, which made me irritable and self-conscious. I began muttering to myself and trying too hard and cursing everyone who stopped and caught my eye; I mean, you'd think the least you could ask of a passer-by would be to pass by.

And then came a more serious setback. As I struggled in un-gainly fashion down a gentle incline, swearing as I banged my ankles against the pedals while trying to get at least one bloody foot on one of the damn things for at least a few hundredths of a second, a bunch of 'colourful locals' – in other words, mouthy drunks – began passing comment on my performance in Scottish accents so thick that, if you did an impression of a Scottish accent like that, you'd be accused of crass stereotyping. The gist of their assessment was that I really needed to build up a bit more speed and let the momentum carry me, rather than inching my way down as if one mistake would send me into a snake-pit. One of them, a sociopathic-looking short-haired man with a bottle of what looked like whisky in his hand, made this point to Darren in the kind of language not normally heard within a stone's throw of a children's playground.

'It's all right, thanks,' said Darren politely. 'He's just taking it very slowly.'

'Did ye no' hear me?' asked the Scot incredulously. 'Wha' I'm sayin' is, is that he needs to go *faster.*'

'Yes, well, I'm a cycling instructor,' said Darren, patiently, 'so I think I'll just . . .'

'Eh, mate!' said our new acquaintance, getting to his feet, '*did ye no' hear me?*'

By now it was evident that the questioning was not really about whether we'd succeeded in hearing this gentleman – I was pretty sure most people in Britain would be able to hear him – but about whether he could turn this into an opportunity to beat, as they say, the living shit out of Darren, and maybe me as well. I was rather keen to leave, now, and as quickly as possible; actually, it was the type of situation where you wish someone had invented a device for getting from A to B by means of a pair of wheels attached to a basic frame. But no such thing came to mind. And moreover, Darren, heroically, and also in my view crazily, was still standing his guard and trying to address this person as if he were an emotionally stable individual with a genuine concern for my future cycling career, rather than what he manifestly was, a lot of pain waiting to happen, and looking as if he wouldn't wait to happen for all that much longer.

'Now, my friend and I are just going to go over here . . .' said Darren, still conciliatory. I know it is cowardly but by this point I had already 'gone over there' and was making plans to go quite a bit further 'over there', specifically, to my flat. The man laid his hand on Darren's sleeve. This was now looking a lot like the start of an episode of *Casualty,* when you see two people enjoying a seemingly innocuous rooftop barbecue or game of golf and think

'Well, unless this is a very atypical episode, one of them's going to be almost dead in a minute.'

'Calm it, mate,' said Darren, removing the guy's hand, but the man held on and we were now on the verge of at best, a little bit of 'handbags', as football commentators call petty violence, at worst, the first time my inability to ride a bike had actually killed a man. The attacker more or less pulled Darren off his feet. I'm not sure I should admit this, but it did flash through my mind that if I could get a photo of this, it would be great for a book. I didn't have the guts for anything of the sort, of course; I simply watched, in my usual crisis-management mode of immobile, rabbit-in-headlights panic. Darren squirmed out of the lunatic's grasp and began leaving, even now not actually running but sort of trotting along, and still wheeling the bike with the tenderness a man might show a horse.

'Bit of bother there,' he muttered, as the curses of the excitable Scot and his pissed-up mates followed us out of the park like gunfire in the distance.

I got a cab home.

Shortly before midnight the same day, I was on the Royal Mile before two hundred and fifty people, about to end the tyrannical grip exerted by buildings upon performers for many generations of the Edinburgh Fringe by beginning 24 hours of comedy out in the glorious open air, with a loud-hailer, standing on a little bollard. A lot of people had been there for half an hour or more and were standing around tenaciously in the unseasonable cold with coats and scarves on. There was an air of expectancy which, as usual at the start of a marathon show, I found both exhilarating and terrifying. For one thing, the room we'd planned to move into for the (always important) 2 a.m. to 9 a.m. slot wasn't big enough to hold all these people; also, the room that had been meant to accommodate us for large tracts of the remaining seventeen hours had been withdrawn hours before, and Corry had managed to talk someone into letting us use a makeshift venue in a tent for the whole of the Tuesday afternoon. I hadn't been in this tent, and, although it would certainly add a bit of authenticity to the whole in-touch-with-nature motif, it might well also add a bit of impossibility to the whole trying-to-create-an-atmosphere-and-not-having-the-whole-audience-pass-out thing.

Also, I hadn't really prepared any actual material. There hadn't been time.

Trying to describe what happened over the next 24 hours is difficult. It's the ultimate example of something that's a lot funnier if you're there, though I'm loath to say 'you had to be there' as I find that a very irritating expression ('Well, I wasn't there; that's the whole point of your describing what happened. This is why talking was invented, so we can comprehend things we don't experience. You don't get newsreaders saying, 'In London last night . . . ah, you had to be there.') Well, I'm digressing. The fact is that the long shows are only really interesting if you're physically present, and even then, only some of the time, and moreover, this was certainly the least consistently funny, by far, of the five times I've done this dubious feat. I ran out of ideas more often, the audience was understandably sluggish for longer periods than usual, and although my idea of wandering around Edinburgh certainly got us all out in the open air, it also made it nearly impossible for newcomers to work out where the show was at any given time.

And yet, taking a look at what happened, you would probably say it was reasonably fun; 85 people witnessed the whole thing, and not all of them can have been mentally unstable. In the course of my quest to show the audience an environmentally friendly good time, we got up to all sorts of high jinks. Among the highlights, I was quite proud of the bit where we all piled onto a specially hired double-decker bus and drove along to a natural beauty site, your correspondent scooting up and down between the lower and upper decks with the loud-hailer, fulfilling my dream of being one of those people who take coach tours and shout at you to look to your left and get a glimpse of the historic Town Hall before everyone shoves you out of the way to take a picture on their mobiles. Admittedly, I have never in reality harboured any dream of doing this job, but if it helps, I've certainly dreamt about it since. When we got there, we were given instructions in tree planting and tree maintenance by the nice, certified GATE people who run the place, and then everyone piled in and started getting their hands dirty. I joined in for a while and managed to rip out some weeds and use the space to shove in a sapling and put a tube on it to stop it from falling over. In between these horticultural moments, and in order to fulfil the basic requirement of a comedy show that the performer should actually be addressing the audience most of the time, I had some fun patrolling the tree-planting ranks with my loud-hailer shouting things like, 'CONTINUE PLANTING', 'KEEP APPRECIATING NATURE', and then, when it was time to leave, 'TIME UP, PLEASE STOP APPRECIATING NATURE.'

It's another of those moments when, if I could have seen myself a year ago typing that sentence back there with the word 'sapling' in it, I would only have been able to assume that 2007 was going to bring me some sort of psychological breakdown. Maybe in a way it has, but, hell, there's a tree in a corner of Scotland that wouldn't be there if it hadn't been for me. Except, of course, that someone else would have planted it. And probably better than I did. (After I'd planted my baby tree, the photographer from the *Scotsman* took a photo of me kneeling next to a tree someone else had planted, because it looked more like it had a chance of surviving the next 24 hours. That's how history is rewritten.)

And of course it isn't a 'corner of Scotland', I didn't spend a month trekking there to replenish a deforested area – I'd been taken to a place only just outside Edinburgh to play at being an environmentalist. But still. It was something. And what was heartening was to hear people, as we left, saying that they'd like to come back and help with more of this kind of thing. I was also delighted by how excited people were to be on the bus, and how sentimental a number of audience members became about the pleasure of public transport and their immediate intention of doing fewer journeys by car. Of course, it's not every bus journey where everyone spends a whole minute counting in a chorus because they're about to celebrate the thirteenth hour together (although if you've ever got the night bus from Central London to Lewisham, where I used to live, you'll probably have got close), nor is it an everyday occurrence for wild excitement to break out on a bus because someone has just spotted former *Play School* stalwart Dave Benson-Phillips advertising his show to bemused passers-by (most of whom, on this occasion, did indeed pass by). Even so, even if it encouraged just one person to go on a bus, it was better than nothing. It was better than driving the audience around in big old 4x4s. It was better than if I'd gone ahead with my original plan for a 24-Hour Jamboree Of Destruction and Wantonness (including Plastic Party and Polluting Hour).

And there were various other bits where the enviro-theme came off at least partly: the bracing walk down Princes Street to a bookshop where I launched my novel (it's both fun and slightly alarming being at the head of a hundred or so people walking – you feel like a cross between the Pied Piper, Hitler, and one of those people who have too many kids and are never quite sure they'll come home with all of them); the singing-a-song-on-the-air-without-power shenanigans; and the mass raffle of ethical goods (which took up nearly forty-five minutes, almost all of which I spent saying over and over again, 'Everyone loves a raffle! Nothing's more fun than a raffle! Isn't this a great raffle!' and so on).

And, oh yes, the small matter of the cycling. Darren, seemingly fully recovered from almost having all his teeth knocked out by a man with a whisky bottle – although to be honest he was seemingly more or less recovered within a minute of it, so perhaps it wasn't the first time – had marked out a cycling arena on the Meadows where we could have bicycle-based fun, if that wasn't, as I had always maintained, an oxymoron. Darren had also rigged up an obstacle course with cones and a tiny little seesaw and narrow bits and ledges and all sorts of other hazards. Of course, having failed to learn to ride, despite all my promises and a fair bit of hauling myself around a park astride a two-wheeled steed, I had about as much chance of traversing this course on a bike as I would have had of completing the obstacle course they used to have on the *Krypton Factor*, with a cargo net, a really really muddy bit, and the world's biggest climbing frame among other perils. (A dismaying number of people no longer remember the *Krypton Factor*. Without wishing to deviate from our topic once again, it was one of the greatest ever quiz shows, subjecting contestants to a range of mental and physical trials undreamed of in these powder-puff *Deal or No Deal* days; and, by the by, its presenter Gordon Burns was the brother of my French teacher.) Anyway, there were plenty of other people prepared to take on this menacing bike odyssey, and we ran a series of time trials while I commentated in an over-zealous manner, getting a taste of what really was my boyhood dream job (and still is really, if anyone reads this and is trying to recruit a sports commentator). Watching people teeter and wobble around the obstacles I had to concede that if I ever did master this shadiest of human arts, possibly, just possibly, it might be a tiny little bit of fun.

But I hadn't, of course, not yet, and so I had to pay the price – both fiscal and emotional, as my conscience and my sense of duty as a jester compelled me to have a go at the course myself. Backed by vehement encouragement from the crowd encircling the temporary course, I mounted a bike and dragged myself, feet on the ground, around the circuit at a pace like that of a snail heading off to something it wishes it hadn't committed to. The course, which had taken other contestants an average of thirty seconds, detained me for a good five minutes, including one pretty hefty fall, which knocked the wind out of me more than you'd expect given that the bike was probably travelling faster when it was sitting in Darren's garage. When finally I had struggled over the finish line, there was a surprise in store for me: Darren had brought a tandem along, and he proceeded to whisk me around the park for a bit while everyone else either cheered and whooped, or feigned enthusiasm, or took this opportunity to wonder to themselves why exactly they had devoted this section of their lives to watching people cycling. The tandem was rather romantic in its way, and as I felt the wind rush past, and pretended that it was me and not my more able companion who was doing the actual riding, I thought I could detect somewhere in my being the first, faint stirrings of an unlikely love affair between myself and the machines I had avoided for more than a quarter of a century. It would be a long, long time, if it ever happened at all, before this relationship was consummated, but at least we had, finally, been properly introduced.

I'd like to mention that TV's Matthew Kelly made a guest appearance near the show's climax and hosted an impromptu revival of *Stars In Their Eyes* with Fringe award winner Brendon Burns and Green Feet headliner Andy Zaltzman as the competing vocalists, but (a) you might not believe me, though it's true, and (b) there is no way, although I've thought about it, that I can really pass it off as having anything to do with the environment.

24-HOUR SHOW SURVIVORS' BLOGS

Sarah: I speak to Mark before the show, in a murderer's alleyway just off the Royal Mile, as a couple of hundred people wait patiently around the corner for him to start proceedings. He is the same colour as the wall he was leaning on and breathing unusually.

Andrew: The key is that it's not supposed to be laughter for 24 hours (who would want that?), it's partly blitz spirit and mostly (particularly the night-time section) like watching a teacher try to keep a class's attention without anything to teach.

Sian: A strange man comes in to fill a gap in the comedy with some contorting. Five sheets to the wind, he strips down to his pants, insults the audience, then grosses everyone out with his dislocating arm trick.

Andrew: Only when he's departed does the audience realise there was actually no need, in terms of the act, for him to have taken off his trousers.

Tom: Mark stops the bus to give a live interview to Radio Scotland. This involves the whole audience walking into a tent and whooping to cues from Sue from Mel & Sue, while a roving mic captures our emotions. The drained, monosyllabic answers we give to questions results in the mic being quickly removed.

Corry: (*producer*) My favourite moment of the 24 hours is the tree planting. It's a shame that the entirety of the huge audience can't fit on the bus, as it's a highlight. The view from Craigmillar Park over Arthur's Seat is stunning. Although everyone is tired they plough into the work and get a vast amount done in the short time that we are there. It is amazing to think that those trees will still be there when we are all gone, it's a real long term reminder of the 24-hour show and the message that Mark's trying to promote.

John: I spend most of this period mulching.

Andrew: I leave for a sleep and my absence is noted. When I get back at 1 p.m., the new venue has actually filled up, but fortunately they're about to head off to The Meadows for an outing, which involves getting people to volunteer to cycle around a small obstacle course. After a decent interval, I step up and hear with some alarm that this is my chance to 'turn from a villain into a hero!'

Tom: Complex social codes are beginning to develop around the respect afforded to individuals based on how much sleep they've had throughout the course of the last 14 hours. For example, seconds are added to cycling competitors' times on the obstacle course if they've had the cheek to get their heads down. If it turns out they've had a full night's sleep, then they get booed all the way around. The status of insomnia is thus ruthlessly upheld.

Sarah: Josie Long wanders in clutching a bottle of champagne and toasting everyone and everything, which is such a glorious and positive moment that bits of rainforest probably regenerate spontaneously anyway.

Tom: The final countdown culminates in a massive roar as the clock strikes midnight. A short band encore is given, with Watson on drums. Lots of boogying on the spot erupts amongst the cramped rows of chairs. Then, exhilarated, happy, sweaty, proud and relieved, we disperse into the night and towards our waiting beds. A fantastic way to use one day in the life of our planet.

Corry: (*producer*) If anyone plans to attend one of Mark's marathon shows, heed this advice: take a holiday the day before and the day after, and SLEEP.

Emily: (*wife*) I hated the whole thing.

Examined in retrospect, the 24-hour show (which, incidentally, also raised a very small amount of money, which I put into our little kitty for events which I regrettably hadn't managed to organise yet) was like most other things I had done since pronouncing myself Crap At The Environment: well-intentioned, silly, attention-grabbing, more sweet than efficacious, but probably just about worth it. And it was fun, and after all, my mission statement had always included injecting fun into the end of the world. And like I said, it was only a day.

We got the train back from Edinburgh to Bristol – another flight I'd succeeded in not making, another small eco-economy. (This was a term I'd coined during the 24-hour show, but it proved not to be very popular because it makes you sound like you're stammering.) I read the papers, something one is prevented from doing while at the festival by an invisible force-field separating everyone there from everything of the slightest importance in the world unless there's a stage and a microphone attached to it. There were acres of debate about ethical shopping, offsets, Britain's carbon targets. In Australia, Kevin Rudd, the challenger to John Howard's throne, was promising to bring Australia into line with the rest of the world (apart from that bit of the map with United States written across it) by ratifying the Kyoto treatment. The climate camp had ended in the way protests usually do, with all sides claiming victory at once. There was a lot going on. This subject had grown tenfold, in terms of coverage, in the time I'd been interested in it; CO_2 was as ubiquitous in the media now as it was in the atmosphere. And, overwhelmingly there were far, far more questions than answers. Everyone was crap. Everyone was confused. There was everything to play for.

The next month would decide whether I managed to raise my engagement in line with the rate at which the planet's problems seemed to be growing, or settled for maintaining my part-time involvement and doing nice little activities and conducting rather spuriously informed interviews on the subject. In three weeks I would be in a room in Australia being lectured by Al Gore. After that, what?

This journey was the opposite of the surprisingly-pleasurable Funrifices that I'd undertaken months ago in the honeymoon period of my CATE days. The train was cramped, slow, and full of idiots, including one of the most awful children I have ever had the misfortune to be trapped with: an obnoxiously conceited little chap of about eleven who addressed a string of food-and-drink-related requests to the harassed train staff, and then, when one of them couldn't be met, reported it to the ticket collector with the words, 'I'm afraid one of your staff was rather snotty.' An *eleven-year-old*. Was this precocious little leech the 'next generation' for whom I was hoping to help keep the planet serviceable by undertaking – and making my wife undertake – this interminable trip?

Well, yes, perhaps it was. But the problem of whether the human race would be fit for the planet in twenty years' time was one that could wait, I guessed, till we'd ensured the planet was fit for human beings. Anyhow, maybe I'd get to discuss it with Al.

As I prepared to go, the BBC announced that it had cancelled Planet Relief, its proposed environmental-awareness night, because they were worried they would look biased in favour of a 'cause'. 'It is absolutely not the BBC's job to save the planet,' said a spokesman called Peter Horrocks, whose name was close to being rhyming slang for his opinion. The BBC had been making annual attempts to tackle poverty for twenty years; how come they'd suddenly decided they weren't allowed to meddle in world issues? And more to the point, how could anyone from such a weighty organisation wash their hands of responsibility in such a brazen way? 'It is not our job to save the planet,' indeed – as if it's anyone's 'job' to care about things, rather than simply a fairly obvious moral imperative. What next? Suspending Sunday night programming because 'it is not our job to put on period dramas'? Why not just give up making shows altogether because it is 'not the BBC's job to provide television?'

Ooh, it made me angry. Angry enough to go to Australia and get ready to save the planet myself.

END OF AUGUST REPORT CARD

Credit: Tried to learn bike-riding despite presence of colourful locals; continued success of voluntary tax scheme; waxed indignant against BBC's pusillanimous stance on climate change; accepted place on course with actual Al Gore; did ever such a long show incorporating outdoor segments; finally starting to reduce meat consumption after being shamed by thin man off the telly; posed with recycling bins.

Debit: 24-hour show, despite being fun, not the most effective piece of propaganda, and also wasted energy in places; still didn't actually learn to ride the fucking bike.

Savings: Acceptable, even if more theoretical than actual.

Status: Increasingly Keen To Stop Being Crap At The Environment.

SARAH'S AUGUST BLOG

This summer has had a very odd atmosphere to it. On the one
hand, 'green' has never been more fashionable. On the other,
there seems to be an awful lot of congratulation going on for
very little change. 'Consciousnesses' may have been raised by
Live Earth, but people seem to be thinking terribly hard about
things, rather than doing them. The word 'offset' is everywhere,
as though life is a giant seesaw, with things and stuff and
consumer goods on one end of it, and all you need to do is drop
a big bag of money on the other side to 'balance things out'.
People are still flying short haul, and buying new shiny things,
but the shiny things had big green stickers on and that made it
'OK'. No one seems to be suggesting that maybe we should all
learn to just press less hard on our end of the seesaw. As ol'
Moonbat said recently, 'Uncomfortable as this is for both the
media and its advertisers, giving things up is an essential
component of going green' – something you're not likely to read
in *Vogue* any time soon.

The other problem with things being fashionable is that, at some
point, they have to become unfashionable. Otherwise we'd all still
be wearing Fido Dido T-shirts. The other day I genuinely
overheard the phrase, 'Ethical's a bit out now, isn't it?', like the
catwalks of Milan had been full of models wearing blood diamonds,
mink coats and mahogany snoods. Yes, green is 'in' but it's in
danger of becoming a fad, meaning people are consuming slightly
different things rather than questioning their consumption.

A popular retailer has started putting little aeroplane stickers on
their food and flowers to show the carbon footprint produced by
air-freighting the goods. Except, flowers grown in Holland
produce five times the carbon produced by Kenyan roses

because of the heating and lighting involved, rendering the whole thing a little pointless. Pointless to everyone, that is, except the retailers, who are selling lots of lovely roses to shoppers jumping on the 'guilt-free' bandwagon, and who may be now under the impression that the non-aeroplaney flowers were picked in a meadow down the road by Shirley Temple. No wonder people are confused. (I say 'people' like I'm not part of it, like I'm not about ready to smash my face into the *Guardian* every time I read some new info that conflicts with something I read yesterday.)

FACTLET: Low-Power Flowers

While Sarah shakes her head in despair at the complexity of working out how many 'carbon miles' are attached to your flowers, veg and so on, it should be pointed out that there is one pretty reliable way to cut through all the arguments, which is simply to buy local, and in season, as much as you can. If, instead of getting flowers from Kenya *or* Holland, you try www.britishroses.co.uk (to mention one source among many), you can be reasonably confident you've got your blooms with the minimum of waste. If roses aren't in season at the moment, well, there are quite a lot of other flowers to choose from. Likewise, rather than trying to unscramble the sometimes bewildering carbon charts to assess the relative merits of Egyptian and Mexican strawberries, you *could* just have something else for dessert. Like the blackberries you picked just down the road in the summer and have frozen.

In the midst of this confusion, and finding myself, like Mark, considered to be some sort of green ambassador without really knowing much, a friend came to me with an ethical shopping dilemma. '[POPULAR HIGH STREET SHOP] is doing T-shirts with the CND logo on, do you reckon they're eco-friendly?' 'I'd imagine not really,' I said. 'I can't see them guaranteeing Fairtrade organic cotton, carbon-neutral import, chemical-free dyes for £6.99. If you want a CND T-shirt why don't you look on the CND website, they might at least have a go at being a bit more ethically produced?' To which she replied, 'Yeah, but they don't do the colour I want.'

I thought this was the best example of 'getting the environment wrong' I've ever come across.

SEPTEMBER

It was just after eight in the morning and I was in a garden at the back of the Melbourne Arts Centre, with a large, well-behaved, but enormously excited crowd. Never, except in a nightmare, would I normally have expected to be conscious, let alone in a garden, at this time on a Saturday morning. But this was only the first jolt of what was all set to be the oddest weekend of my life.

To add a melodramatic twist to this already peculiar scenario, I nearly didn't get there. During the attenuated West End run which led up to the Australia trip, I started getting chest pains, which is something that periodically happens; I once had a pneumothorax, which can be the result of a little hole in your lung, and ever since then my lungs have given me, as they say, some grief, normally as a kind of hint at times when I am doing too many things. This pain was as intense as any I'd had since it first happened five years ago, and I ended up in an ambulance at four in the morning, breathing oxygen through a mask, with paramedics asking me, 'How much does it hurt between one and ten, where ten is the worst pain you've ever known?' Just when I thought I'd escaped the scrutiny of the Edinburgh Fringe, we were back to reviewing things. ('I reckon eight out of ten, four stars. If you only get one respiratory problem this year, consider this one.')

If, as I was convinced, this pain was a recurrence of the pneumothorax, I wouldn't be allowed to fly, in all likelihood, for some weeks afterwards, and the whole Al Gore rigmarole would vanish like the improbable thing it had always seemed from the start. After a super-efficient Eastern European doctor had run an ECG on me and done a chest X-ray and so forth, there followed a tense pause while Emily heroically tried to cheer me up, assuring me that everything would be all right and I would probably still get to go to Australia. This was an impressively selfless line to take, given that she didn't much want me to go to the other side of the world, and given that I, less heroically, was sitting on the bed in an NHS dressing-gown feeling so sorry for myself – even with the howls and moans of the much more afflicted all around me – that if the entire hospital had collapsed on top of us, I would have muttered, 'Oh great, now this as well.' But, as often, Emily was right and I was wrong in my pessimism; the pain was just a bit of an inflammation which I could counter with antibiotics and so forth – I could go after all, I could still save the planet. I was on the West End stage within twelve hours and, a week after that, off to the Lucky Country again.

The first day of the course had been an introduction, largely, and a chance to meet the other one hundred and fifty people. They were drawn from all kinds of socio-economic and professional backgrounds, and pretty much united only by the fact that everyone was convinced of the need to act now to halt climate change, and prepared to take the fight to unfriendly, sceptical or politically hostile audiences. There were members of conservation organisations from all over Australia and New Zealand. There were people who worked for ethical farming groups, in green youth schemes, or in sustainability programmes. There was a girl who'd walked from Brisbane to Sydney, over a period of nine weeks, to raise awareness of the issue. There were anti-deforestation campaigners, members of pressure groups, nature photographers. And, also, me and a girl from *Home and Away*.

During this first day, I made only a handful of faux pas, including getting a nosebleed during the screening of *An Inconvenient Truth* which they arranged to get us all in the mood, and having to sit there with blood all over my hands for an hour because I was at the front, and I didn't feel I could distract everyone from the dangers of rising global sea levels just because I was unable to regulate the flow of liquids through my own nose. In the evening reception – local wines, a vegetarian buffet with snacks served on tiny squares of recycled tissue – we heard speeches by former graduates of the course who described the way in which it had changed their lives. Then we got our first glimpse of the big man himself. He appeared suddenly, like the Pope on a balcony overlooking us all, to give us a rousing first talk, in a *coup de theatre* which the organisers had only slightly undermined by, every five minutes for the preceding hour, saying things like, 'We're encouraging people not to leave *just* yet because there *might just be* a special guest in a minute . . .'

And now this was the big moment, the main day of our Gorification (on the Sunday we'd learn more about the mechanics of giving presentations and so on). There was what I can only describe, and I think I'm using this word for the first time outside Scrabble, as a 'hubbub'. I couldn't remember such a charged atmosphere outdoors since Emily and I honeymooned in Kenya and had to sleep in a tent on an isolated game reserve. The roaming lions were poorly segregated from the frail paddock of tents containing pasty tourists who, after coming all this way to get close to animals, were now wishing they were a bit further away. Our safari guide sent us to bed with the comforting words, 'There is a guide with a gun posted by the gate,' then added, with a chuckle, 'But, of course, he is only one man!'

In the wild, as we learned on that long, stomach-churning night in Northern Kenya, baboons warn each other of the presence of predators with a shrill, melancholy moan which echoes around the trees. In much the same way, large masses of people now alert each other to developments with the insidious chk-chk sound of a photo being taken on a mobile phone. At about half past eight, around the back of the Arts Centre, this sound began to spread inwards from the far corner of the garden. People were holding their phones aloft in one hand like birds fluffing up their feathers. Through this path of raised arms came a large, solid dark figure, flanked by minders. As you got nearer you could see he had a black shirt and a black suit on – the combination of a man who really means business – and steely grey hair slicked ruthlessly back over the scalp. He stopped to shake hand after hand, looking each person in the eye with a stare so searching that, as he came our way, I shuffled backwards and let a more gutsy individual have a go. Motioning the crowd to press in even closer around him, the former Vice-President Gore took up a position next to a tree and began to speak. He spoke, in fact, more or less for the next ten hours straight.

Years of lecturing have given Gore a portentous manner and a powerful, swooping voice, a combination which gives weight to his most trivial utterance; indeed, quite early in his address he went off on a wry digression about how he doesn't like bananas, and it sounded as though he was describing a large-scale terrorist threat. Luckily, he is also surprisingly funny, and humane, with an oratory skill, vigour and charisma surpassing anything I'd ever seen before or expect to see again. From a comedian's viewpoint it was an fantastic master-class in holding the attention of an audience. Just a month before, I'd congratulated myself for doing a two-hour stretch of comedy outside with a loud-hailer, but Gore's efforts made me look, yet again, like a puny charlatan.

Plus, I didn't have any moments in my show where I could casually say, 'Bill Clinton and I were talking about this . . .' or 'I have to leave tomorrow to do the keynote speech at the United Nations.' Still, as the old phrase goes, if you're going to be shown up, at least make sure you're shown up by the former Vice-President of the United States. I hope next time I'm convincingly beaten at Twister, it's by Al Gore.

It's hard to describe exactly how Mr Gore made such an impression on his audience. Some of it is probably down to the range of his learning, which allows him to wring interest from areas of science I would have crossed the street to avoid a year ago. He wove in quotes from Gandhi, Plato, Martin Luther King, Theodore Roosevelt, Mark Twain and Dire Straits. (The Roosevelt quote referred to the need for strength of conviction – 'You can't blow an uncertain trumpet' – which seemed a pretty good description of my time in the infant school recorder chorus.) It was an object lesson in the ancient craft of Making A Boring Thing Interesting: however dense and esoteric a lecture may have become, all the speaker has to do is mention someone famous and there is a part of any listener's brain that automatically goes, 'Aha, I've heard of that person. I shall enjoy this next bit.'

Then there was the way Gore conveyed the urgency of the task in hand. This was partly done by means of shamelessly Churchillian rhetoric. As in the film, he commented upon the Bush administration's fixation upon terrorism, to the exclusion of all other concerns, by pointing out that even a fractional sea-level rise could see the rebuilt Twin Towers disappear under water. He even used a line from Churchill himself to draw parallels between pre-war apathy towards the Third Reich and the present scepticism about climate change. I wasn't sure whether he was saying my dad was a Nazi.

But the be-very-afraid tone was undergirded by a lot of hard facts, some of them supplied by a couple of Australia's leading climatologists who sat to one side as a support team. They would sometimes pop up and show an alarming map of Australia's temperatures over the past ten years, or a newspaper cutting about drought-hit local wildlife. TIME IS RUNNING OUT FOR EMU, one said, and although it was probably on the cards once Rod Hull died, it still sent a shudder through the room (for the record, the bustard and the white-fronted chat are also among those under threat, but there wasn't a cheap gag to be had about those). At other times, they would step in to clear up questions from the floor so tough that not even Gore was confident answering them. When this happened, he would say something wry like, 'That question is so easy, I'm going to let one of the others answer it.' It got a laugh every time.

Again, as in *An Inconvenient Truth*, Gore also injected his central argument with a considerable poignancy by describing how his then-tiny son (also called Al) had nearly been killed when Big Al let go of his hand for a second and he charged into the road, and how, in the weeks that followed, the possibility of losing his child forced him into a total reassessment of his priorities in life, just as the death of his sister from lung cancer caused his parents to abandon their lifelong involvement in the tobacco industry. This motivation-by-personal-hardship once again moved me to reflect how privileged my life has been, and how difficult it is to fight really hard for a cause, any cause, without the impetus of some truly meaningful life experience. Against the emotional impact of Gore's personal motivation to action, and the profundity of his love of nature, I really still only had good intentions to offer. I suppose what I'm saying is, people who've undergone awful misfortune don't know how lucky they are.

But if there was one reason for the talk's inspiring qualities, it was the emphasis upon optimism, rather than gloom. The 'take-home' message – as jargonistas like to say – was that, while the planet was on the verge of being shafted (and again I'm para-phrasing here), there was still hope. And the hope lay with the actions of ordinary people. And those ordinary people could be motivated by still ordinary, but now trained-up, people like us. And if we didn't do it, in fifty years the next generation would wonder what the hell we were playing at. There were 'tipping points' throughout history and we could help to shove humanity towards this one. From a man whose commitment to reaching this 'tipping point' is so strong that his own wife is called Tipper, this was a powerful message indeed.

When, finally, he came to the end, the now exhausted audience was invited to ask questions. Nearly every time I've ever been in a situation like this, whether at school, university, or the handful of occasions in my life I've been to a lecture on something out of pure curiosity like an adult might, the sentence 'I'll now take questions' has struck the audience much the same as 'Who would like to see me get naked?'. Traditionally, a teacher, lecturer or equivalent is forced to raise a hand and try to say, 'Actually, can *I* ask some-thing?' without it sounding like a humiliating defeat for everyone present. I recall, after a spellbindingly dull lecture at school about what it's like to work in a mosque, a desperate teacher had to ask four consecutive questions before being allowed to say, 'Well, let's show our gratitude to Mr Iqbal.' But this time, many hands shot up, even though I couldn't believe I was the only person in the room thinking, 'This is tremendously interesting, but I really would like to leave now.'

Gore fielded twenty questions at least, ranging from, 'People are always saying that water vapour is a bigger contributor to global warming than CO_2, what should I say to them?' (the answer is to be found the next time I do one of those dialogues between me and some other people) to, 'Will you please stand for President again?' (this got a round of applause, but Gore, who must have been expecting the question, simply smirked and said he had fallen out of love with politics and could do more good this way). Disappointingly, no one asked him to elaborate on his enmity towards bananas.

Finally, it was time to go. Our mentor thanked us. People started to clap and whistle. An eager little chap sitting not far from me sprang to his feet to start a standing ovation, clapping with his hands above his head like people do at rock concerts. Very rapidly, to my left and right, other people began to get to their feet. Personally, I've always disliked the convention of the standing ovation because of the embarrassing pressure of having to make out you enjoyed yourself slightly more than you really did. Once the next person has got up, staying in your own seat is tantamount to saying, 'Actually, I thought it was shit'. I had a standing ovation once for a gig which I'm pretty sure only about ten people actually enjoyed. There's a cunning parallel to be drawn here with the way that people's lifestyle choices influence each other, and the ramifications of that for our environment, but let's not try to be too flash. I'll simply record that, in this case, for the first time in my life, I felt unembarrassed about getting to my feet.

It was only as Gore's monolithic frame departed through the doors and the applause finally died away, replaced by the distinctive hum of a crowd that's just witnessed something special, that it dawned fully upon me that, a year after mocking the efforts of the doomed flight-disrupters at Heathrow, I had now completed my metamorphosis into one of them, at least in spirit. Had there been a plane waiting to take off when we came, somewhat dazed, out into the courtyard, I'm fairly sure I would have thrown myself in front of it. It's probably lucky that there wasn't; it would have seemed a rather inconsistent gesture given that I was still relying on a plane to get me home.

But before that, the following day, I was one of a handful of people fortunate enough to chat with Al Gore one-to-one. The word 'chat' suggests a jaunty exchange in the queue for lentils, but, of course, I was as nervous as I've ever been about a conversation, apart from when I proposed. I'm normally unfazed by celebrities, because I have a job which brings me into contact with quite a number of them for a brief time each, and anyway, fame is not of itself very interesting in an age which has spawned so many reality shows that all but about twenty of us have now appeared on one. But there are always a few people with whom the prospect of a meeting provokes a surge of adrenalin, and the concomitant thought, 'I hope I don't make too much of a tit of myself here.' I had already met most of my heroes without damaging my self-respect too seriously (Jarvis Cocker, Bristol City manager Gary Johnson), or am unlikely ever to meet them because they're dead (Geoffrey Chaucer) or don't really exist (Lisa Simpson). But this was another level. This was possibly the most learned and in all likelihood the most inspirational individual I'd been at close quarters with. *And* the most famous. And bear in mind that I don't throw this kind of accolade around lightly, given the competition: I mean, I've met Tony Hadley.

I was pushed forward gently by the course's organisers with my little heart thumping as if I were about to play chess against someone from Exxon and the prize was the planet. I introduced myself.

'I'm a comedian,' I said meekly, wondering about my T-shirt – had it been ethically produced? Would Gore suddenly rip it off me with a bear-like roar of fury?

'A comedian,' said Al Gore, thoughtfully.

There was a pause which probably came in at about two seconds, but in the circumstances felt about as long as it would have taken a medieval monk to copy out the Bible.

'Yes . . .' I went on, hesitantly. 'I'm hoping to do a, er, sort of a comedy version of your lecture show, now that the training's finished . . .'

'A comedy version?' echoed Gore, in surprise. We eyed each other. Come on, I thought, he may be about to win the Nobel Prize, but you were nominated for Perrier Best Newcomer at the 2005 Fringe. And he'll be well aware of that.

'Imeanobviouslynotchanginganyofthescienceordistortingthe-messagebutjusttryingtomakeitaccessibletopeoplewholikecome-dy,' I elaborated in one breath.

But he was nodding now, and looked interested. I relaxed a bit. I wasn't going to be invited to play tennis with the Clintons, but nor would I be 'asked to leave' by a minder in an even darker suit than Mr Gore's. Gaining confidence, I mentioned that I was impressed with the way he'd managed to include 'humour', as people who don't like comedy call comedy, in the previous day's speech. It was no doubt good for Al Gore's confidence to get this nod of approval from me as well, and the conversation was now much less strained.

He confided that some of the jokes in his lecture felt 'pretty thin' now. 'I've been doing them a long, long time,' he said in a pensive voice, and there was an odd, brief moment of what felt like professional complicity between us: I imagined him trooping away from Jongleurs in Nottingham muttering, 'Stag parties never like the CO_2 material.'

Then he said, 'Well, good luck with that, good luck,' and shot me square in the eyes with one of those piercing looks that seemed to reinforce the encouragement while simultaneously communicating: 'Don't do anything silly, will you?' And it was all over.

And as I walked away from the Arts Centre that evening, with my brain feeling as if it had been squeezed in a vice for three days, but a somehow enjoyable vice (no pun intended with Mr Gore's former office), I reflected that I could learn something from that microsecond of weariness in my mentor's voice as he looked back over the thousands of times he'd given his lecture. This, after all, was – as I mentioned earlier on – a man who had famously once been Crap At Public Speaking. One of the main factors in his election defeat was the lingering perception that he lacked warmth and couldn't really communicate his passions (that, and a loophole in the American electoral system allowing his opponent to win the election despite probably not actually getting as many votes as Gore). This was a man who'd been lampooned on *The Simpsons* by giving a character a talking Al Gore doll, who repeated, in an expressionless voice: 'You are hearing me talk.' Somehow he had not only overcome this apparent impediment but transcended it utterly. I, on the other hand, had always been good at the talking, but rubbish at every other area of environmental activity. Surely I could take inspiration and, by approaching from the opposite direction, arrive at the same destination as Mr Gore. I thought about texting him to share this further discovery of the bond between us but, somehow, I'd neglected to take his number.

It was about now that I ran into the acquaintance who quizzed me on whether climate change was a myth. Here was my first chance to put into action the enormous reserve of conviction and hard scientific knowledge I'd stockpiled over the past three days. This was the first little moment in the next stage of my emergence from the cocoon as a butterfly of conservationism.

You've already read what happened next; I did the usual thing. I umm-ed and ahh-ed and only managed to admit that I even believed in global warming after a large amount of backtracking and mumbling. By now I was accustomed to the fact that every time I experienced some sort of epiphany, or felt that I was making any sort of progress, it was immediately followed by a moment when I disappointed myself. So this time I didn't brood on how Crap At The Environment I still was, after everything. I started to consider how I would answer someone who asked me similar questions in three, six, twelve months' time. I began thinking about how I was going to leave the Crap behind altogether.

Back at my friend's house, with my eyes barely open, I tried to sum up some of the contents of my teeming brain in a blog:

It's difficult to explain what it was like being one of the 150 or so people who took part in Al Gore's climate change course. It already feels like it can't possibly have happened. The whole experience had a dreamlike quality, largely because it was such an unlikely situation for me to find myself in. But I'm almost certain I'm not making it all up.

My job now will be to take Gore's legendary slideshow (which we were all given a copy of) and make a comedy show out of it. My ultimate aim will be to do what he does, travelling around giving presentations, but giving it a comic slant. Gore has done his talk about 3000 times and it's shit-hot. He is such a persuasive speaker that if he urged everyone to put buckets on their heads and hit them with spoons, there'd be no complaints. Whereas I imagine my first 40 or so presentations will be fumbling affairs where I keep panicking and just saying the word 'carbon' over and over again. But I'll get there.

I have to go to bed now. My head is still full of graphs of CO_2 emissions, words like 'sequestration', and slides of melting ice shelves. But while these things have always filled me with a certain sense of futility, Gore's course has made me feel like the message is actually one of hope rather than despair. Good. I'd better get on with doing some things.

END OF SEPTEMBER REPORT CARD

Credit: Attended course with actual Al Gore.

Debit: Had to fly there; squandered first chance to display Gore-given motivational skills.

Savings: None, given long-haul flight, but huge potential for future.

Status: Crap, But Enlightened.

SARAH'S SEPTEMBER BLOG

Early in this month, I received an invitation to what promised to be 'a new kind' of eco-venture. In my capacity as a flim-flam sort of journalist, I was invited to the opening night of 'Club4ClimateChange'. Now as we all know, there's nothing more fun than a number instead of a word. How down with the kids is that? What next, replacing the Cs with K's? Kool! So, the KKK (maybe not, then) was billed as a glittering event in London's West End which would 'bring a breath of fresh air to the Capital's party circuit by producing a party powered with bio-diesel . . .' What? What futuristic magic is this? The breathlessly excited press release went on: 'At 8 p.m. the mains power will be transferred to a climate-friendly generator, which the stars will fill up with bio-diesel as they arrive. One objective of the event is to publicise the significant carbon emission reductions that are possible by simply switching this equipment to "cleaner" fuels given that many are already capable of using renewable fuels.'

Now, we're all just crazy about the stars. OMG, celebs! So celebrities topping up generators with bio-diesel just about spins my propeller in every way possible. The bumph that came with the invite did make all the right sort of noises about having a stab at being an entirely green and well-intentioned event. It would raise funds and – yep – 'awareness' for the Clean Planet Trust. It even had a neat little slogan: 'Make A Difference On The Dance Floor!' Yeah! We're gonna save the world!

It was only inside the quite horrible 'top London nitespot' (I didn't see any celebrities with cans of diesel on the way in, though the night was young at that point) that it transpired that maybe, just maybe, the evening's green credentials were perhaps a tiny bit insincere. Apart from the nice ladies in gold bikinis handing out ice creams (symbolising the genuine threat of global warming to decent clothes-wearing people), and male break-dancers in their pants and big clock necklaces (symbolising it's *time* to start thinking about the planet, I'm assuming), it was hard not to notice a couple of glaring schoolboy errors. The MASSIVE ice-sculptures, for instance, or the 'green' canapés 'prepared on the premises to minimise "food miles"' that were proudly sponsored by an extremely cheap and cheerful supermarket. Nothing wrong with Lidl, their 8p bread has got me through some hard times, but generally when your USP is 'we're cheap as fuck' it's safe to assume it's not all locally sourced and organic as hell. 'Prepared on the premises' doesn't really mean anything.

ICE SCULPTURES for God's sake. Oh yeah, and for no reason at all, every surface was strewn with fresh rose petals. I'm really not being picky here; it was like they'd gone out of their way to be deliberately, laughably wasteful and unnecessarily bad for the environment as possible. There was a jacuzzi, an indoor swimming pool, and a HUGE chocolate fountain for stars like Aisyleen from *Big Brother* to dip strawberries and marshmallows into, great piles of pre-packaged food everywhere from Holland and South Africa, and yet more ice 'luges' you could lick vodka from.

Before you think I'm being a terrible snob, and lord knows how much fun that can be, please don't think I'm dismissing the venture on the grounds of taste. There's nothing wrong with this kind of clubbing, if you like that sort of thing; who am I to judge, and anyway it keeps the sort of people I hate away from the sort of places I like. And for the record, I liked Aisyleen on *Big Brother*, she was 'spunky'. It's just very, very odd and a bit depressing that this 'Klub' was hanging its hat on this 'green' angle – did anyone who paid the full £50 for a ticket to get in really turn up hoping to be part of the future of eco-clubbing, or were they there, as seemed transparently obvious, for a go on the chocolate fountain and the chance to see a Cheeky Girl? I hate being all cynical when people are trying their best, but in this case, they totally weren't. It was so bleakly spray-on, such a 'will this do?' attempt to cash in on an issue that people do, generally, seem to actually give a fuck about . . . well I found it very hard to choke down my many-umbrella'd vodka cocktail, I can tell you. Ho ho.

Apparently the biggest of the many ice sculptures was meant to represent the melting polar ice caps, which, yeah, it did admittedly, but probably with a bit too much literalness to be a decent metaphor. 'You know how mankind is unnecessarily using all this energy and it's melting the icecaps? Well, as symbol of that wastefulness we've unnecessarily used a huge amount of energy to make this thing out of ice, and now we're going to watch it melt.' 'I'm sorry, I don't quite get it, can you create another visual metaphor for how we're polluting the planet with just these old petrol-soaked tyres and some matches?' 'No I'm afraid Alicia Douvall has just turned up and I'm going to wank myself raw. For the planet's sake!'

Anyway, after about 90 minutes of watching coked-up city brokers trying to fuck the pole-dancers and shuffling about to

Sexxxyback, it was all a bit much. In sheer befuddlement I shoved fistfuls of chocolate into my handbag and then ran out into the night going 'whaaaat?'. My boyfriend and I sort of rolled around the street, clutching our bellies and gasping with laughter and making comparisons to the Green Field at Glastonbury.

So what did I learn from my clubbing adventure? Well, it's a bit disingenuous to try and claim your club night is all about the environment when it's really mainly about looking at tits and chocolate fountains and having someone hand you little paper towels when you go to the toilet. But also, y'know, if bio-diesel really is a more ecologically friendly way of powering nightclubs, and you really must have nightclubs to contain all the ghastly terrible things that go on in nightclubs, probably it's quite a good thing to keep using it. I just don't want to be there to see it.

Part Four

October, November, December and Beyond:

In Bloom

OCTOBER

A week and a bit later, in the middle of a once-bright afternoon that was just beginning to get a bit wintry, in a park tucked around the back of Melbourne's city centre, I prepared to address my fellow humans on the subject of the environment for the first time. The event was called the Big Switch Off, and the idea was to put the spotlight on the need for energy conservation, as one newspaper either ironically or rather ill-advisedly described it. The organisers had made no such mistakes. Not only was there no artificial lighting because we were making use of well-known galactic body 'The Sun', there wasn't even any electricity involved. The tiny stage was powered by being plugged into a bus which in turn ran off bio-diesel.

It was going to be my first ever carbon-neutral performance, unless you counted my apprenticeship spent toiling around comedy clubs so basic that they didn't have proper equipment, and if you wanted to be amplified, you more or less had to tell your jokes to a person who would repeat them in a slightly louder voice. So this was a landmark event, of sorts, in my metamorphosis into mini-Gore. I was more nervous than excited, though; there were various indications that this might also be my first ever laughter-neutral performance.

The main worry was that I was the comedian on a bill which otherwise consisted largely of folk musicians. Being the lone comic at any event is something of a poisoned chalice, the poison being people's quite understandable bafflement. An audience that has just been listening to a motivational speaker describing his experiences of life as a hostage in Iraq, or a renowned chamber musician giving a beautiful rendition of a funeral march, is not likely to be in the mood for high-spirited banter about Hillary Clinton. The only thing worse is when there's no 'bill' at all, as happens when you're booked to be the sole entertainment in the middle of some company's black tie dinner, and when you spring to your feet with the microphone in the middle of the sorbet course, people look at you as if you are a member of the waiting staff who's got carried away and decided to try out some gags.

The other thing with comedy is that it really does require people to be facing the same way and sitting more or less in silence. Both of these requirements were going to be impossible to meet on this occasion; the members of the Big Switch Off crowd – which was dwindling as the temperature began to drop – were spread out over a big grassy bank and mostly playing Frisbee, chatting, lying in a narcotic haze, making sure their kids didn't run off with bogeymen, and so forth. This is all very well if you're a folk band and can just plough through the indifference with a mighty screech of your fiddles, but as a comedian it's somewhat harder to ignore the fact that people aren't listening. Al fresco gigs allow people too much freedom, basically. Stand-up comics are tyrants whose art relies heavily on the fact that the audience is trapped in a cramped, dingy room with them, and hence have no more attractive option than to listen to a man talking about sex or the Government. As soon as people have the option to drift about, they will. Keen as I now was on the environment, in other words, I didn't really want my audiences getting anywhere near it.

(This need for confinement, incidentally, is the main reason that big stadium-sized comedy shows have never really taken off in the way that was predicted. There was a time, around the beginning of the nineties, when the cult success of people like Newman and Baddiel prompted many commentators to speculate that 'comedy was the new rock and roll'. But in the end people realised they were better off watching stand-ups on DVD than in a big stadium, and 'the new rock and roll' turned out to be bands playing music almost the same as the old rock and roll, but with shorter hair.)

It was only when I got onto the stage, greeted by whatever the word for a quarter of a smattering of applause is, that I began to realise a still more intimidating obstacle lay between me and my goal of saving Australia and/or the world over the next twenty minutes. Most of the people clustered around the stage, the percentile of the audience I actually stood a chance of making an impression upon, had something in common which set them aside from my usual demographic. In brief, they were tiny. They weren't proper people. They were kids. The collection of eyes turned expectantly upon the stage for my first ever stab at environmental preaching belonged almost exclusively to two-to-eight-year-olds and their parents, whose faces scanned me warily for the thousands of dangers which a newcomer presents to a small, vulnerable being. Especially a newcomer with a microphone and an impish expression.

As I stumbled through my introduction, it did occur to me to wonder if I ought to be here at all. Such questions arise fairly often in a comic's career, both in relation to one's worthiness to be on stage and to be in the human race at all, but it was particularly potent in this case. The fact was that in order to do this gig, I had broken off a ten-day run of gigs in and around Sydney. To put it less equivocally, I had flown back from Sydney to do this gig. I had *flown* from Sydney. I had taken a *domestic bloody flight* to do a 'green' gig. Had I learned nothing from Gore?

The seemingly paradoxical answer was: actually, yes, it was because of him that I'd decided to take this on. When it was first offered to me, around the time I was about to start the training course, my initial reaction had been that it would be impossible to justify the flight (even though the organisers promised to offset it and so on). What changed my mind was the Gore-inspired feeling that I had to start being bolder and backing myself to make some difference by positive action, rather than merely by trying to keep quiet and do as little as possible (though there was still a definite place for that). Mr Gore, after all, ran up enormous carbon expenses with his tireless traversing of the globe to promote his cause. Did any serious environmentalist consider Gore a plague on the planet? No, because the end justified the means: he had badgered any number of world leaders, got all sorts of initiatives underway, raised the awareness of probably tens of thousands of people, including people as resistant as I used to be.

As I stood there trying to 'play' the (both numerically and physically) tiny crowd on this increasingly draughty afternoon, however, the true gap between me and my new guru became clear to me. The end could only be said to justify the means if I made some sort of impression on at least a few people. The blank-faced kids and their shivering minders looked on impassively. What Would Al Do? Having seen the repertoire of techniques at his disposal, I had little doubt that in such a situation he would have some child-pleasing Plan B whereby his slideshow turned into a magic show and he wrestled some ethically sourced balloons into the shapes of animals, before departing on a unicycle singing songs from *Charlie and the Chocolate Factory* (the Gene Wilder original, of course, not the lurid Johnny Depp remake). I, like most people who don't have kids, don't entirely understand them, and –

much as I like their company, under the supervision of more capable adults – am terrified of trying to amuse them. There's an occasional comedy club for children which has tried to book me more than once, and while I applaud the effort, I'd honestly be happier with an audience of dogs. At a 'family gig' in deep Wales once, a nine-year-old shouted out a racist joke which I inadvertently repeated, in an attempt to diffuse the situation, and ended up losing my fee and being accused of hate crimes. (It was true in a way; for some time afterwards I hated racist kids from Merthyr.)

Nonetheless, this panicky train of thought provided me with a possible escape route from this sticky gig. Wasn't the whole nucleus of Al's inspirational message, one of the biggest emotional hooks that he hung his huge-brain-sized hat on, the fact that we were doing this for the kids, for the fabled 'youth' who, even though one sometimes heard them implicated in iPod/trainers-related crimes, were famously the future? Looking into the saucer-like, confused eyes of my juvenile listeners, I threw caution to the wind and began trying to involve them in some audience participation, disregarding the old rule of stand-up: 'Never work with children, animals, in a field, in the middle of a Sunday afternoon, on a stage powered by fertiliser, with material that's largely about the parlous state of the planet.'

By persistent bantering I learned some of their names (one was called Zak, another a Polish name I failed to catch even the third time). I say 'bantering', though 'banter' by definition is meant to include more than one person; 'banter' with only one participant is more normally labelled 'abuse'. Inch by inch, I gained the trust of the diminutive folk and began to bring them into the gig. Once we were friends, I started to use them to focus my ranting. 'This is why the environment is important!' I rambled, semi-coherently, gesturing at the youngsters and their nonplussed parents. 'We're doing it for people like Zak. Otherwise . . . (what was it Gore said?)

otherwise they will ask us what the hell we were doing.' Zak applauded this sentiment and a kid who had been throwing grass at me momentarily let up. I had now gathered slightly more listeners around me and I banged on for a considerable time, becoming bolder as I went. Of course, this was preaching to the converted – most of the people who'd consider attending an event devoted to energy conservation were likely to be fairly clued-up anyway; it was unlikely they were Shell executives who would go away saying, 'That thin, animated man was right; we should really clean up our act.' And my address was hardly the polished presentation we'd been trained to give: as I'd predicted in that blog, there were quite a few moments where I began saying something like, 'You see, the thing about greenhouse gases . . .' and then forgot what I was trying to say, and ended up settling for something like, '. . . is that you have to be a bit careful.'

Still, as I left the stage to perhaps half a smattering of applause, I reflected that this was a start. It hadn't been a great gig or a great talk on climate change. But it had been both of those things at once, and that alone was some sort of achievement.

That afternoon, my friend Bec cooked me kangaroo. This was another stage in my crusade against my own red-meat-lust. Since that chastening meal with old goody-two-shoes Amstell and my increasingly non-animal-killing wife, I'd been steadily, though not spectacularly, getting my consumption down, by such expedients as eating fish and vegetables, filling up on bread, and occasionally just spending my lunch break eating a bowl of Shreddies and whimpering in self-pity. Kangaroo, though, seemed to represent a perfect compromise: it was still red meat, but its production caused far less carbon emissions than beef, which, as we have already learned, puts the 'meat' into 'methane' (doesn't quite work, but if you look at the words quickly it's close enough). It was a sacrifice with almost no actual hardship at all involved. The word 'Funroofice' was suggested by Sarah to define a Funrifice involving the eating of a marsupial. It seemed a pretty important thing to have a word for.

Of course, all this would count for little if old Skippy didn't turn out to taste nice, but luckily, the kangaroo was delicious. It's a bit richer than beef but very lean at the same time. I wish I was eating a nice chunk even now, to be honest. On the contrary, however, the success of this gastronomic experiment left me with a bitter-sweet feeling, because such a handy solution to the ongoing problem of my beef-mania was not to be found in the UK. Of course, you *can* buy kangaroo steaks in certain establishments in London, from the same sort of gourmet 'outlets' that sell über-fashionable treats for food snobs like fillet of endangered panda or peregrine-falcon-on-a-stick, but I sensed that what moral high ground I'd gain from eating roo rather than cow in Britain would be swiftly lost if the roos in question had been transported across the earth. The only solution, I supposed, was for me to introduce kangaroos into my native country and breed them in order to eat them. I was as surprised as anyone to be contemplating being a farmer, and a non-mainstream farmer at that, but it was scarcely any odder than contemplating myself as I was now: a climate change campaigner.

Two days before my return to England, I was lounging around in Sydney's beautiful Botanic Gardens trying to stock up on some pleasant memories of nature to take back with me to what would soon be a cold, forbidding country. I watched a strange lanky bird strutting about the park with an odd, hunched gait, poking at things with its long pencil-like beak. I became quite attached to this scrawny creature, it reminded me of something; towards the end of our time together it struck me that, embarrassingly, I was pretty sure it reminded me of *me*. For all I knew, this charming bird could be a bustard or any one of many other birds whose names sounded like stifled curses. The astounding diversity of wildlife had been wasted on me for so long, because I could barely tell a fish from an elk, but the course, and the past months generally, had sharpened my awareness of it, and it felt now like one of those gifts that you only know you've got when it's gone. Like the TV series *Morph*, or the Wispa bar. It was another reminder that the 'climate crisis' wasn't just about some projected apocalypse, but the – sometimes quite brisk – erosion of what was around us now at this minute.

The bird, which looked much too clumsy to get off the ground, suddenly took flight and I watched it soar for a few seconds until, as if chartered by some special company called Symbolism Airlines, a passenger plane roared over the horizon and reminded me that I would soon, once again, be in the skies chugging out greenhouse gases like a supervillain.

There was, however, hope of making amends for the trip – other than by preaching Gore's message in the future – by means of a cunning 'offsetting' scheme devised by CATE member, John. He suggested a project whereby everyone involved in CATE made a journey by foot which they would otherwise have taken by car or other fuel-guzzling machine. If enough people did this, we might eventually, collectively, be able to tot up all the carbon savings to make a figure roughly equivalent to the 'carbon miles' I'd used getting out to Australia and back. This sounded like a good idea; it would be a symbolic 'offsetting' of the damage done by my travelling, and, moreover, a chance to get lots of people walking around, a worthwhile aim in its own right. When Andy, of Self-Sufficientish fame, thought through the idea in more detail, the figures were admittedly a little daunting:

Right then: I have just worked out John's idea. It is 10,562 miles from Heathrow to Sydney airport. Or 21,124 miles there and back.

If everyone who is member of CATE – 1137 of us at the last count – were to offset his flights, we would need to walk twenty miles each (instead of taking another form of carbon-producing transport) making a total of 22,740 miles. This would certainly offset the plane journey there and back and allow a little leeway for error and travel to and from the airports.

Twenty miles per person was no great task, in theory. In practice, however, we knew quite a number of the 1137 CATE members to be armchair fans whose wardrobes, to use an American coinage, did not include 'partici-pants', or slipped-through-the-net spammers posting occasional messages like, 'Wow I can't believe we went to high school with this girl! She's so hot!' Bona fide CATE members were going to have to pitch in a good deal more than twenty miles each, therefore, especially as Andy's meticulous calculations had even allowed for 'travel to and from the airports'. But the response to this idea, which I christened the CATEwalk (a play upon the word 'cakewalk', meaning something very easy or effortless; I hoped this would encourage people), was huge; it provoked far more comments than any other blog since the site began. People as far apart as Stoke Newington and Western Australia promised to use Shanks' pony, as they used to call walking in old detective novels, over distances ranging from Lucinda's half-mile trot to work (which she'd always previously done in a car) to the fifty miles in a single week cycled by Hugo. Out in the sticks in New South Wales, Cat pledged to make the treacherous trip to school by bike: 'Cycling down the mountain could be fun! Just have to make sure I don't die!' Paws 'did the whole twenty miles in one go, even though I got chased by a swan at one point'. Meanwhile John, who'd started the whole thing in motion, pointed out that you could also chalk up the miles by cancelling or side-stepping journeys altogether. He notched up a saving of twenty-two miles in the first week by 'placing my trust in sub-contractors rather than going to see them on the site myself'. It was another example of doing something positive simply by doing less.

After the first week of the CATEwalk, we had collectively not travelled 172 miles by car. This was some way short of the 22,740 target, for sure, but the thought of people scuttling this way and that on nothing but the legs God gave them was a balm for me as the captain switched off the seatbelt sign, the attendants came rushing down the aisles with trolleys of un-economically produced snacks, and – with a certain inevitability – Al Gore's face appeared on the in-flight entertainment system in front of me. I settled back and tried to think about more ways I could do more by doing less, and do more by doing more.

END OF OCTOBER REPORT CARD

Credit: Did carbon-awareness gig largely to kids; non-meat-eating going surprisingly well; CATEwalk encouraged mass car-journey evasion; saw a bird and thought about nature.

Debit: Still so much more to do . . .

Savings: Noticeable, at least in terms of food miles.

Status: Planning To Be Better At The Environment.

SARAH'S BLOG: SPECIAL EDITION

Freecycle: A love story

Freecycle is basically a 'global recycling network', where people within communities can advertise stuff they want to get rid of, and in turn people request stuff they want. It's like recycling, and entirely free, and there's very little in this world that makes me happier than a clever compound word. Freecycle. It originated in Tucson, Arizona, as a local project to promote waste reduction, and by 14 August 2007, the membership stood at 3,354,732 across 4,001 communities. It's a fiendishly simple set up – you go to www.freecycle.org, find your local group and sign up to a Yahoo! Communities group. After that, you get a daily bulletin for your area. I signed up thinking it would be good to get rid of some old books and clothes, maybe see if anyone was advertising a telly stand (mine's wobbly and currently propped up with Trivial Pursuit and Buckaroo). But it was more, so much more.

I am, unashamedly, the sort of soppy bugger who can get weepy over an advert in a newsagent's window that reads 'wedding dress for sale – never worn'. For voyeurs of the human condition, Freecycle is addictive. Every day in your inbox you get a heartbreaking insight into a whole bunch of lives you would otherwise never have known about. Some of it's mundane ('steel bedframe, good condition'), some bittersweet ('designer suits, laptop, golfclubs to be collected asap', clearly a cuckolded wife getting rid of hubbie's possessions before he gets back from a 'business trip'), and some bizarre (the woman offering a nearly full sack of wholemeal pasta to the first respondent). What's most touching though, are the requests – on the whole polite and entirely reasonable, only occasionally do you get a cocky type demanding a specific model of mobile phone or a new mountain bike. My personal favourite was from a man looking for 'yellow sou'westers and a gong (or other device for making thunderous noises)' – presumably someone mounting *Birdseye! The Musical*.

Every time I've used Freecycle I've had some heartwarming or odd experience, like the bed-ridden old lady who sent her husband round to collect a bag of books – when I asked what he looked like (just in case a local murderer decided to pop round that afternoon) she described him as 'a little balding fat man in a silly flashy car' with such affection in her voice that when he turned up on my doorstep, I wanted to cuddle him. Or the time a lady from a local women's refuge came round for a bag of clothes and I said, 'Do you want these coats, even though it's summer?' She said breezily that it was fine as most of the recipients were out on the streets as 'sex workers. You know, prostitutes.' Which left me with the vague worry that one day I'd walk up Brick Lane and see dozens of prozzies dressed up like me.

NOVEMBER

Whether it was a coincidence or not, very soon after I arrived back home full of tales about my encounter with, and education/brainwashing by, Mr Gore, he received a burst of publicity greater even than when he won the Oscar. While there was a chance that his renewed media exposure was a direct result of his new association with me – as had happened to Lily Allen, who became a celebrity weeks after we appeared on *Never Mind The Buzzcocks* together – there were two factors that probably played a greater part. The first was that a teacher was fighting a court case contesting some of the claims of *An Inconvenient Truth*, and trying to stop it from being shown in schools. The second was that Al Gore had won the Nobel Prize. This made him the first Nobel winner I could count among my acquaintances, unless someone like Johann had picked one up and was just being outstandingly modest about it.

The fact that these two news stories came hot on one another's heels, and were given pretty much the same amount of coverage in the press, neatly summed up for me the way that – getting on for a year after his film had persuaded me to take action – a great big chunk of the country still couldn't make up its mind whether Al was a genuine crusader, a cynical politician, a deluded pseudo-scientist or what. You would have thought that receiving a Nobel Prize would lend him some pretty strong scientific credibility, but the media were inevitably attracted by the court case and the prospect that everything he'd stood for might prove inaccurate. One paper I read devoted more space to a photo of the teacher who was filing the court case than they did to reporting the fact he'd won the prize at all. Of course, this is hardly unusual – we're all more interested in people's failings than their successes. It reminded me of the joke that in London, if someone walked on water, people would say, 'Look at that, he can't even swim.'

But it was annoying. I was pretty sure that the judge would rule that *An Inconvenient Truth was* fit to be shown in schools, and that, by and large, it represented the view of almost all mainstream scientists; and sure enough that was exactly what happened (for a slightly more in-depth examination of the case, see the next chapter). Once it had been in the papers, though, it would always be in the back of people's minds that they'd heard there was 'something a bit dodgy' about the whole climate change palaver. The 'no smoke without fire' mentality of the cynical British public means, for example, that people always remember that such-and-such a celebrity was accused of some sexual misdemeanour, but rarely recall how the case actually turned out. Even if the charges are dropped twenty minutes after the arrest, the accuser turns out to be a paranoid schizophrenic and the celebrity in question goes on to save a dozen orphans from drowning, there will always be people in the pub muttering, 'I'm sure there was *something* in it' and, 'I've always thought his eyes were a bit funny.' Given that one of the main focuses of the course had been the urgency of the situation, it was frustrating to think that any saving-of-the-world precipitated by Gore's award would have to wait another few months while everyone um-d and ahh-ed over this latest controversy.

The mixed coverage of Al Gore's eventful fortnight made me realise once more that if you want people to do unglamorous things like help stop the world from melting, what they call the 'battle for hearts and minds' is crucial. It was with this on my mind that I decided now was the time to put into action a plan which had been suggested by our online community ages ago: a celebrity-recruitment campaign, in which I would revive the tradition of the CATE challenges with some high-profile participants. Proud as I was of things like the CATEwalk and the ongoing hands-on stuff that people like Sarah were continuing to occupy themselves with, part of my role as a Newly Trained Version Of Al Gore was to promote the cause as far and wide as possible, and nobody does that like celebrities. If I could get a few even moderately famous people to out themselves as CATE and take on a challenge in the public eye, there could be a considerable knock-on effect. People will always copy celebrities. If you look at the public figures who emerged in 2007, and the general trends that emerged during the year, the parallels are obvious. To use our familiar example of Lily Allen, she had barely swaggered ironically into the charts when people everywhere started to wear those hideous big white glasses; no sooner had Gordon Brown come to power than people started granting independence on monetary policy to the Bank of England.

I decided the most eye-catching thing I could do would be to get an open letter in the national newspapers appealing to the great and good to get involved. In all honesty I was hoping for the great, but if they weren't available, at least the good might be able to help me out.

Collating the best suggestions from website readers, I drew up a list of special, sparkly challenges which would appeal to celebs. It was important to get the balance right: there was no point in making all the challenges spectacular things like moving into a new solar-power-driven house, because then the ordinary person on the street would say, 'Well, it's all right for *him*, *he* can afford it.' Equally, it would be pointless setting challenges – like cooking with a microwave instead of an oven – so mundane that celebs, who famously crave attention, would consider it beneath them. I also had to get the tone right. I wanted it to be entertainingly insolent, so there was more chance of newspaper editors picking it up and printing it, but not so out-and-out disrespectful that an influential celebrity – like the Pope or Jimmy Carr – would take offence and send a man to have me taken out.

This was what I eventually sent out.

AN OPEN LETTER TO BRITAIN'S CELEBRITIES IN THE LIGHT OF AL GORE'S NOBEL PEACE PRIZE

Dear great and good,

Hope it's all going well. I enjoyed your show on TV/downloaded your single/wore clothes from your range/cried when you went out of Wimbledon/campaigned for your release from jail/have always just admired you in general.

Two things:

Firstly, whatever you make of this Al Gore business, most people agree that the environment is in trouble. It would be nice to do something about it without giving up too much of your time. But what?

I'm a comedian; you may have seen me on such satirical treats as *Mock The Week*. I have set up an organisation called Crap At

The Environment, which, as the name suggests, is for people who are not very green at all, but keen to do slightly better before we all find ourselves under water. I now want to recruit some more important people to take on some challenges alongside me.

Indeed, even if you're not famous at all, but influential in some field or other, I would love you to pledge to do one or more of these things. If you're a captain of industry, for instance. Or the speaker in the House of Commons. Or Alan Bean, the fourth man on the moon.

Here are the challenges:

Switch to a green energy supplier. This will actually save you money in the long run, which might come in handy given the famously fickle nature of fame. Wanted: **50**.

Decorate a canvas bag with your own design, be pictured using it, and auction it off for environmental charities. Wanted: **50**.

Only use taxi firms which deploy 'green', e.g. hybrid, cabs; and vow to use trains/buses instead of domestic flights. Go on. I have. No one needs to fly within the UK. Wanted: **30**.

Hijack the airwaves to promote eco-friendly living. Mention it on your radio show. Do an 'unplugged' performance. Slip it into a *Parkinson* interview. Do a stand-up routine about it. Mention it in the Queen's Speech if you are the Queen. Wanted: **10**.

Wear only second-hand clothes for a week. Wanted: **10**.

Give up your private jet! Now this requires a celebrity of considerable stature, both in terms of status and morality. Wanted: **1**.

Do some other noteworthy thing of your choosing. Become a vegetarian. Edit your film on a single computer instead of a whole suite. Hold a high-profile dinner party with locally sourced ingredients. Use your imagination. You must have a lot of imagination or you wouldn't be the great and good. Wanted: **infinite**.

I'd be very grateful if you would join in this modest, but genuine, attempt to do something worthwhile.

Mark Watson

I had never composed an 'open letter' before; I normally associated the phrase with magazines such as *Chat* or *That's Life!* which published diatribes by middle-aged women including phrases like, 'Wherever you are, Keith, I want you to know that I have recovered from what you did and forgiven you.' (There's a discarded copy of *That's Life* on the train seat opposite me as I write this, and its front cover story is 'HE CHOPPED UP MY DAUGHTER . . . THEN WENT BACK FOR SECONDS'. 'That's life!' seems a remarkably philosophical response to an incident like that.) I was unsure of the procedure for delivering my missive to Fleet Street. I hadn't written to a newspaper since I was twelve, when I put pen and paper to inform *The Times* of my concern that Sky TV was taking football coverage away from terrestrial channels. The letter, which began, 'As a twelve-year-old football fan . . .', was never published. In the end, I emailed the challenge to the letters pages of *The Times, Telegraph, Independent, Guardian, Sun* and *Mirror*.

The response was dramatic, to say the least: when I checked my email the following morning, there were emails in my inbox from all six papers. Excitedly, I opened the one from *The Times*, which was first to reply. It said, 'Unfortunately, we cannot accept submissions to the letters page without a full postal address.' The others all said the same. This had no doubt been made perfectly clear, if I'd just bothered to read the small print a bit more carefully, so it was my own fault; but I couldn't help wondering why, in an age of virtual communication, newspapers were 'unable to accept' a message that hadn't come from a proper house, as if they were the *Beano* and needed to know where you lived in case you won the Dennis The Menace fun pack for Star Letter. One of the key points about email is that it removes the need for old-fashioned formality and bureaucracy. Whatever next: people refusing to acknowledge text messages unless they begin with 'Dear Sir or Madam'? Nonetheless, I gritted my teeth and re-sent the letters. The gauntlet had been not so much thrown down to celebrities as dropped uneasily in the corner of the room, but at least it was out there.

What I had to be careful to avoid, this time, was becoming so zealous in my missionary activity that I forgot all about doing the little things myself. Accordingly, I signed up to The Nag (www.the-nag.net). This, as you've already heard, is an ideal resource for CATE people: a site which, every month, gives you a very gentle reminder to do something worthwhile like putting a brick in your cistern or getting energy-efficient light bulbs, and provides you with all the web links and other information you could require to take these steps. It's like living with a very well-informed, but non-pushy environmentalist, whom you only meet once a month. My first Nag assignment was to start buying more local goods, supporting small-scale, ethical produce, which would help to push the price down: the 'voting with your money' which Sarah mentioned earlier. This struck a particular chord because part of my pledge, made at Green Feet, had been to use farmers' markets more regularly, and this was proving much more difficult in practice than my other commitments to switching-things-off and non-taxi-use. At The Nag's suggestion I therefore signed up to receive a weekly box of local produce from a company called Abel & Cole.

Very shortly afterwards they left a box (covered in instructions on how to re-use it) on our doorstep full of goodies ranging from the genuinely alluring (plump apples, sweet-smelling carrots) to the unattractive-but-undeniably-good-for-you (leeks, things that looked like leeks) right down to the 'probably won't use this, in all honesty' (butternut squash). Emily cooked up some of the carrots that same night and was full of praise for how fresh and free of pesticides they tasted. I nodded wisely and pretended I was into vegetables. The next day, though, she produced a big pot of parsnip and apple soup.

This was a revelation. It was so tasty that I had it for lunch three days running. On the third day, when I began to get hungry in the run-up to lunchtime, I realised I was *looking forward to vegetables* for the first time in years. Thanks to The Nag, I had rediscovered my love of parsnips.

I'd almost forgotten, but in the days when I lived at my parents' and my mum would cook Sunday lunches, I used to wolf down parsnips like they were going out of fashion, which indeed they were. Or maybe they were never *in* fashion. People seem to consign them, quite unfairly, to the mental larder of chunky, featureless veg like turnips and swedes which school caterers dumped onto your tray, in the knowledge they were so rarely eaten that they might well be able to use the same portion again tomorrow. In fact, a parsnip has no place alongside these work-manlike roots. It is closer in spirit to the carrot, or to a sexed-up, slinky version of the potato. Even the name 'parsnip' sounds somehow feminine and seductive to my ears.

In a better world, I mused, shovelling the soup down with a bagel from a local bakery (I'd been using Tesco less and less in favour of small shops on our road, as an ethical by-product of my general CATE activities; the plastic bag war was the final nail in the coffin), in a fairer world, as I say, parsnips would occupy the iconic place in culture that potatoes do. Had they enjoyed the cultural head-start that spuds had, being brought back like a delicacy by Sir Walter Raleigh and having their profile raised constantly by association with such institutions as Mr Potato Head, maybe we would be eating mashed parsnip and parsnip waffles now, and the lyrics to classic songs would go, 'You say parsnip, I say parsnip', and football pundits, instead of saying a player 'went down like a sack of spuds', would say, 'He went down like a canvas bag full of lovely, succulent parsnips grown in the UK.' The parsnip, instead of languishing in the vegetable aisle next to fellow stragglers like the cabbage, would be in every kitchen in the land, being curried, or parboiled in a roast, or fried with a little maple syrup or honey, or just sitting there in the pantry, white and knobbly but with a heart of brilliant gold, providing a morale boost each time the door was opened.

Lord, I love parsnips.

But this recrudescence of an old gourmet love was only one of a number of culinary discoveries I was making as my campaign to ease off on the red meat continued. A combination of my (slightly) increased adventurousness, my wife's ingenuity and encouragement, and my desire to contribute to a worldwide fall in methane emissions led to encounters with all manner of wholesome (both morally and nutritionally) dishes. Perhaps I couldn't become the vegetarian, let alone vegan, that hardcore critics would have me be, but I was at least less dependent upon eating murdered creatures than I once had been. I now, in conjunction with Sarah and my wife, present a brief guide to the ways you can cut down on red meat and still enjoy your dinner. I shall also play the roles of notable foodies Gordon Ramsay and Jamie Oliver.

THE CATE GUIDE TO EATING SLIGHTLY LESS MEAT WITHOUT HAVING A SLIGHTLY LESS GOOD LIFE

* 'Ooh, I fancy a bit of spaghetti bolognaise.'

Mark: Why not try using a soya-based meat substitute, like Quorn, instead of mince? In all honesty, as someone who has spent an estimated 30 per cent of his waking life eating beef, it's not easy to tell the difference between something like cooked Quorn and actual mince.

Emily: Also, Quorn and other meat replacements are a lot less fatty. You don't end up with a massive load of animal fat in your frying pan.

Jamie Oliver: Yeah, it's all about how you cook it, innit? You might think 'Cor, bloody hell, I don't fancy soya meat when I could be eating proper meat,' but you cook it up in a nice sauce with real tomatoes and a little bit of herbs and what-have-you and bish bash bosh, you could be eating the real thing.

* 'Ooh, I really fancy that nice meaty feeling of chowing down on a bit of lamb or something.'

Sarah: There are a couple of vegetables that are nearly as exciting as meat. Mushrooms and aubergines have that proper 'flesh' feeling to them; you can wrench out their guts and stuff them with nice things like the sluts they are. Also, carrots, drizzled with maple syrup, in the oven for 45 minutes at gas mark 6. Oh, momma.

Gordon Ramsay: Yeah just get some fucking aubergines, stuff the little bastards with . . . hang on, what's going on over there? What are you doing? This is a *kitchen*! It's a fucking *kitchen* and you're *blowing your nose*! *Fuck* me!

* 'Ooh, I'm in Australia and I don't half fancy a lovely bit of steak.'
Mark: I don't know if you were reading a bit earlier, but I was talking about kangaroo. It's really nice and, because kangaroos don't fart like cows do, kangaroo meat provides a carbon-free alternative to beef.
Jamie Oliver: Yeah, yeah. Get a little bit of roo, do it with a nice green salad like this, chuck some couscous in – there we go, lovely jubbly – and if you taste a little corner of it like this . . . mmm . . . if it tastes sort of really nice, that means you've done it properly.

* 'Ooh, I really fancy a pasty from Greggs for lunch. I mean, what else can you have that fills you up nicely and is warm, and doesn't take long to prepare?'
Mark: Soup, mate! That's what! Get some vegetables . . . may I recommend parsnips? (Pause) Um, sort of a *bit* like swedes but really much more like what a potato would be like if it was almost sexually attractive. Right, knock up a bit of soup by adding in apples, ginger . . .
Gordon Ramsay: Yeah, put a bit of fucking gin-fucking-ger in the fucking soup, that'll give it a bit of a punch. No one here has balls. I'm not seeing anyone with real testicles.
Mark: . . . take it to work, heat it up in your nice energy-efficient microwave, off you go.
Jamie Oliver: Bish bash bosh.
Mark: Precisely.

* 'Ooh, I really fancy some protein. I'd be seriously underweight if I didn't eat steaks and things.'

Mark: Speaking as a repulsively scrawny individual myself, I can safely say this is something of a myth. You can get protein heaps of other ways than the flesh of a fallen beast. For a start, you can try things like beans and lentils. Lentils are a bit of a joke because they're often associated with vegetarian austerity but they are surprisingly tasty.

Jamie: Yeah. Try curried lentils, a bit of dhal, oh my God, that's nice.

Mark: Also, if you're looking to put on a bit of weight, for example to become more 'buff', you can always just get your day's recommended protein from a protein shake, of the kind sold at gyms, health shops and other places frequented by the buff of the nation.

* 'Ooh, I really fancy avoiding meat here, but I don't like fish. Don't like the taste of it.'

Mark: It might be that you need to try different kinds, because some fish taste totally different from others. Since trying to ease off on red meat, I've tried barramundi, fancy prawn dishes, monkfish, swordfish . . . it's a different experience each time. Emily's the person to talk to, really.

Emily: Yes. Monkfish in particular is an unexpected treat. It's easily as good as any meat.

* 'Ooh, I really, really, more than anything fancy a nice, slightly bloody but tender, so-big-it-barely-fits-on-the-plate rump steak.'

Mark: Well, fair enough. Me too. I don't think it's realistic for most people to transform themselves into out-and-out vegetarians. It may be possible, but the effort of will required is a lot to ask, especially of someone like me or you who loves food so much that they could be carrying out brain surgery and would still be distracted by the thought 'Mmm, I've got a nice rack of lamb marinating for later.' What most people *could* do is consume quite a bit *less* red meat without it casting a cloud over their existence. I hope I've demonstrated that here.

Gordon Ramsay: You fucking have.

So the boxes from Abel & Cole kept coming, parsnip and apple soup kept accounting for two of my five-a-day, and I kept actively seeking out alternatives to red meat, even if my eventual choice was no greater a sacrifice than, say, ordering chicken breast with added essence of beef. I estimated that over the course of November I ate one-third less red meat than in February (even though February is a shorter month). Of course, these figures are somewhat speculative, as I couldn't remember every meal I'd had in either month; indeed, I might be better off calling it a 'guesstimate' except that some people take very violently against that neologism. But I was eating far less of it than I used to, that was for sure, and that had to be good: as well as meaning my diet hinged less upon the meat industry, I was perhaps less easy prey to the various health traps for the prolific beef-eater (increased risk of cancer, heart disease, having awfully ruddy cheeks, etc). Everyone was a winner.

Before November was out I'd had my second go at doing a prototype Al-Gore-style rally. Again, the audience was youthful; again, the venue was unusual: this time, my sisters' school (Red Maids, in Bristol); and again, I felt woefully under-prepared. The background to this latest peculiar gig was that my sisters – who are in what used to be known as the lower sixth, these days it's probably Year 23 or something – were involved in a sort of Young Enterprise-type contest where two 'businesses' formed from members of the year group went head-to-head to make the most money. My sisters' group were selling, as their product, canvas bags, which meant that I felt justified in coming to their school and doing a 'fundraising' gig whose principle rationale was to ensure they would raise enough 'funds' to blow their rival team out of the water.

I asked people from the CATE site to suggest slogans for canvas bags; the best would be emblazoned on a bag and given to the winner. This accolade went to someone who put forward Gandhi's famous quotation 'You must be the change you wish to see in the world'. It's a bit cheeky using someone else's wisdom to win a contest, but Gandhi was a famously mild individual who, I was confident, would not have begrudged our winner her bag. The youth-friendly slogan 'GLOBAL WARMING – SO NOT HOT', a runner-up, was plastered onto a banner which would stand by the side of the stage as I did my stuff. Despite having sisters who are officially youths, I wasn't sure whether 'the kids' would be moved by this, or whether they still said things were 'so not hot', but it was hard to know without being immersed in their culture. I knew certain television commissioners who claimed to 'target the 14-21 demographic' with their programmes, but this is normally thinly disguised media-speak for 'Our shows are largely aimed at morons, but hell, they're cheap to make and I go skiing for eleven weeks a year.' Still, no one seemed to look at me askance, or 'dis' me as they say these days.

The actual gig was a ramshackle affair, the pattern of which was that I kept starting to talk about the environment, and then chickening out because it was easier to do jokes. To be fair to me, it had been billed as a 'comedy night', people had paid actual money, and I didn't want to fail to deliver on their expectations and leave my sisters looking like low-down shysters and possibly being run out of town, or at least out of the Sixth-Form Common Room. To be unfair to me, it was another indication that I was some way short of reaching anywhere near the level of mastery of the subject that would make me a worthy disciple of Al's. It was only a matter of months until I'd be expected to start giving the presentations I was contracted to do, and I'd had no time yet to prepare more than the tiniest morsels of material, still less to learn the skills of PowerPoint and cherry-picking-operation.

The event was certainly a success inasmuch as – like the 24-hour show – it made people think about the environment more than they would have done had they spent the same amount of time watching a show concocted to give Graham Norton something to do, or ten-pin bowling, or any of the other distractions with which people apparently fill their lives if I'm not there to beguile them. It was – like the Big Switch Off gig in Melbourne – a bigger contribution to the climate-change-awareness campaign than I would ever have expected to make a year before. But, as Live Aid had demonstrated, 'raising awareness' is more than just a matter of getting a lot of people in the same place. It demands genuine passion and genuine authority. It would be some while yet before I possessed the latter at least.

As for passion, well, the least you could say now, as the year drew on towards its end, was that the idea of the environment meant more to me now than it ever had done in the past. As the train pulled out of Bristol, I compared the way things were now with the way they'd been a year ago, before the dawning of my interest in this issue (if the future of the planet is an issue). Even if I'd wasted quite a bit of time on hare-brained initiatives, it was true to say my lifestyle habits had been altered, even if only marginally, and the same could be said of a number of people who'd joined in with me. I hadn't Pimped all the Patches I intended to (but I was talking to Sian about doing the community gardening plan, definitely, in 2008); I hadn't been able to replace all my light bulbs (even though I was a hell of a lot more careful about when I switched them on, and for how long); I hadn't cut out red meat (though I had cut down); I hadn't shunned all forms of aviation (but I'd flown significantly less and offset the rest); I hadn't learned to ride a bike, quite (but I was getting there). And by the end of November not one paper had printed my open letter, not even in its repackaged form with my full name, address and bank details (but it had caught the eye of a few people via the website). Summing up all these not-quites and their hopeful parentheses, it had been in some ways a year of failures, but honest failures at least – and, better still, failures with successful by-products.

This was a starting point, at least, as Stephen Fry remarked online at about this time – not in relation to me, I should be clear, but as regards the environment in general. In his own blog, which he presumably began to keep himself occupied as he was bored with only being an actor, film star, novelist, game show host, comedian, wit and astronaut, Fry said that he was 'trying to try' when it came to green matters, and likened it to Pascal's Wager: if global warming turns out to be nonsense, we won't have done any harm; if it's not nonsense, we *will* have done a lot of good. I wasn't going to argue with Fry, Gore and Blaise Pascal. I, too, would keep trying to try.

END OF NOVEMBER REPORT CARD

Credit: Continuing to espouse green living to 'the youth'; open letter written to celebs; discovering more and more alternatives to red meat, including ordering locally produced organic vegetables; 'trying to try'.

Debit: Stopping short of pushing message to 'the youth' too hard; open letter not published; 'trying to try' not the same as 'trying', or the stage after trying.

Savings: Respectable, thanks to Abel & Cole deliveries.

Status: Inching Towards Being All Right At The Environment, But A Lot Of Ground Still To Make Up In 2008.

SARAH'S NOVEMBER BLOG

We've come a long way. There's a brick in my cistern and a song in my heart.

I'm reading the green news in the paper now and feeling like it somehow applies to me personally. When I read that the hair dye I've been merrily using for years was produced by a company that got the lowest ethical score possible from *Ethical Consumer* magazine, I stopped buying it. Instead I switched to a henna made by a far less fee-fi-fo-fum company, made of all natural ingredients (less damaging to the water table). It's more fiddly and annoying than the stuff that comes packaged with its own little science kit and gloves, and has the consistency of Glastonbury mud that demands to be ground into your carpet with your slippers no matter how much you think you've wiped up every drop, but there's no denying the teeny sense of 'sticking it to the man' with every application.

But these are tiny things, and as Mark's curmudgeonly-but-probably-a-bit-right friend Johann says, 'selfish'. Were my actions having any influence on others, or was I just isolating myself from 'normal' people who drive cars and eat New Zealand apples and buy £8 skirts made in Bangladesh? I'll be honest, I don't feel isolated. I feel like a part of something.

Mark mentioned in one of his early blogs his cynicism about the war march and I can't say I entirely agree – if people are prepared to give up a Sunday lie-in on a freezing February, they're probably going to remember those frosty fingers and sitting through Miss Dynamite when it comes to election time. Similarly, a few dozen tampons a year flushed into the ocean is nothing compared to the tonnes of awful industrial pollutants dumped by commercial companies, but any girl who's bought a mooncup in an attempt to 'do her bit' is going to have this thought in the back of her head:

'I didn't faff about with a weird cornet-shaped bit of rubber just for those bastards to merrily carry on pumping that crap into the sea.'

She then boycotts that company's products, and writes to her MP, and her kids grow up thinking it's not normal and OK to chuck horrible things into the only water we've got. Standing in my bathroom as a tepid cowpat cooled on my head, there was a part of me that knew my effort was a (literal) drop in the ocean but I still felt part of something bigger.

I'm old enough to remember when people smoked in cinemas and on buses, unthinkable these days – it's quite gratifying to think that every little old lady who tutted at a youth pulling on a Woodbine did in her own way make a difference. So is it all a 'narcissistic distraction' as Johann would have it, or does all the collective under-breath tutting have its own tipping point – a 'tutting point' if you will?

I'll be honest, I don't know. I do know that I've got no idea how to stop China building factories or Chelsea mums insisting a 4x4 is vital to transport a tiny child half a mile up the road. We think of people who make big decisions as faceless shadowy 'they' people, but they are still people. People who read papers and have children who ask questions and are as much a part of society as the rest of us.

So while Mark was busy doing massive, sexy big glamorous things in Australia, I got back in touch with Sandra, from the school down the road, and offered her some help. When I posted a CATE blog asking for volunteers, there was a heartwarming deluge of people offering plant advice, garden centre discounts, and mainly just the willingness to get their hands dirty for the cause. When the weather is nicer, we're going to raise some money, get some tools and build a conservation garden. In a tiny corner of Hackney, a handful of kids will have access to plants and animals and see for themselves the wonderful tiny fragility of the environment. And hopefully some lovely things will grow from that.

DECEMBER

I'm writing this on December 31st 2007. The sun, whose effects upon the earth I have spent an unexpectedly large part of the year contemplating, has set for the final time. In Australia, where some of my greatest CATE adventures took place, it's 2008 already.

I'm at my parents' house in Bristol, and, for my final meal of the year, I have just eaten butternut squash. There could hardly be a more dramatic symbol of the way in which this year has removed me from my comfort zone of thoughtless consumption, and, more specifically, studious avoidance of weird-looking vegetables. A couple of weeks ago I took Emily to Acorn House, the greener-than-green restaurant run by one of my fellow 'dragons' from the British Library's fun day back in May. To find such an ethically minded establishment in the grimy brothel-complex of King's Cross was like falling in love with someone while visiting a prison. There was a bowl full of apples at the front desk, there were jars of appetising-looking spreads on shelves along the walls, the water and wine all came from Britain or (at a push) France, and the menu was full of delicious fare that almost certainly had a clear conscience, carbon-wise, as it breathed its last. I kept expecting Arthur Potts Dawson to leap out and snap, 'It's all so small-scale!' when we said we didn't have room for dessert, but he was nowhere about. I think I read he was launching other restaurants elsewhere in the country. Certainly this one was full on a cold, cheerless Monday night, so it looks good for Potts Dawson as he continues to offer guilt-free feeds to media types ducking out of Soho in their lunch hours to impress clients, or show prostitutes a good time *à la Pretty Woman.*

Speaking of food, I forgot to cancel the Abel & Cole order, so, in our flat in London, brown boxes are now piling up on our doorstep. Even before Christmas, the weekly vegetable invasion had been threatening to overwhelm us. It was all well and good when I was at home, but in weeks which took me out of London, Emily's soup-making energies sagged under the realisation that she would have to eat it all herself. Just a few days ago I received a charming voicemail message from someone who not only had a melodic voice, as you might expect from a person who made a living promoting right-and-proper grocery shopping, but was even called Melody. 'I just heard from our driver that he noticed your box from last week still outside your flat,' she said. 'Please do give me a call just so we know all is well.' I was touched by the personal concern implied by her tone, and briefly beguiled by the idea of a middle-class murder mystery which begins when the victim's neighbours' suspicions are aroused by the pile-up of organic veg on the doorstep. When I rang Melody back, she told me (pleasantly) that the boxes we'd left out for recycling had been rotted by rain, because of my carelessness in not covering them, so as well as all that wasted food, I had wasted the packaging. Even in the midst of GATEness I had succeeded in remaining a bit crap. I changed our weekly order to a smaller box.

Shortly before Christmas we threw a party with the theme of 'local produce' and a good number of our friends turned up with

Suffolk cider, white mulled wine brewed in Somerset, fancy crisps hand-cut in Northamptonshire and so on, and caroused in the shadow of our locally grown Christmas tree which we'd already arranged to have collected for recycling in the New Year. On the mantelpiece sat our party piece, a Christmas card with a touching family portrait on the front, which I made a good job of repeatedly brushing past, or coughing in the vicinity of, and then in response to the solicited questions, shrugging nonchalantly and saying, 'Oh, that . . . just a Christmas card from Al Gore. You know.'

On Christmas Day itself, in response to my appeal for ecologically agreeable presents, Emily gave me – among other things – a goblet made from a wine bottle, and two notebooks whose covers were made respectively from old circuit boards and car tyres. In my own gift-buying I tried to get 'experience'-based presents which would involve doing Fun Trips rather than purchasing flashy, but short-lived Things. I took my brother and wife to the World Darts Final and also planned a romantic January trip to Paris on the newly carbon-neutral Eurostar (for the wife not the brother). In addition my siblings and I bought my sister Lucy a day of paintball, combining the low carbon cost of the 'virtual gift' with the electricity-bypassing good-old-fashioned-romp outside. I've since heard from various friends that paintball is draining, painful and frightening, but the beauty of presents is that you don't have to use them yourself.

Over the course of the festive period I fielded a good many questions from family and friends, many of whom were only just catching up with the idea that I was into the environment these days, since, being my family and friends, they rightly considered it beneath their dignity to read my blog. Probably three-quarters of the questions were about how slick Al Gore's hair is and how firm his handshake was, but there was also quizzing on what I'd been doing, what I planned to do in the future, whether it was 'wrong' or 'bad' to do this and that, and, of course, the old favourite of whether this whole global warming was in fact a load of crap. To summarise a few of the most frequently (as they say) asked questions:

Cynic: So – saved the world yet?

Mark: Not quite.

Hardcore environmentalist: Is your carbon footprint lower than it used to be, though?

Mark: Well, yes. I took far fewer flights this year than last, and more to the point, a lot fewer flights than I was scheduled to. I cut down significantly on taxi use. I reduced the 'food miles' racked up by my taste for foreign delicacies and Antipodean wines, and also took steps to cut my intake of red meat when I learned how much carbon that was responsible for. I introduced a system of fining which led to my being far more vigilant about leaving appliances on standby. While it's hard to make precise calculations, here are my figures for 2007, using the same calculator as I used before:

END-OF-YEAR REPORT CARD, SPECIAL EDITION

CARBON-OFF: Mark v. The rest of the nation: The rematch

	MARK IN 2006	MARK IN 2007	UK AVERAGE
Home	2.21	1.67	2.0
Appliances	0.4	0.37	0.68
Travel	3.69	2.24	1.8
TOTAL	6.3	4.28	4.48

Obviously, this is not an indestructibly reliable guide, but since I used the exact same calculations as before, it does seem to suggest a pretty big reduction (about one-third) in my emissions; still bad, maybe, but not *too* bad for someone who travels as much as I do. (I could have made my figures look prettier by factoring in offsets I bought, but I decided to steer clear of this, what with all the controversy about that.) Most encouragingly, if actonCO2.direct-gov.uk is to be trusted in all this, I am now below the national average, and so claim my revenge on those who defeated me earlier in the year. Unless the national average has also gone down since I first used the website. Which I suppose it must have done, as I'm part of the nation. Hmm. Well, anyway. Not bad.

Editor of this book: What about getting your electricity from a green supplier? What about replacing your light bulbs, by finding an electrician who can grapple with your weird wiring?

Mark: No. As of the end of December, I have not sorted these things out. I have written to my landlady about changing to a green tariff, but it's not been sorted yet. And there are a lot more things I could do. For example . . .

Well-intentioned watcher of *Channel 4 News*:   In spite of progress made around the world this year . . .

Mark: Oh, I was talking to someone else.

Well-intentioned watcher of *Channel 4 News*:   Oh, sorry.

Mark: No, it's fine.

Well-intentioned watcher of *Channel 4 News*:   I was going to say – obviously there have been encouraging signs this year in world politics, for example the ratifying of Kyoto by the new Australian Government; I saw that on *Channel 4 News*. But aren't global carbon emissions still far outstripping the targets half-arsedly set by world leaders, which, in any case, were always inadequate? And if so, isn't it pointless trying?

Mark: I'd agree that globally, there are enormous socio-political changes which have to happen before we have a realistic chance of arresting CO_2 levels. And I admit those changes, however eagerly anticipated by Monbiot and others, seem a long way off. Just before Christmas you could see Jeremy Clarkson – I'm sorry to mention him once more – advertising his latest tome on posters on the Underground with the slogan: 'THE ONLY WAY YOU'LL GET ME ON PUBLIC TRANSPORT!' Clarkson's books sell many thousands of copies a week, which is why I've used him several times as an example. In order to gain a foothold anywhere near big enough to start making an impact on the voting public, the environmental lobby needs spokespeople who can also sell thousands of books a week. There is no such person at the moment. But who knows?

Bookworm: Are you slyly suggesting you could be that person?

Mark: Unfortunately not, because I still don't have green credentials to match Jeremy's anti-green credentials, and also, not many people, relatively speaking, read my books. What I can do is continue trying, in my small way, through comedy.

Bookworm: Oh that's good – I like comedy as well as books. How exactly will you do that?

Mark: I'll answer that in my closing remarks, in a moment, just after I've dealt with these last few people.

Mild xenophobe: You didn't really answer the last question. What's the good of us getting rid of our cars and all this other playing-silly-buggers if China continues to dump a million tonnes of crap a second into the atmosphere, and everyone in America has a car the size of Chessington World of Adventures?

Mark: One of the things I've learned is that it is all too easy to absolve yourself from personal responsibility by shaking your head helplessly and gesturing in the direction of 'all those foreign bastards'. Al Gore, while admitting that China has enormous carbon output because of all its coal-based industry, also reeled off about twelve ways in which their environmental policy outperforms that of the West. Notably, their minimum legal fuel-efficiency standard for new cars is far higher than manufacturers in the USA get away with. In the past week it's been on the news that their government is enforcing an outright ban on plastic bags . . .

Well-intentioned watcher of *Channel 4 News*:   Yes, I saw that.

Mark: . . . which is something our own Prime Minister has talked about, but seems incapable of getting round to.

Mild xenophobe: This is all very well, but the Chinese are still building factories at the rate of ten in the time since I began this sentence.

Mark: True, but it might be worth asking *why* it is that their economy is growing so fast and their production is so prolific. A large part of it has to do with the fact that we, in the West, have moved a lot of our production out there, because it's cheaper, and we are basically letting China serve as our 'smokestack', as one economist put it recently. If we complain about 'the Chinese' belching out greenhouse gases, but continue to buy into industries that rely heavily on Chinese industry, that's like walking into a butcher's shop, saying, 'God, it stinks of meat in here, what's the matter with these people?' and then walking out with a massive leg of lamb and placing an order for ten more.

Mild xenophobe: OK, so what about those Yanks with their inefficiently large country that they insist on driving round, and their consumerist culture which is very different indeed from the frugality that marks the British middle classes?

Mark: Well, on the subject of the USA: after seeing *An Inconvenient Truth*, Arnold Schwarzenegger this year not only had his Hummer converted to run green, but rushed through harsh carbon-curbing legislation which has reduced the state's current, and projected, emissions so drastically that California was actually held up as a model for Australia by Al Gore and his people. This is a famously sybaritic state governed by a supposed idiot who made his name impersonating muscle-bound superheroes, and in very little time they turned around their collective carbon footprint. I didn't know this until recently – I ridiculed the idea of Hollywood stars caring about the planet, for example, as recently as the February chapter – and I shouldn't think many other people in the UK do either. I'm not saying that giant swathes of the States aren't an environmental disaster, but I do think it's worth tidying up our own act, both personally and as a nation, before pointing too many smug fingers across the ocean.

Cynic: On the subject of Al Gore, I saw on the net that that teacher proved his film was mostly lies, and that schools are being forced to show *The Great Global Warming Swindle*, a dissenting view, in the interests of balance.

Mark: Not really. The film's errors made the headlines, not surprisingly, but the judge actually found that 'Al Gore's presentation of the causes and likely effects of climate change in the film was broadly accurate.' He went on to issue the caveat that the film's science was used to score political points. All this isn't an unconditional nod for Gore, of course, but personally, I don't care if the film is seen as having a political agenda or as being a self-promotional tool for Al Gore; those considerations don't diminish the core facts of the movie. If someone tells you there's a sniper in your garden pointing a rifle at your patio, and then mutters 'probably bloody gypsies', you might not like their politics, but the fact is that if you ignore them and, sure enough, you do get shot while doing a Sudoku under your parasol, you will have to concede that their key facts were right even if the presentation was lacking. As for the inaccuracies in the film which *were* identified by the court case, they are all details relating to specific climatic phenomena, and not one of them comes close to invalidating the central message. You can split hairs as much as you like over the science, and you won't get much of an argument from me because I still don't have the expertise to adjudicate in a battle of proper climatologists, but I'd be astonished if anyone can read the findings of the case and honestly say that, in their opinion, Al Gore is no longer worth listening to. As for *The Great Global Warming Swindle* – well, if you want to talk about inaccuracies, it was heavily criticised by the scientific community for falsifying data; two of the main scientists who give evidence in it went on record to say the film misrepresented their views; thirty-seven climate scientists signed a letter to protest at its release on DVD; its creator, Martin Durkin, had been publicly lambasted for his previous documentaries, including *Against Nature*, which was so misleading Channel 4 had to make a public apology for it during prime-time. Plus, when Durkin received a detailed, critical email about the show from geneticist Armand Leroi, which was copied to several other prominent scientists, he sent an email back to the lot of them addressing the entire critique with the single phrase: 'You're a big daft cock.' I'm not making this up; this is the man the anti-Gore media lobby has as its flagship. And the court case did not in fact recommend that anyone showed his film in schools, let alone make it mandatory.

Indecisive sort::   But if Gore *is* wrong . . . ?

Mark: Well, as has become obvious during this book, there are two separate issues really. Climate change is one thing, ethical living is another. Participating in the second one may help to combat the threat of the first. But if such a threat doesn't really exist, all things being equal, it must still be better to live ethically than not. It clearly makes sense to concentrate on renewables rather than fighting wars over fossil fuels; it's nicer to breathe clean air than polluted air; it is better for almost everyone if people shop locally and favour small businesses over multinationals; it's healthier to walk or ride a bike than to drive a car; you save money by turning lights off; recycling and discouraging waste helps to bring about a more equitable, less throwaway society. A surprising number of people would be happier if they spent less time coveting expensive goods produced on the other side of the world. Most of the lifestyle changes advocated by people who are Good At The Environment, in other words, stand up quite clearly as things which are also Good In General. If the global warming business turns out, in spite of everything, to have been a massive hoax or an even more massive misunderstanding, chances are we will still have made a number of improvements to our lifestyles. That's good enough for me, for now.

Bookworm: One more thing. Ages ago, near the start of the book, you made a passing reference to the 'ozone layer' and promised to return to it.

Mark: I'm glad you mentioned that, as it provides me with a good opportunity to use a specific example which encapsulates some of what I have been talking about over these pages.

Bookworm: Great. I love it when people do that.

Mark: As you'll know if you have seen *An Inconvenient Truth*, the hole in the ozone layer is an example of how big, intimidating ecological problems can, indeed, be addressed by public action. As you might remember, in 1985, a hole was discovered in the ozone layer – caused largely by the presence in the atmosphere of manmade compounds like CFCs, from aerosols – and everyone got quite excited about it, not in a good way. For many of us this was our first taste of green issues, and even – if we were young enough at the time – the word 'environment'. Nowadays the business of the hole in the ozone layer very rarely comes up, and in fact I've heard it referred to as another one of those 'green scares' that come up from time to time and are put to bed once the hippies run out of homespun cloth to write slogans on. But in fact, the reason it rarely comes up is that, following public alarm over CFCs and the ozone hole, a piece of legislation (the Montreal Protocol) was very swiftly agreed on, and passed, by politicians who'd been spurred into action by the fact that the public was demanding something be done about this. Virtually all countries in the world signed up to phase out CFC production, and by 2003, scientists announced that the depletion of the ozone layer was slowing down for the first time. It'll take a long time before all those CFCs leave the atmosphere, and there could well be more complications, and I'm sure the science is a lot more awkward than just 'right, stop spraying cans of stuff on yourself and that nasty hole will go away' – but the point is, people got alarmed, politicians were forced to act, and large law changes came into being very quickly. So it's no use just saying, 'Well, politicians will never listen anyway.' Arguably, it is a citizen's duty to make sure they do. It would be nice if, because of the actions of ordinary people, in another couple of generations, cynics were saying, 'Yeah, there used be all this hoo-hah about global warming. You don't hear so much about *that* these days!'

Cynic: I shall prepare such a speech right now.

On that note, what's around the corner for me? I'll continue to do small things in my own life and medium-sized things in the CATE community. I'll sort out the shortcomings of my current rented property, and by the end of the year, I hope to have bought a new house lit entirely by energy-saving light bulbs, and also looked into solar power, insulation and cladding and all the other things I can't do while still a tenant. I'll continue my self-taxing, continue offsetting, and so on. I am talking to CATE people about ideas like the fete, the film festival, the Pimp My Patch, which we didn't quite nail last year.

And then there will be bigger stuff. With the 'open letter' still having failed to force its way past all the competitors into an actual newspaper, I've been busily targeting celebrities in person, which is a lot slower, but should yield some great-and-good challenges very soon. Barely three months from now, it looks like I'll be doing the first of my Gore-trained presentations in the Melbourne Town Hall, supported by the Australian Conservation Foundation, and attended by up to 1500 people. Even typing that sentence made my fingers go clammy. And whether it goes well or not, my diary's already filling up with more engagements, either to give my Gore lecture or to talk on other aspects of the environment. If I can get the lecture right – in almost no time, given the schedule of other things I'm committed to – it is an amazing opportunity to bridge the gap between entertainment and eco-information in a way no one's really done so far. If not, I will look like a prat.

Either way, after that I guess it's onwards and upwards into the realm of drastic lifestyle changes. That's right: I've already booked a bike lesson for February. Who knows, by the time you read this, I might have made a newspaper pot.

Further Surfing

There are many great books – as well as many dull ones – you can read on this subject, including the ones I've mentioned, and the details are below. However, in keeping with the slightly-lazy-but-well-meaning theme of Crap At The Environment, I thought a bibliography of websites was more likely to be useful. Even then, it is difficult to pick from the many many sites I've used extensively over the past year. This selection merely represents sites that have either been of particular use in CATE activities, or in writing this book. But you know how to use Google. You can probably compile a better list yourself. I might put some blank spaces for you to expand on this list, like in kids' books where it says, 'Draw your own monster here.'

BOOKS

Heat by George Monbiot, published by Penguin 2006
Six Degrees by Mark Lynas, published by HarperCollins 2007

WEBSITES

www.timesonline.co.uk
You can navigate from here to *The Times'* excellent Eco Worrier blog by Anna Shepard. Also try Leo Hickman's similar regular feature in the *Guardian*.

www.freecycle.org
Meet interesting, or odd people, and trade things with them.

www.actonco2.direct.gov.uk
Take the carbon footprint test for yourself.

www.changeiscoming.org.uk
A mine of unintimidatingly presented climate-related information.

www.theclimateproject.org
Al Gore's organisation.

www.planestupid.com
Online headquarters of those people who try to stop planes taking off. Even if you think this is an idiotic idea, the site is interesting.

www.selfsufficientish.com
Be inspired, or psyched out, by the living-mostly-off-the-land exploits of Andy and Dave. Also, buy their book, *The Self-Sufficientish Bible*, published by Hodder in May 2008.

www.therainforestsite.com
One of these sites where you can click every day and save a bit of the rain forest. I've been doing this for ages now. It's a lot easier than brawling with loggers.

www.passionfortheplanet.com
A DAB radio station mixing music (actual music, not whale noises and stuff) with low-pressure environmentally-friendly-ism.

www.thenag.net
Sign up and get the politest of monthly reminders, along with all sorts of good-humoured advice on how to actually do it.

www.wannaveg.com
This is for you if you like the idea of dabbling in part-time vegetarianism.

www.emptyroads.com
A nice site promoting fun that doesn't involve getting into cars.

www.monbiot.com
The personal site of this fanatical climate change campaigner and general left-wing powerhouse, with a large archive of interesting articles.

www.hippyshopper.com
Despite the perhaps off-putting name, this is a valuable site for ethical fashionistas.

www.seat61.com
Admirable, remarkably thorough site, letting you know how to get almost anywhere without flying. Also contains a lot of non-boring travel information. A lot of fun to read even if you've no intention of actually going to Albania by boat.

www.greenelectricity.org
Switch to a green tariff faster than you can say 'This will also save me money in some cases.'

www.energysavingtrust.org.uk
Greening up your home.

www.ethiscore.org
A site a bit like the *Which?* magazine of the green world, providing things with 'ethical scores', which is nice as everyone likes competitions with winners and losers, and there's no reason environmentalists should escape just because they're often quite chilled-out.

www.foe.co.uk
Friends of the Earth. Sappy-sounding organisation, but in fact a robust body with exemplary principles. Not a foe at all.

www.facebook.com
Facebook groups:
   Crap At The Environment
   Online Environmental Action
   Buy It Naked
. . . and far too many to list – just search for 'environment'. You know.

Oh, also,

www.myspace.com/crapattheenvironment and, under reconstruction now, www.crapattheenvironment.co.uk.

Write in your own websites below:

Acknowledgements

Extracts from *Heat* (George Monbiot) published in 2006 by Penguin appear by kind permission of the publishers.

Extracts from people's Crap At The Environment blogs appear either by their kind permission, or at the very least, without their out-and-out resistance. I'd like to thank everyone who joined in with CATE, either on the site, or in the real, physical world.

A huge amount of information and enlightenment has been lifted from the websites listed above, and from others on the miraculous shortcut to knowledge and misinformation that is the Internet.

I owe an enormous debt of thanks to Al Gore's Climate Project and to the Australian Conservation Foundation for allowing me to go on the course, and also for the use of various materials and for quite a few other crucial pieces of help.

I'd like to acknowledge the help of Andy and Dave, the Self-Sufficiency Twins, in particular, for their remarkable knowledge and approachability. Thanks also go to Alex Bonham and Tara Gladden for their inspiration and indefatigability. And Patrick Walsh for agenting. And my wife for putting up with this.